Practical Electronics

Volume III

Embedded Systems with PIC18 Microcontrollers

Dr. T. VEERAMANIKANDASAMY

Associate Professor
Department of Electronics and Communication Systems
Sri Krishna Arts and Science College
Coimbatore – 641008, India

Practical Electronics

Volume III

Embedded Systems with PIC18 Microcontrollers

ISBN: 9789334105094 (Paperback)

Cover image by Dr. T. Veeramanikandasamy
(Credit: unsplash.com)

Second Edition 2024

About the Author

Dr. T. Veeramanikandasamy is an Associate Professor of Electronics and Communication Systems at Sri Krishna Arts and Science College in Coimbatore, India. He earned his doctoral degree in Electronics from Bharathiar University, Coimbatore, India. With more than eighteen years of teaching experience at both undergraduate and postgraduate levels, his expertise lies in the fields of Embedded Systems and Nanomaterials Characterization. He has successfully guided five scholars in obtaining their M.Phil. degree under his supervision.

Dr. Veeramanikandasamy has authored seven subject books with ISBN and edited two conference books with ISBN. He has published over 16 research articles and holds 2 patents in the domains of Electronics and Materials Science. Additionally, he has presented more than twenty research papers at national and international conferences and delivered twelve technical lectures across various institutions.

As a Life Member of the Indian Society of Systems for Science and Engineering (ISSE), he remains actively involved in the academic community. Dr. Veeramanikandasamy also holds a certification as an Embedded Software Engineer, issued by the Electronics Sector Skills Council of India. He has obtained a professional certification in Data Science with Python from IBM. Moreover, he has developed several student enrichment courses covering topics such as Embedded Systems, Digital Systems Design using VHDL and Verilog, Digital Signal Processing, Programmable Logic Controller, IoT, and Machine Learning with Python.

PREFACE

Laboratory experiments are an essential component of science and engineering education. The purpose of this book is to provide organized experiments that help learners better understand the laboratory aspects of electronics. It includes fifty-one laboratory experiments specifically for PIC18 microcontrollers, designed to aid students in grasping theoretical principles and gaining insights into the design and implementation of both software and hardware for embedded systems.

The book offers comprehensive and clear explanations of PIC18 assembly language programming using **MPLAB® XC8 PIC® Assembler (pic-as)** and embedded C programming. Each experiment is presented as a complete module, featuring the aim, algorithm, program, circuit diagram, and results. The results section includes sample inputs and outputs for each experiment, facilitating easy verification.

The primary audience for this book consists of undergraduate and postgraduate students in science and engineering. The advanced technologies covered in this book are applicable in various sectors, including communication electronics, consumer electronics, automotive electronics, industrial controls, medical electronics, and other relevant fields.

This book aims to:

- Promote experiential learning among students.
- Provide practical knowledge to understand the operation of systems.
- Illustrate the relationship between software and hardware in embedded systems.

If you find any errors or have suggestions for improvement, please contact the author at veeramaniks@gmail.com. Errors will be corrected, and suggestions incorporated in the next edition.

- Dr. T. Veeramanikandasamy

CONTENTS

PRACTICAL ELECTRONICS

(VOLUME III)

EMBEDDED SYSTEMS WITH PIC18 MICROCONTROLLERS

1. Introduction to PIC18 Microcontrollers

The PIC microcontroller was developed by General Instruments in 1975. General Instrument's Microelectronics division developed a very successful 16-bit microprocessor called the CP1600. While the CP1600 was a good CPU, it had low I/O performance. To address this, the 8-bit PIC MCU was developed in 1976 to improve the overall system performance by offloading I/O tasks from the CPU (PIC1650, an NMOS chip).

In 1985, General Instrument sold their Microelectronics division, and the new owners canceled almost everything, but they introduced EPROM to produce a programmable controller. In 1989, the Microelectronics division was renamed Microchip. Initially, PIC stood for Programmable Intelligent Computer, but it later came to stand for Peripheral Interface Controller. Microchip is headquartered in Chandler, Arizona, US.

In 1993, Microchip Technology launched the 8-bit PIC16C84 with on-chip EEPROM, which could be programmed using a serial programming method. The improved versions of the PIC16C84, featuring on-chip flash memory, are the PIC18F84 and PIC18F84A, released in 1998.

Microchip is widely known for their line of PIC Microcontrollers,

- 8-bit MCUs - PIC10, PIC12, PIC14, PIC16, PIC18

- 16-bit MCUs - PIC24, dsPIC
- 32-bit MCUs - PIC32MX, PIC32MZ

Computer software MPLAB IDE

- MPLAB Xpress
- C and C++ compilers
- Code libraries

The "C" suffix implies that the chip uses EPROM memory (OTP).

- PIC12C; PIC16C; PIC17C; PIC18C

The "F" Suffix implies that the chip has reprogrammable Flash memory.

- PIC10F -- in super-tiny 6 pin packages
- PIC12F -- in tiny 8-pin packages
- PIC14F; PIC16F; PIC18F; PIC24F; PIC24E; PIC24H
- dsPIC30F; dsPIC33F; dsPIC33E

The PIC18 is based on a 16-bit instruction architecture incorporating advanced RISC architecture. The PIC18F is the highest performer among all 8-bit PIC families, with benchmark nanoWatt low power consumption. The PIC18 core is integrated with modern communication protocols like USB, CAN, LIN*, and Ethernet (TCP/IP protocol) to communicate with local and/or internet-based networks. The PIC18 family has two series: the PIC18 "J" series and the PIC18 "K" series.

The Microchip has introduced six different lines of 8-bit MCUs:

PIC12XXX	: 8-pin, 12- or 14-bit instruction format
PIC14000	: 28-pin, 14-bit instruction format (= PIC16XX)
PIC16C5X	: 12-bit instruction format
PIC16CXX	: 14-bit instruction format
PIC17	: 16-bit instruction format
PIC18	: 16-bit instruction format

PIC18 family share the same instruction set and the same peripheral function design (better upgrade path). PIC18 MCUs implement 77 instructions. Out of which 73 instructions are 16 bits, and the remaining four are 32 bits.

The PIC18 MCUs provide the following peripheral functions:

- Parallel I/O ports with high current sink/source 25mA/25mA

- Timer functions (Three 16-bit timer/counters & One 8-bit timer) including counters, Two Capture/Compare modules (Capture 16-bit, max. resolution 6.25ns/Compare 16-bit, max. resolution 100ns), real-time interrupt, and watchdog timer
- Pulse width modulation (PWM)
- SPI (3-wire) and 12C serial interface
- Universal Synchronous/Asynchronous Receiver Transmitter (USART)
- A/D converter with 10-bit resolution
- Analog comparator
- Low-power operation mode
- SRAM and EEPROM
- EPROM or flash memory
- Controller Area Network (CAN)

1.1 PIC18 Bus Structure

- *Address bus*
    - 21-bit address bus for Program Memory
    - Addressing capacity: 2 MB
    - 12-bit address bus for Data Memory
    - Addressing capacity: 4 KB
- *Data bus*
    - 16-bit instruction/data bus for Program Memory
    - 8-bit data bus for Data Memory

1.2 PIC18 Registers

The PIC18 SFR Registers are categorized into:

- CPU/ALU SFR Registers
- Peripheral SFR Registers

These registers are implemented as RAM in the data memory space from 0xF80 to 0xFFF. PIC18 MCU has CPU registers from 0xFD8 to 0xFFF.

CPU/ALU SFRs:

- WREG: working register
- ID: Instruction Decoder

- STATUS: Status register
- BSR: Bank Select Register (4-bit)
- FSR: File Select Register
- PC: Program Counter
- Stack Pointer
- Table Pointer and Table Latch
- PRODH and PRODL: Product Registers

Working Register (WREG):

- 8-bit Working Register (equivalent to an accumulator)

Bank Select Register (BSR) (0 to F):

- 4-bit Register
- Only low-order four bits are used to provide MSB four bits of a12-bit address of data memory

File Select Registers (FSR):

- FSR0, FSR1, and FSR2
- FSR: composed of two registers (FSRH and FSRL)

FSRH (4-bit)	FSRL (8-bit)

- Used as pointers for data registers and associated with index (INDF) registers
- Holds 12-bit address of data register
- Instruction decoder (ID) – when the instruction is fetched it goes into the ID to be interpreted – tell the processor what to do 16-bit instructions

Program Counter (PC):

- 21-bit register functions as a pointer to program memory during program execution

Table Pointer (TBLPTR):

- 21-bit register used as a memory pointer to copy bytes between program memory and data memory

Stack Pointer (SP):

- Register used to point to the stack

Stack:

- 31 word-sized registers used for temporary storage of memory address during execution of a program

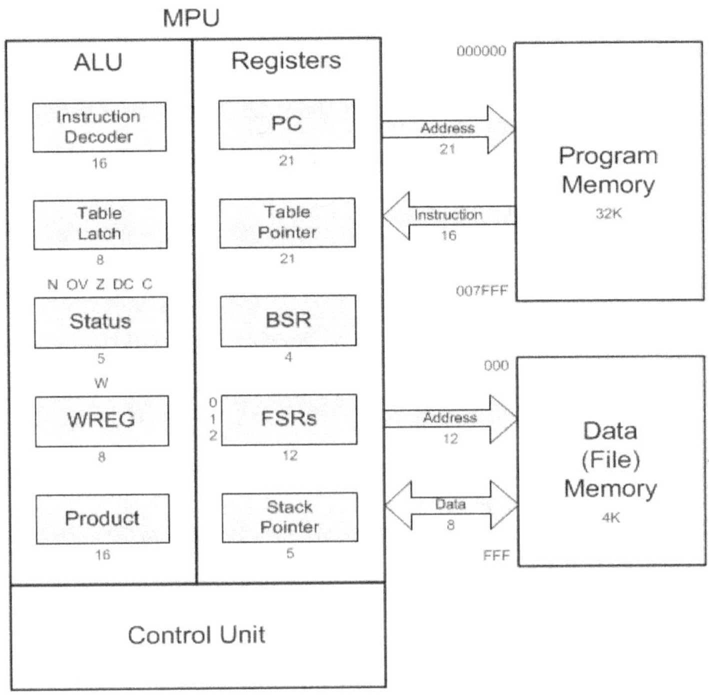

Fig.1. Blocks of PIC18F devices

Power On Reset (POR):

- The Power On Reset will hold the device in reset until a minimum Vdd voltage threshold is met and the oscillator is stable

Brown Out Reset (BOR):

- The PIC MCU will reset when the Vdd drops below a brown-out threshold voltage.

Power-Up Timer (PWRT):

- The PWRT is used to allow the Vdd voltage of the PIC MCU to stabilize, with a 72 millisecond delay.

1.3 PIC18F Memory Organization

- Memory consists of a sequence of directly addressable "locations".

- A memory location is referred to as an information unit. PIC18 holds eight bits of information
- Address and content of memory register is referred as,
  0x22 - Memory address
  [0x22] - Memory content
- PIC18 MCU has a 21-bit program counter that is divided into three registers: PCU, PCH, and PCL
- Only the PCL register is directly accessible to the user
- Both the PCH and the PCL are 8 bits & PCU is 5 bits

PCU	PCH	PCL	= PC
5-bit	8-bit	8-bit	= 21

There are three types of memory in PIC18 enhanced microcontroller devices:

- Data RAM
- Data EEPROM
- Program Memory

1.3.1 *Data memory*

- Some chips only have SRAM, while others may have both SRAM and EEPROM. EEPROM stores permanent data.
- Each location in the data memory is also referred to as a register or file register.
- The PIC18 MCU supports 4096 bytes of data memory.
- It requires 12 bits of address to select one of the data registers.
- SRAM data memory begins at the 12-bit address 0x000 and ends at the 12-bit address 0xFFF (4K).
- Data memory is often divided into two sections.
- General Function Registers (GFR) or register file locations
  - 000 - 0xF7F locations
  - GPRs are used to hold dynamic data when executing a program
- Special Function Registers (SFR)

  - o 0xF80 - 0xFFF locations (upper 128 bytes)
  - o Used by the CPU and peripheral modules for controlling the desired operation of the MCU
- 4096 file registers are divided into 16 banks
- Each Bank having 256-byte
- Only one bank is active at any time
- BSR<3:0> used to select the banks
- Half of bank 0 and half of bank 15 form a virtual (or access) bank that is accessible no matter which bank is selected
- Access Bank: The Access Bank consists of the first 96 bytes of memory (00h-5Fh) in Bank 0 and the last 160 bytes of memory (60h-FFh) in Block 15

The Access Bank is utilized by core PIC18 instructions that incorporate the Access RAM bit (the 'a' parameter) within the instruction. When 'a' is '0', the instruction is compelled to utilize the Access Bank address map, completely disregarding the current value of the BSR. Conversely, when 'a' is '1', the instruction employs the BSR and the 8-bit address included in the op-code for the data memory address.

d-bit refers to destination

d=0, the result will move to working register (W) d=1, the result will go into data memory

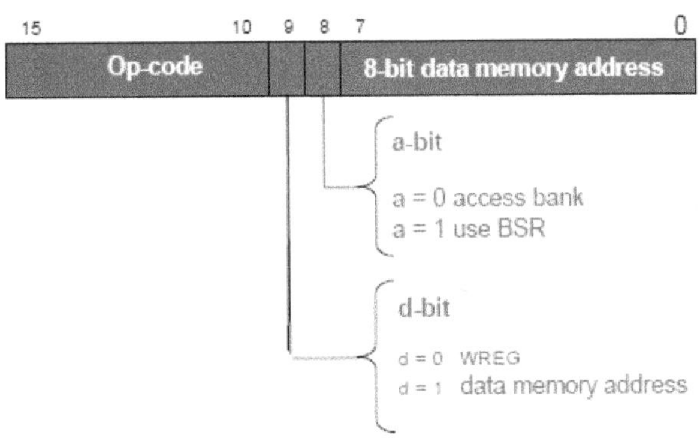

a-bit determines if we are accessing the access bank or other BANK

a=0, access bank is selected

a=1, other bank will be selected

Ways to access data registers from the MPU:

- Access Bank
    - Directly accessible (default BSR<3:0> = 0000)
- Direct using Bank Select Registers (BSR)
    - Bank address (4-bit MSB) + Instruction (8-bit LSB)
- Indirect using File Select Registers (FSR)
    - FSR contains the address of the data register
    - MPU uses FSR to access data registers

1.3.2 *EEPROM Data Memory*

- The data EEPROM is a nonvolatile memory array
- Size: 256 bytes or 1024 bytes
- Data EEPROM is readable and writable during normal operation
- It is used for long-term storage of program data
- It is not directly mapped in either the register file or program memory space, it is indirectly addressed through the Special Function Registers (SFRs)
- Four SFRs are used to read and write to the data EEPROM:
    - EECON1 (Control register 1)
    - EECON2 (Control register 2)
    - EEDATA (Data register)
    - EEADR (Address register)

1.3.3 *Program Memory*

- PIC18 has a 21-bit program counter and hence is capable of addressing the 2-MB program memory space
- PIC18C have on-chip EPROM program memory
- PIC18F devices have on-chip flash program memory
- PIC18 devices have two interrupt vectors (Reset & Low/High priority interrupts),
    - The address 000000h is assigned to the reset vector
    - The address 000008h is the starting address of the high-priority interrupt service routine. 16 bytes are allocated
    - The address 000018h is the starting address for the low-

priority interrupt service routine, no default size

- User program should follow the low-priority interrupt service routine (ISR)

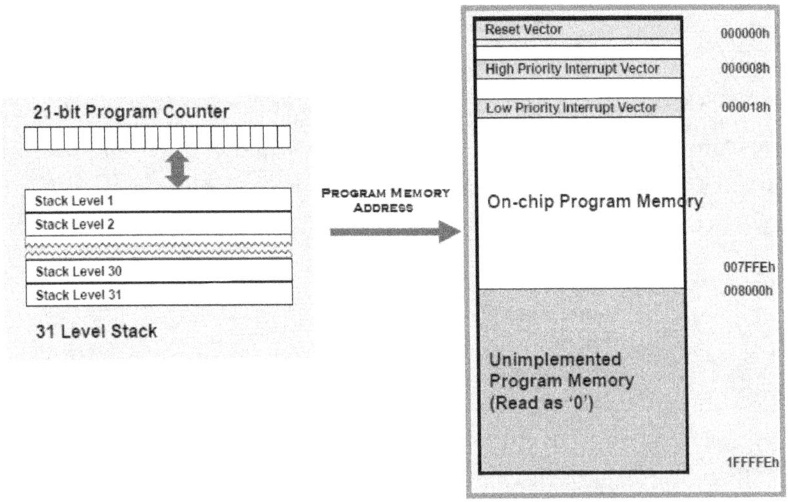

Fig.2. Program memory organization

1.3.4 *Table Read and Table Write Operations*

- In order to read and write program memory, there are two operations that allow the processor to move bytes between the program memory space and the data RAM
  - Table Read (TBLRD)
  - Table Write (TBLWT)
- The program memory space is 16 bits wide, while the data RAM space is 8 bits wide. Table reads and table writes move data between these two memory spaces through an 8-bit register (TABLAT)
- Control Registers
- Registers are used in conjunction with the TBLRD and TBLWT instructions. These include the,
  - EECON1 register
  - EECON2 register

- TABLAT register
- TBLPTR registers

1.4 PIC18 Clocking Scheme and Instruction Cycle

The clock input, whether from an internal or external source, is internally divided by four to generate four non-overlapping quadrature clocks (Q1, Q2, Q3, and Q4). The program counter is incremented on every Q1; the instruction is fetched from the program memory and latched into the Instruction Register (IR) during Q4. The instruction is decoded and executed during the subsequent Q1 through Q4 cycles.

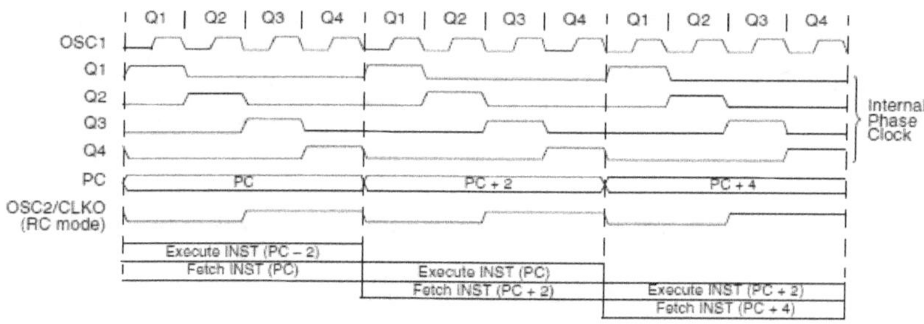

Fig.3. Clocking Scheme

If XTAL frequency = 20 MHz, then instruction cycle time is 0.2μs or 200ns (= 20MHz/4 => 5MHZ & 1/5MHZ = 0.2μs)

Most instructions execute in one instruction cycle (200 ns). During branching or call operations, if a condition is true or the program counter (PC) changes, it takes two instruction cycles (440 ns for a 20 MHz crystal oscillator).

Osc Type	Crystal Freq	Typical Capacitor Values Tested:	
		C1	C2
XT	4 MHz	27 pF	27 pF
HS	4 MHz	27 pF	27 pF
	8 MHz	22 pF	22 pF
	20 MHz	15 pF	15 pF

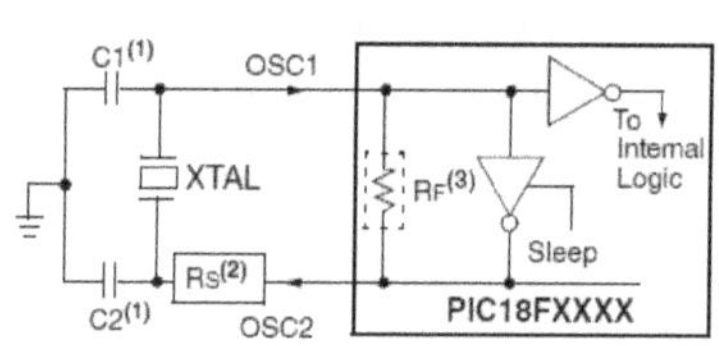

Fig.4. Typical Capacitor Selection for Ceramic Resonators

1.5 PIC18 Pipelining

The PIC18 features a two-stage pipeline: Instruction fetch and Instruction execution. Instruction fetch takes one instruction cycle, while decode and execution take another instruction cycle. However, due to pipelining, each instruction effectively executes in one cycle.

Fig.5. Two-stage pipelining

A fetch cycle begins with the Program Counter (PC) incrementing in Q1. During the execution cycle, the fetched instruction in the Instruction Register (IR) is decoded in Q1 and executed across Q2, Q3, and Q4 cycles. Data memory is read in Q2 (operand read) and written in Q4 (destination write). This allows the processor to overlap the execution of multiple instructions, achieving higher instruction throughput.

2. Instruction Set of PIC18 Microcontrollers

2.1 Instruction Format

The instruction format is grouped into five basic categories,

- Byte-oriented file register operations
- Byte-to-byte Operations
- Bit-oriented file register operations
- Literal operations
- Control operations

Format for byte-oriented operation instructions:

15 — 10	9	8	7 — 0
opcode	d	a	f

d = 0 for result destination to be WREG register.
d = 1 for result destination to be file register (f)
a = 0 to force Access Bank
a = 1 for BSR to select bank
f = 8-bit file register address

Syntax:	ADDWF f {,d {,a}}
Operands:	$0 \le f \le 255$ $d \in [0,1]$ $a \in [0,1]$
Operation:	(W) + (f) → dest
Status Affected:	N, OV, C, DC, Z
Encoding:	`0010` | `01da` | `ffff` | `ffff`
Description:	Add W to register 'f'. If 'd' is '0', the result is stored in W. If 'd' is '1', the result is stored back in register 'f' (default). If 'a' is '0', the Access Bank is selected. If 'a' is '1', the BSR is used to select the GPR bank (default).

Format for byte-to-byte operation instruction:

There is only one instruction that uses this format: movff f 1, f2

This instruction allows to move data from one file register to another.

15 12	11 0
opcode	f (source file register)

15 12	11 0
1111	f (destination file register)

f = 12-bit file register address

MOVFF	Move f to f
Syntax:	MOVFF f_s,f_d
Operands:	$0 \le f_s \le 4095$ $0 \le f_d \le 4095$
Operation:	$(f_s) \rightarrow f_d$
Status Affected:	None
Encoding: 1st word (source) 2nd word (destin.)	 `1100` | `ffff` | `ffff` | `ffff`$_s$ `1111` | `ffff` | `ffff` | `ffff`$_d$
Description:	The contents of source register 'f_s' are moved to destination register 'f_d'.

Format for bit-oriented file register operation instructions:

This format uses an 8-bit field (f) to specify a file register as the operand.

15 12	11 9	8	7 0
opcode	b	a	f

b = 3-bit position of bit in the file register (f).
a = 0 to force Access Bank
a = 1 for BSR to select bank
f = 8-bit file register address

BCF	**Bit Clear f**
Syntax:	BCF f, b {,a}
Operands:	$0 \le f \le 255$ $0 \le b \le 7$ $a \in [0,1]$
Operation:	$0 \rightarrow$ f<b>
Status Affected:	None
Encoding:	1001 | bbba | ffff | ffff
Description:	Bit 'b' in register 'f' is cleared. If 'a' is '0', the Access Bank is selected. If 'a' is '1', the BSR is used to select the GPR bank (default).

Format for literal operation instructions:

A literal is a number that is operated on directly by the CPU.

15 8	7 0
opcode	k

k = 8-bit immediate value

MOVLW	**Move Literal to W**
Syntax:	MOVLW k
Operands:	$0 \le k \le 255$
Operation:	$k \rightarrow W$
Status Affected:	None
Encoding:	0000 | 1110 | kkkk | kkkk
Description:	The eight-bit literal 'k' is loaded into W.
Words:	1
Cycles:	1

Q Cycle Activity:

Q1	Q2	Q3	Q4
Decode	Read literal 'k'	Process Data	Write to W

Example: MOVLW 5Ah

After Instruction
W = 5Ah

Format for control operation instructions:

These instructions are used to change the program execution sequence and making subroutine calls.

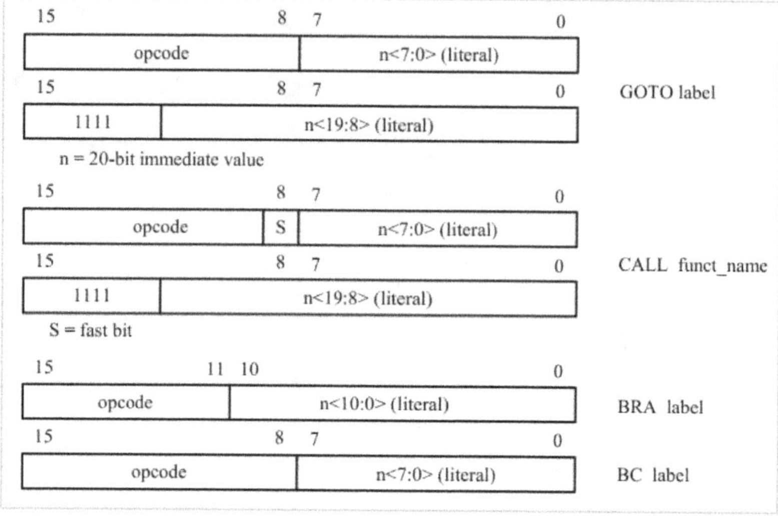

2.2 PIC18 Addressing Modes

An addressing modes is to specify the operand to be operated on. The PIC18 MCU provides following five addressing modes

- Register direct addressing mode
- Immediate addressing mode
- Inherent addressing mode
- Indirect addressing mode
- Bit-direct addressing mode

Register Direct Addressing Mode

PIC18 devices use an 8-bit value to specify a file register (data memory register) as an operand. The register may belong to either the access bank or other banks. This 8-bit value serves as the least significant 8 bits (LSB) of the data memory address, while the most significant 4 bits (MSB) come from the BSR register. For registers in the access bank, the bank value in the BSR register is ignored.

movwf 0x45, A

- copied the contents of the WREG register to the memory location 0x45 in the access bank (A=0 or c)

movff reg1, reg2

- copied the contents of the register reg1 to the register reg2

Immediate Addressing Mode

The actual operand is provided in the instruction. There is no need to access any memory location.

addlw 0x20

- ADDs the hex value 20 to the WREG register and places the sum in the WREG register

movlw 0x15

- loads the hex value 15 into the WREG register

movlb 3

- places the decimal value 3 in the lower four bits of the BSR register

Inherent Addressing Mode

The operand is implied in the op-code field. The instruction does not provide the address of the implied operand.

movlw 0x20

- places the hex value 0x20(operand) in the WREG register. The destination WREG is implied in the opcode field

andlw 0x13

- performs an AND operation. WREG is implied

Indirect Addressing Mode

A special function register is used as a pointer to the data memory location. This can be useful for data tables in data memory and for software stacks.

There are three indirect addressing registers:

- FSRO, FSR1, and FSR2
- To address the entire data memory space (4096 bytes)

Two 8-bit registers are used to store the 12-bit data memory address.

- FSRO: FSR0H and FSR0L
- FSR1: FSR1H and FSR1L

- FSR2: FSR2H and FSR2L

After placing the address of the file register in one of the FSR registers, the data can be read from or written to the following registers: INDF0, INDF1, and INDF2.

For instance, if an instruction writes a value to INDF0, the value will be written to the file register whose address is indicated by FSR0H:FSR0L.

movwf INDF0

- copies the contents of the WREG register to the data memory location specified by the FSR0 register.

Bit-Direct Addressing Mode

PIC18 MCU has five instructions to deal with an individual bit. These instructions use three bits to specify the bit address.

BCF PORTB, 3, A

- integer 3 specifies the bit to be cleared or bit address. clears bit 3 of the PORTB

BSF PORTA, 4, A

- integer 4 specifies the bit to be set or bit address. sets bit 4 of the PORTA

2.3 PIC18 Instructions

The PIC18 includes 77 instructions.

- 73 one-word (16-bit) long
- 4 two-word (32-bit) long

They are divided into seven groups

- Move and Load instructions
- Arithmetic instructions
- Logical instructions
- Branch, Call and Return, and Skip instructions
- Bit manipulation instructions
- Table read and write instructions
- Machine control instructions

2.3.1 *Move and Load Instructions*

```
MOVLW     8-bit    ; Load an 8-bit literal in WREG
MOVWF     F, a     ; Copy WREG in File/Data Reg
                     if a=0/c, F is in Access back
                     if a=1/F, Bank is specified by BSR
MOVFF     Fs, Fd   ; Copy from one Data Reg to another Data Reg
```

2.3.2 *Arithmetic Instructions*

```
ADDLW     8-bit    ; Add 8-bit number to WREG
ADDWF     F, d, a  ; Add WREG to File/Data Reg
                     Save result in W if d=0
                     Save result in F if d=1
ADDWFC    F, d, a  ; Add WREG to File/Data Reg with carry
                     Save result in W or F
SUBLW     8-bit    ; Subtract WREG from literal
SUBWF     F, d, a  ; Subtract WREG from File/Data Reg
SUBWFB    F, d, a  ; Subtract WREG from File/Data Reg with borrow
INCF      F, d, a  ; Increment File/Data Reg
DECF      F, d, a  ; Decrement File/Data Reg
COMF      F, d, a  ; Complement File/Data Reg
NEGF      F, a     ; 2's complement of File/Data Reg
MULLW     8-bit    ; Multiply 8-bit and WREG
                     Save result in PRODH-PRODL
MULWF     F, a     ; Multiply WREG and File/Data Reg
                     Save result in PRODH-PRODL
DAW                ; Decimal adjust WREG for BCD
```

2.3.3 *Logical Instructions*

```
ANDLW     8-bit    ; AND literal with WREG
ANDWF     F, d, a  ; AND WREG with File Reg
                     Save result in WREG or File Reg
IORLW     8-bit    ; OR literal with WREG
IORWF     F, d, a  ; OR WREG with File Reg
                     Save result in WREG or File Reg
```

```
XORLW      8-bit     ; Exclusive-OR literal with WREG
XORWF      F, d, a   ; Exclusive-OR WREG with File Reg
                       Save result in WREG or File Reg
```

2.3.4 *Branch Instructions*

```
BC       n          ; Branch if C flag=1
BNC      n          ; Branch if C flag=0
BZ       n          ; Branch if Z flag=1
BNZ      n          ; Branch if Z flag=0
BN       n          ; Branch if N flag=1
BNN      n          ; Branch if N flag=0
BOV      n          ; Branch if OV flag=1
BNOV     n          ; Branch if OV flag=0
GOTO  address       ; Branch to 20-bit address unconditionally
```

* n is + or – 64 words

2.3.5 *Call and Return Instructions*

```
RCALL     nn        ; Call subroutine within + and - 512 words
CALL      20-bit, s ; Call subroutine
                      If s=1, save W, STATUS and BSR
RETURN, s           ; Return subroutine
                      If s=1, retrieve W, STATUS and BSR
RETFIE, s           ; Return from interrupt
                      If s=1, retrieve W, STATUS and BSR
```

2.3.6 *Increment/Decrement and Skip Instructions*

```
DECFSZ     F, b, a  ; Decrement File Reg and skip the next instruction
                      if F=0
DECFSNZ    F, b, a  ; Decrement File Reg and skip the next instruction
                      if F≠0
INCFSZ     F, b, a  ; Increment File Reg and skip the next instruction
                      if F=0
INCFSNZ    F, b, a  ; Increment File Reg and skip the next instruction
                      if F≠0
```

2.3.7 *Bit Manipulation Instructions*

```
BCF       F, b, a  ; Clear bit b of File Reg (b=0 to 7)
BSF       F, b, a  ; Set bit b of File Reg (b=0 to 7)
BTG       F, b, a  ; Toggle bit b of the File Reg
RLCF      F, d, a  ; Rotate bits left is File Reg through carry
                     Save result in WREG or File Reg
RLNCF     F, d, a  ; Rotate bits left is File Reg
                     Save result in WREG or File Reg
RRCF      F, d, a  ; Rotate bits right is File Reg through carry
                     Save result in WREG or File Reg
RRNCF     F, d, a  ; Rotate bits right is File Reg
                     Save result in WREG or File Reg
```

2.3.8 *Test and Skip Instructions*

```
BTFSC     F, b, a  ; Test bit b in File Reg and skip the next
                     instruction if it is cleared
BTFSS     F, b, a  ; Test bit b in File Reg and skip the next
                     instruction if it is set
CPFSEQ    F, a     ; Compare File Reg with WREG, skip if F=W
CPFSGT    F, a     ; Compare File Reg with WREG, skip if F>W
CPFSLT    F, a     ; Compare File Reg with WREG, skip if F<W
TSTFSZ    F, a     ; Test File Reg, skip if F=0
```

2.3.9 *Table Read and Table Write Instructions*

```
TBLRD*    ; Read program memory pointed by TBLPTR into TABLAT
TBLRD*+   ; Read program memory pointed by TBLPTR into TABLAT
            and increment TBLPTR
TBLRD*-   ; Read program memory pointed by TBLPTR into TABLAT
            and decrement TBLPTR
TBLRD+*   ; Increment TBLPTR and read program memory pointed by
            TBLPTR into TABLAT
TBLWT*    ; Write TABLAT into program memory pointed by TBLPTR
TBLWT*+   ; Write TABLAT into program memory pointed by TBLPTR
            and increment TBLPTR
```

TBLWT*- ; Write TABLAT into program memory pointed by TBLPTR and decrement TBLPTR

TBLWT+* ; Increment TBLPTR and write TABLAT into program memory pointed by TBLPTR

2.3.10 Machine Control Instructions

CLRWDT ; Clear Watchdog timer

RESET ; Reset all registers and flags

SLEEP ; Go into standby mode

NOP ; No operation

3. PIC18F4550 Microcontroller

The PIC18F family combines high performance and integration with the ease of an 8-bit architecture. The PIC18F4550 is a popular microcontroller from Microchip Technology, featuring high-performance enhanced flash and USB capabilities, utilizing nano-Watt technology.

3.1 PIC18F4550 Microcontroller - Features

- High-Performance RISC CPU
- 32 KB Flash Program Memory; 1,000 erase/write cycles Enhanced Flash Program Memory
- 2048 Byte SRAM Data Memory
- 256 Byte EEPROM Data Memory; 1,000,000 typical erase/write cycles EEPROM Data Memory
- Source code compatible with the PIC16 and PIC17 instruction sets
- USB V2.0 Compliant with up to 12 Mb/s at Full Speed and Supports up to 32 Endpoints
- Two External Clock modes, up to 48 MHz with Internal Oscillator support; Secondary Oscillator using Timer1 @ 32 kHz; Dual Oscillator options
- 16-bit wide instructions, 8-bit wide data path
- Three External Interrupts; Priority levels for interrupts
- 8 x 8 Single-Cycle Hardware Multiplier

- Power-On Reset
- Power-up Timer (PWRT) and Oscillator Start-Up Timer (OST)
- Watchdog Timer (WDT) with its own On-chip RC oscillator
- Programmable code protection
- Power-Managed Modes: Run: CPU on, peripherals on; Idle: CPU off, peripherals on; Sleep: CPU off, peripherals off
- Wide Operating Voltage Range (2.0V to 5.5V)
- Single supply 5V In-circuit Serial Programming
- In-Circuit Debug (ICD)
- 35 I/O pins with individual direction control; 25 mA/25 mA sink/source current support
- 40-pin DIP
- 10-bit, up to 13-channel Analog-to-Digital Converter module
- Dual Analog Comparators
- Enhanced USART module
- Enhanced Capture/Compare/PWM (ECCP) module

3.2 Pin diagram of PIC18F4550

MCLR/VPP	Master Clear (Reset) input/ Programming voltage input
RA0-RA6	Digital PORTA I/O pins
AN0-AN12	Analog inputs (13 channels)
RE0-RE3	Digital PORTE I/O pins
CVREF	Comparator voltage reference
VREF- & VREF+	A/D reference voltage
T0CKI	Timer0 external clock input
C1OUT/ C2OUT	Comparator 1 & 2 outputs
RCV	External USB transceiver RCV input.
SS/LVDIN	SPI slave select input/ High/Low-Voltage Detect input
CK1SPP	SPP clock 1 output
CK2SPP	SPP clock 2 output
OESPP	SPP output enable output
VDD	DC positive supply
VSS	DC negative supply

VUSB	Internal USB 3.3V voltage regulator output
OSC1/CLKI	Oscillator crystal input 1 or external clock source input
OSC2/ CLKO	Oscillator crystal input 2 or CLK oscillator output
RC0-2, RC4-7	Digital PORTC I/O pins
RD0-RD7	Digital PORTD I/O pins
T1OSO	Timer1 oscillator output
T13CKI	Timer1/Timer3 external clock input
T1OSI	Timer1 oscillator input
CCP2	Capture 2 input/Compare 2 output/PWM 2 output
UOE	External USB transceiver OE output
CCP1	Capture 1 input/Compare 1 output/PWM 1 output
P1A	Enhanced CCP1 PWM output, channel A
P1B	Enhanced CCP1 PWM output, channel B
P1C	Enhanced CCP1 PWM output, channel C
P1D	Enhanced CCP1 PWM output, channel D

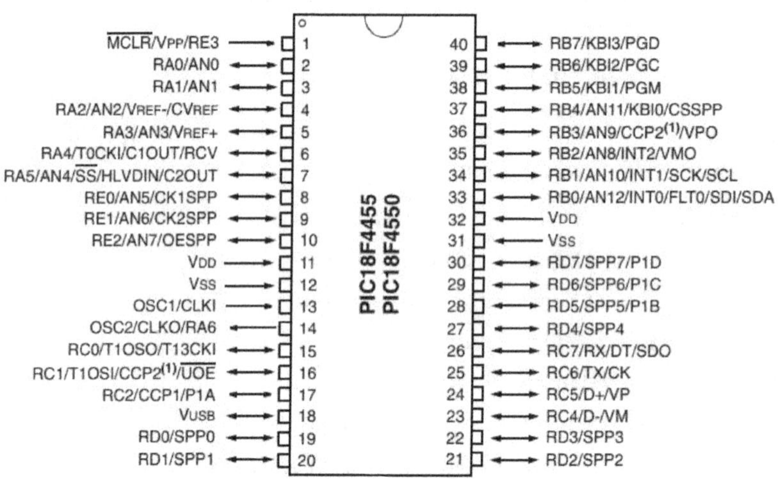

Fig.6. Pin diagram of PIC18F4550

SPP0-SPP7	Streaming Parallel Port data
D-/D+	USB differential minus/plus line (input/output)
VM	External USB transceiver VM input
VP	External USB transceiver VP input
TX/RX	EUSART asynchronous transmit/receive

CK	EUSART synchronous clock
DT	EUSART synchronous data
SDO	SPI data out
RB0-RB7	Digital PORTB I/O pins
INT0/INT1/INT2	External interrupt 0/1/2
FLT0	Enhanced PWM Fault input
SDI	SPI data in
SDA	I2C data I/O
SCK	SPI Synchronous serial clock
SCL	I2C Synchronous serial clock
VMO	External USB transceiver VMO output
VPO	External USB transceiver VPO output
KBI0/KBI1/KBI2/KBI3	Interrupt-on-change pin
CSSPP	SPP chip select control output
PGM	ICSP Programming enable pin
PGC	In-Circuit Debugger and ICSP programming clock pin
PGD	In-Circuit Debugger and ICSP programming data pin

3.3 Essential Circuitry for the PIC18F Microcontroller Experiments

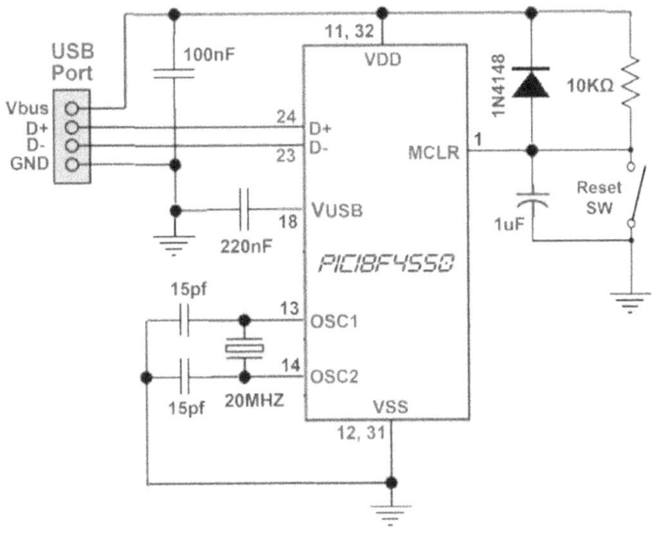

Fig.7. Basic Circuit for PIC18F4550 Microcontroller Experiments

4. Software Development Tools

MPLAB® X Integrated Development Environment (IDE) is an expandable and highly configurable software program that incorporates powerful tools for discovering, configuring, developing, debugging, and qualifying embedded designs for PIC microcontrollers and digital signal controllers. MPLAB X IDE seamlessly integrates with the MPLAB development ecosystem of software and tools, many of which are available for free.

A typical software development cycle begins with writing an application program using a text editor. This program is then translated into executable code or HEX code with the help of an assembler or compiler. MPLAB X tools are compatible with Windows, Linux, and macOS operating systems. MPLAB X IDE also provides an Integrated Programming Environment for production-level programming. It supports the open-source AVR® MCU and SAM MCU GCC compiler. MPLAB X IDE facilitates in-circuit debugging and programming of PIC®, dsPIC®, AVR, SAM, and CEC flash microcontrollers (MCUs) and microprocessors (MPUs) using MPLAB ICD 4, MPLAB PICkit™ 4, and MPLAB Snap. Microchip Studio is a software development tool that incorporates all the features and functionality of Atmel Studio, tailored for AVR® and SAM devices. The MPLAB cloud tools ecosystem offers a comprehensive online solution for users of all skill levels to discover, configure, develop, and debug embedded applications based on PIC® and AVR® microcontrollers (MCUs).

4.1 PIC18 Assembly Language Programming

The source file (.s) is created using the text editor in MPLAB® XC8 PIC® Assembler. The assembler converts the .s file into machine language and generates object and error files. We check the error file for mistakes, then correct them in the .s file before assembling again. The linker processes one or more object files and produces a hex file, a list file (lst), a map file, an intermediate object file, and a debug file. The list (lst) file displays both binary and source code information. The map file illustrates the memory layout, highlighting used and unused memory locations.

A program written in a sequence of statements (mnemonics) to perform the desired operations.

PIC18 assembly program consists of three types of statements:

- Assembler directives: Assembler commands that are used to control the assembler: its input, output, and data allocation
- Assembly language instructions: PIC18 instructions - use up to 77 different instructions
- Comments: Two types of comments in an ALP
    - Explains the function of a single instruction or directive
    - Explains the function of a group of instructions or directives

Each line of the source file may consist of up to four fields.

- Label
- Mnemonic
- Operand(s)
- Comment

Label

Labels must begin in column 1 and be followed by a colon (:), space, tab, or the end of the line. They must start with an alphabetic character or an underscore (_) and can include alphanumeric characters, underscores, and question marks. Labels can be up to 32 characters long and are case-sensitive.

Mnemonic

An assembly instruction mnemonic or assembler directive that must begin in column 2.

Operand Field

Follows the mnemonic field. Operands must be separated from mnemonics by one or more spaces or tabs. Multiple operands are separated by commas.

Comment Field

The comment field is optional and serves documentation purposes.
It starts with a semicolon.

Structure of PIC18 Assembly Language Program

```
ORG      0x0     // Starting address of program
GOTO     Start   // Branch by Start
ORG      0x08    // Vector address of high priority interrupt
RETFIE           // Return from ISR
ORG      0x18    // Vector address of low priority interrupt
RETFIE           // Return from ISR
Start:           // Main function of program - starts

[Statements]

END
```

4.2 Compilers for PIC Microcontrollers

The popular compilers for programming PIC microcontrollers include MPLAB XC8, MPLAB XC16, MPLAB XC32, Mikro C, and PIC CCS. The MPLAB XC compilers are Microchip's official compilers, with the assembler (pic-as) included as part of the XC compiler suite. These compilers are free to use and can be downloaded from Microchip's official website. The MPLAB XC compiler lineup consists of:

- MPLAB XC8 supports all 8-bit PIC® and AVR® microcontrollers (MCUs)
- MPLAB XC16 supports all 16-bit PIC MCUs and dsPIC® Digital Signal Controllers (DSCs)
- MPLAB XC32/32++ supports all 32-bit PIC and SAM MCUs and MPUs

4.3. Getting Started with MPLAB IDE

The MPLAB IDE desktop includes several key elements:

- a menu bar at the top
- a toolbar below the menu
- a workspace where various files, windows, and dialogs can be displayed, and a status bar at the bottom

A step-by-step procedure for creating a new project with MPLAB X IDE:

i. Double click on MPLAB X IDE icon (Version v5.45)

(If you have project(s) in project window, Go to File menu → Close all projects)

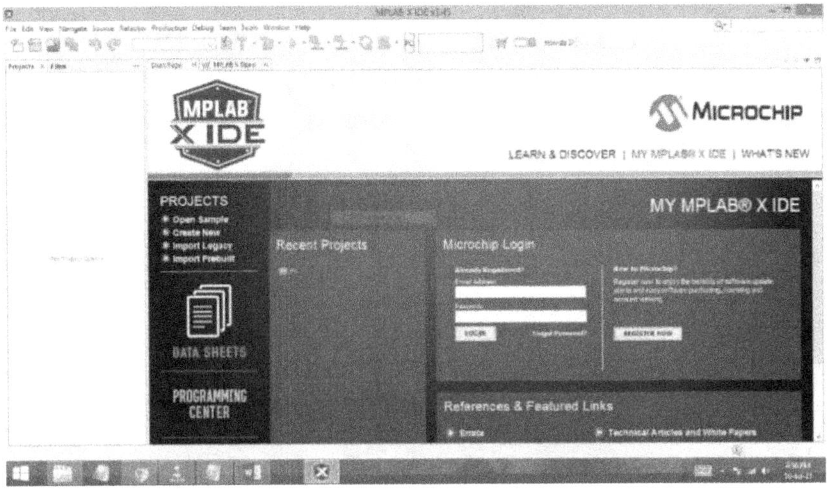

ii. To create new project in MPLAB X IDE

File → New project

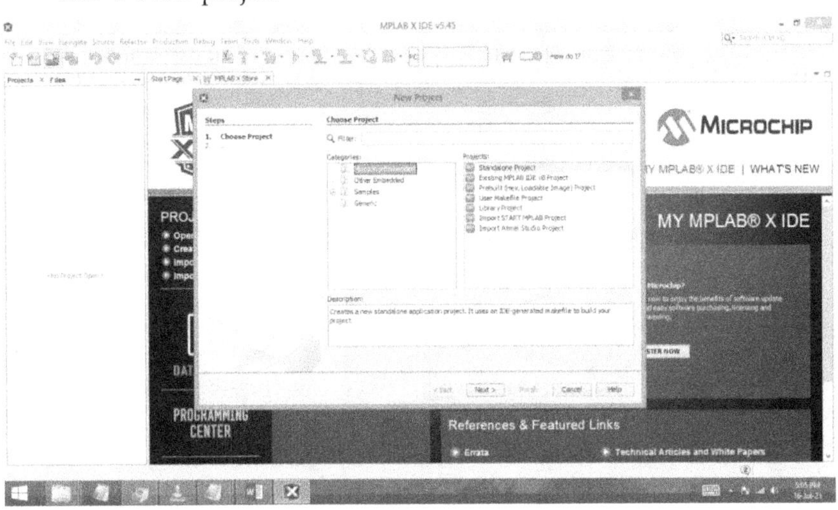

Categories: Microchip Embedded

Projects: Standalone project / any other options

iii. ***Select Device***

Family: Midrange PIC

Device: PIC18F4550

Tool: Simulator / PICkit3 / PICkit4

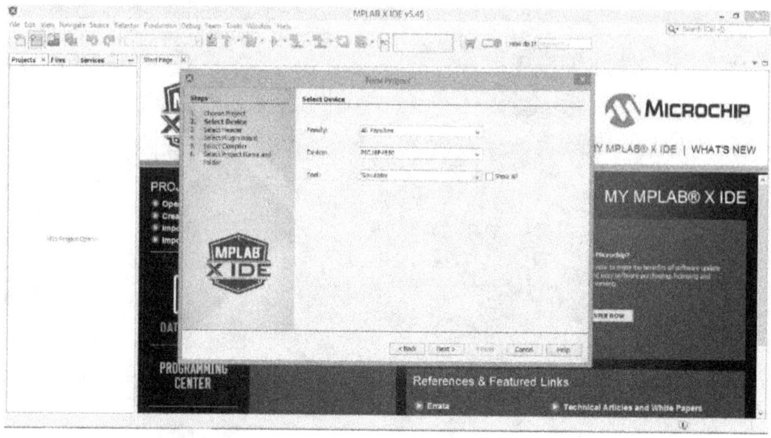

iv. ***Select Compiler***

For ASM CODE: pic-as (version number) like pic-as (v2.31)

For C CODE: xc8 (version number) like XC8 (v2.31)

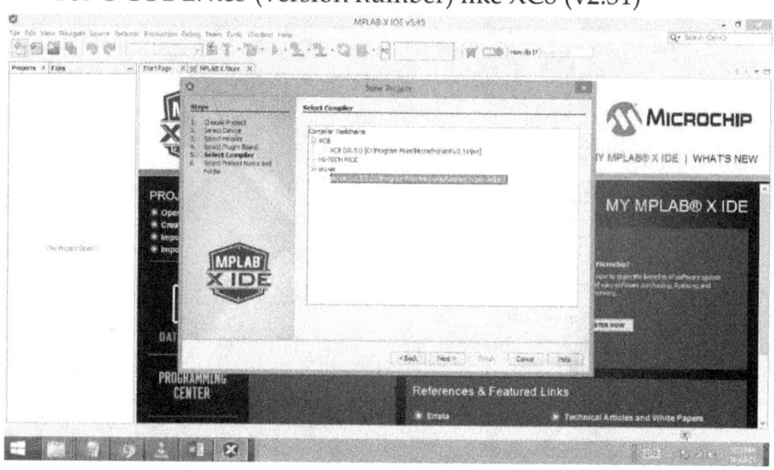

v. ***Select Project Name and Folder***

Project Name: ******

Project Location: *******

Project Folder: *******

Check set as main project

Encoding: ******** (ISO-8859-1)

Finish

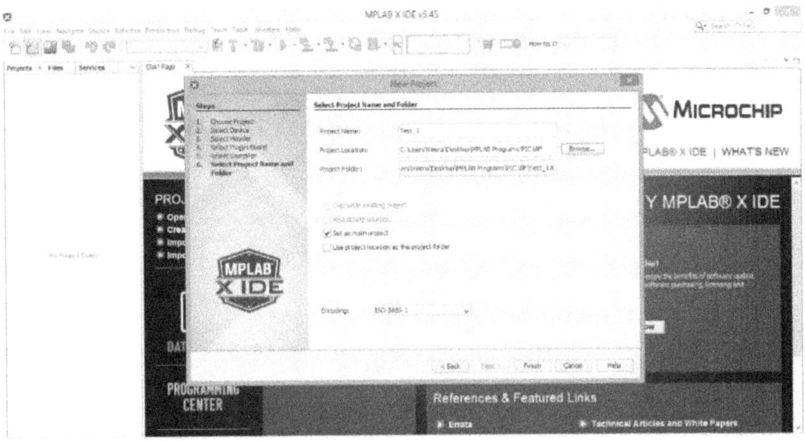

vi. To create a source file, go to File menu and click on new file

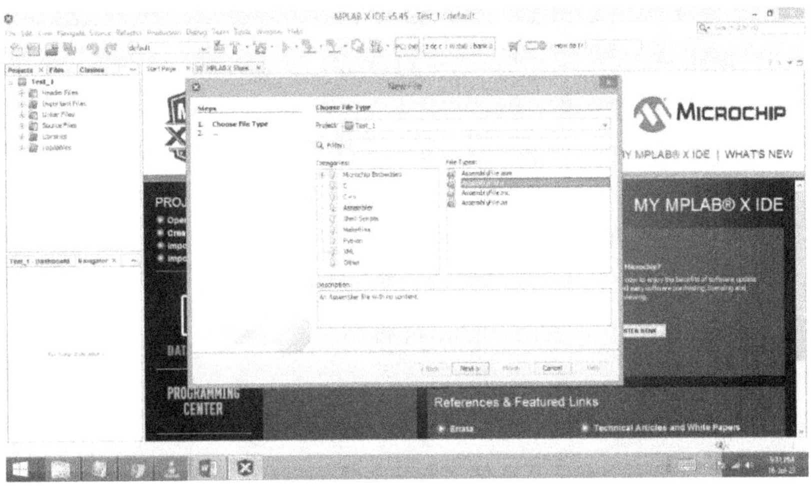

Categories:

For Assembly Language Program, choose Assembler

For C Program, choose C

For Python, choose Python and so on.

File Types:

Choose the file with proper extension (.s/ .c / .inc)

vii. ***Set the file name (Test_1.s) and location. Click on Finish.***

Add the source file (Test_1.s) to the project.

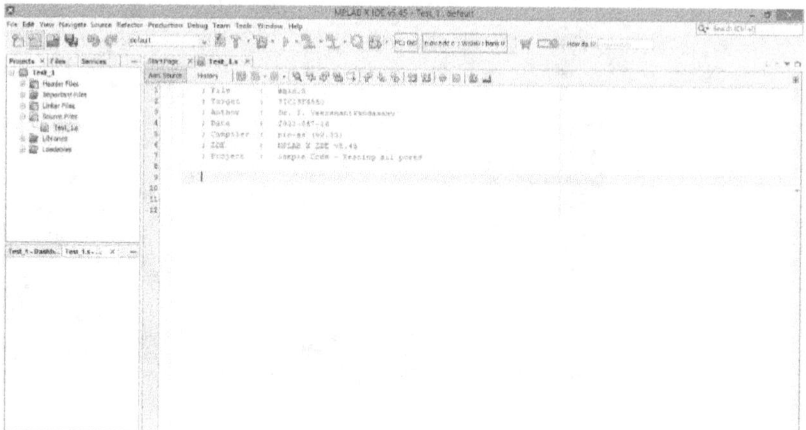

viii. ***Go to Production menu and select "Set Configuration Bits"***

Detail of PIC18F4550 Configuration Bits

Oscillator Selection bits

OSC = LP LP oscillator
OSC = XT XT oscillator
OSC = HS HS oscillator
OSC = RC RC oscillator
OSC = EC EC oscillator w/ OSC2 configured as divide-by-4 clock output
OSC = ECIO EC oscillator w/ OSC2 configured as RA6
OSC = HSPLL HS oscillator with PLL enabled/Clock frequency = (4 x FOSC)
OSC = RCIO RC oscillator w/ OSC2 configured as RA6

Oscillator System Clock Switch Enable bit

OSCS = ON Oscillator switching is enabled
OSCS = OFF Main oscillator is source

Power-up Timer Enable bit

PWRT = ON PWRT enabled
PWRT = OFF PWRT disabled

Brown-out Reset Enable bit

BOR = OFF   Brown-out Reset disabled
BOR = ON   Brown-out Reset enabled

Brown-out Reset Voltage bits

BORV = 45   VBOR set to 4.5V
BORV = 42   VBOR set to 4.2V
BORV = 27   VBOR set to 2.7V
BORV = 25   VBOR set to 2.5V

Watchdog Timer Enable bit

WDT = OFF   WDT disabled
WDT = ON   WDT enabled

Watchdog Timer Post-Scaler Select bits

WDTPS = 1   1:1
WDTPS = 2   1:2
WDTPS = 4   1:4
WDTPS = 8   1:8
WDTPS = 16   1:16
WDTPS = 32   1:32
WDTPS = 64   1:64
WDTPS = 128   1:128

Stack Full/Underflow Reset Enable bit

STVR = OFF   Stack Full/Underflow will not cause Reset
STVR = ON   Stack Full/Underflow will cause Reset

Low-Voltage ICSP Enable bit

LVP = OFF   Low-Voltage ICSP disabled
LVP = ON   Low-Voltage ICSP enabled

Background Debugger Enable bit

DEBUG = ON Background Debugger enabled. RB6 and RB7 are dedicated to In-Circuit Debug.
DEBUG = OFF Background Debugger disabled. RB6 and RB7 are GPIOs.

Code Protection bit

CP0 = ON   Block 0 (000200-001FFFh) code protected
CP0 = OFF   Block 0 (000200-001FFFh) not code protected

Code Protection bit

CP1 = ON   Block 1 (002000-003FFFh) code protected
CP1 = OFF   Block 1 (002000-003FFFh) not code protected

Code Protection bit

CP2 = ON	Block 2 (004000-005FFFh) code protected
CP2 = OFF	Block 2 (004000-005FFFh) not code protected

Code Protection bit

CP3 = ON	Block 3 (006000-007FFFh) code protected
CP3 = OFF	Block 3 (006000-007FFFh) not code protected

Boot Block Code Protection bit

CPB = ON	Boot Block (000000-0001FFh) code protected
CPB = OFF	Boot Block (000000-0001FFh) not code protected

Data EEPROM Code Protection bit

CPD = ON	Data EEPROM code protected
CPD = OFF	Data EEPROM not code protected

Write Protection bit

WRT0 = ON	Block 0 (000200-001FFFh) write protected
WRT0 = OFF	Block 0 (000200-001FFFh) not write protected

Write Protection bit

WRT1 = ON	Block 1 (002000-003FFFh) write protected
WRT1 = OFF	Block 1 (002000-003FFFh) not write protected

Write Protection bit

WRT2 = ON	Block 2 (004000-005FFFh) write protected
WRT2 = OFF	Block 2 (004000-005FFFh) not write protected

Write Protection bit

WRT3 = ON	Block 3 (006000-007FFFh) write protected
WRT3 = OFF	Block 3 (006000-007FFFh) not write protected

Configuration Register Write Protection bit

WRTC = ON	Configuration registers (300000-3000FFh) write protected
WRTC = OFF	Configuration registers (300000-3000FFh) not write protected

Boot Block Write Protection bit

WRTB = ON	Boot Block (000000-0001FFh) write protected
WRTB = OFF	Boot Block (000000-0001FFh) not write protected

Data EEPROM Write Protection bit

WRTD = ON	Data EEPROM write protected
WRTD = OFF	Data EEPROM not write protected

Table Read Protection bit

EBTR0 = ON Block 0 (000200-001FFFh) protected from Table Reads executed in other blocks

EBTR0 = OFF Block 0 (000200-001FFFh) not protected from Table Reads executed in other blocks

Table Read Protection bit

EBTR1 = ON Block 1 (002000-003FFFh) protected from Table Reads executed in other blocks

EBTR1 = OFF Block 1 (002000-003FFFh) not protected from Table Reads executed in other blocks

Table Read Protection bit

EBTR2 = ON Block 2 (004000-005FFFh) protected from Table Reads executed in other blocks

EBTR2 = OFF Block 2 (004000-005FFFh) not protected from Table Reads executed in other blocks

Table Read Protection bit

EBTR3 = ON Block 3 (006000-007FFFh) protected from Table Reads executed in other blocks

EBTR3 = OFF Block 3 (006000-007FFFh) not protected from Table Reads executed in other blocks

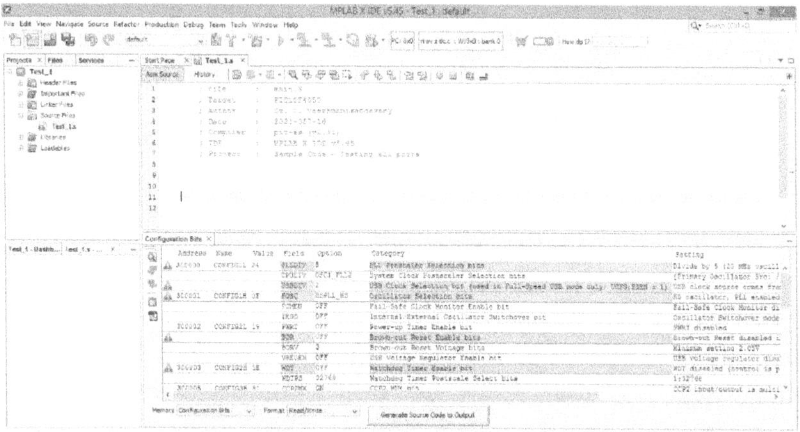

Click on Generate Source Code to output.

Copy the codes and paste it in .s editor file.

Boot Block Table Read Protection bit

EBTRB = ON Boot Block (000000-0001FFh) protected from Table Reads executed in other blocks

EBTRB = OFF Boot Block (000000-0001FFh) not protected from Table Reads executed in other blocks

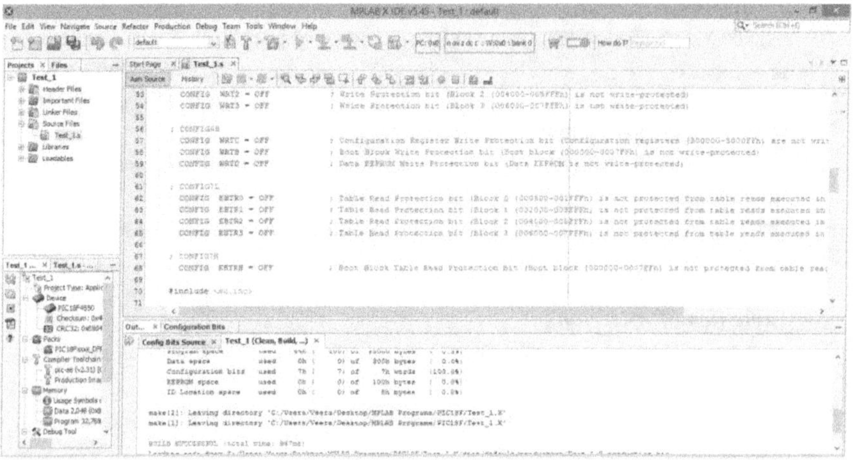

Right click on Project Name (Test_1) --> Set Configuration --> Customize
Select pic-as Assembler under Categories --> Additional options
Copy the below line and paste it in the **additional options** box,
-Wa,-a -Wl,-presetVec=0h,-phi_int_vec=08h,-plo_int_vec=18h -Wl,-Map=main.map
Click on Apply and OK.

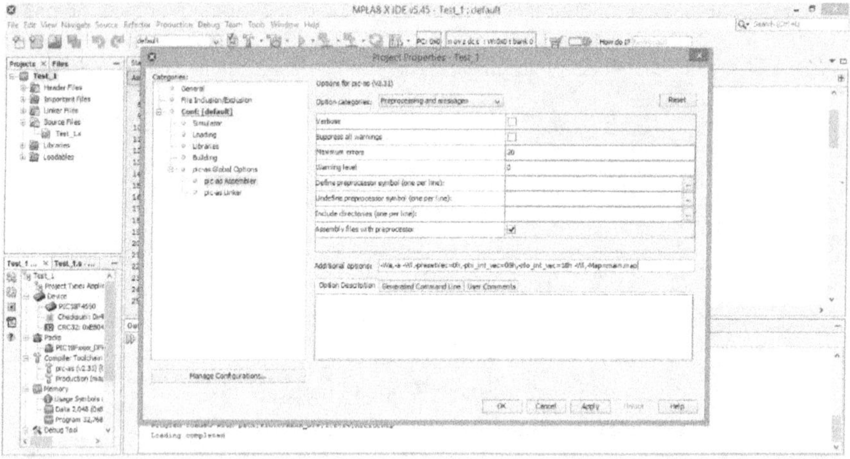

ix. *Create your program in editor after the config lines.*

(a) Assemble Language Program - Sample Code Example

```
; File            :  sample.s
; Target          :  PIC18F4550
; Author          :  Dr. T. Veeramanikandasamy
; Date            :  2021-08-16
; IDE             :  MPLAB X IDE v5.45
; PIC Assembler        :  pic-as (v2.31)
; Project         :  Sample Code to test all GPIO ports

; PIC18 Configuration Bits Setting
config PLLDIV = 5, CPUDIV = OSC1_PLL2, USBDIV = 2, FOSC =
HS
config FCMEN = OFF, IESO = OFF, PWRT = OFF, BOR = OFF,
BORV = 3, VREGEN = OFF
config WDT = OFF, WDTPS = 32768, CCP2MX = ON, PBADEN =
OFF, LPT1OSC = OFF
config MCLRE = ON, STVREN = ON, LVP = OFF, XINST = OFF
config CP0 = OFF, CP1 = OFF, CP2 = OFF, CP3 = OFF, CPB =
OFF, CPD = OFF
config WRT0 = OFF, WRT1 = OFF, WRT2 = OFF, WRT3 = OFF,
WRTC = OFF, WRTB = OFF, WRTD = OFF
config EBTR0 = OFF, EBTR1 = OFF, EBTR2 = OFF, EBTR3 = OFF,
EBTRB = OFF
#include <xc.inc>

PROCESSOR  18F4550
pagewidth  132
radix      dec

; Reset Vector of Processor 18F4550
psect  resetVec, global, reloc=2, class=CODE, delta=1
resetVec:
   goto   main
```

```
; High Priority Vector is at 000008h
psect  hi_int_vec, global, reloc=2, class=CODE, delta=1
goto   HighISR
psect  HighIsr_code, global, reloc=2, class=CODE, delta=1
HighISR:
   return 0

; Low Priority Vector is at 000018h
psect  lo_int_vec, global, reloc=2, class=CODE, delta=1
goto   LowISR
psect  LowIsr_code, global, reloc=2, class=CODE, delta=1
LowISR:
   return 0

; Main Program
psect  main, global, reloc=2, class=CODE, delta=1
org 0x100
main:
         C1 equ 0x20
         C2 equ 0x21
         C3 equ 0x22
         bcf GIE                  ; Disable Global Interrupts
         movlw   0x0F             ; Setting Port A as GPIO
         movwf   ADCON1, c        ; Move WREG to ADCON1
         banksel TRISA            ; Select bank for TRIS A.
         movlw 0x00               ; Setting all ports as output
         movwf TRISA, c           ; by writing '0' to the respective
         movwf TRISB, c           ; TRIS registers.
         movwf TRISC, c
         movwf TRISD, c
         banksel PORTA            ; Select bank for PORT A
   again:
         movlw 0xff               ; Writing '1' to all ports
```

```
        movwf PORTA, c
        movwf PORTB, c
        movwf PORTC, c
        movwf PORTD, c
        call delay              ; Generate 1 sec delay
        movlw 0x00              ; Writing '0' to all ports
        movwf PORTA, c
        movwf PORTB, c
        movwf PORTC, c
        movwf PORTD, c
        call delay              ; Generate 1 sec delay
        goto again
delay:                          ; 1 second delay
        movlw 6
        movwf C1, c
        movlw 24
        movwf C2, c
        movlw 167
        movwf C3, c
  loop:
        decfsz C3, f, c
        goto loop
        decfsz C2, f, c
        goto loop
        decfsz C1, f, c
        goto loop
        return
END     resetVec
```

(b) C Program - Sample Code Example

```
// File      :  sample.c
// Target    :  PIC18F4550
// Author    :  Dr. T. Veeramanikandasamy
// Date      :  2021-08-16
```

```
    // IDE         :  MPLAB X IDE v5.45
    // Complier    :  XC8 (v2.31)
    // Project     :  Sample Code to test all GPIO ports
// CONFIG1
#pragma config PLLDIV = 5, CPUDIV = OSC1_PLL2, USBDIV = 2,
FOSC = HS, FCMEN = OFF, IESO = OFF
// CONFIG2
#pragma config PWRT = OFF, BOR = OFF, BORV = 3, VREGEN =
OFF, WDT = OFF, WDTPS = 32768
// CONFIG3H
#pragma config CCP2MX = ON, PBADEN = OFF, LPT1OSC = OFF,
MCLRE = ON
// CONFIG4L
#pragma config STVREN = ON, LVP = OFF, ICPRT = OFF, XINST =
OFF
// CONFIG5
#pragma config CP0 = OFF, CP1 = OFF, CP2 = OFF, CP3 = OFF, CPB
= OFF, CPD = OFF
// CONFIG6
#pragma config WRT0 = OFF, WRT1 = OFF, WRT2 = OFF, WRT3 =
OFF, WRTC = OFF, WRTB = OFF, WRTD = OFF
// CONFIG7
#pragma config EBTR0 = OFF, EBTR1 = OFF, EBTR2 = OFF, EBTR3 =
OFF, EBTRB = OFF
#include <xc.h>

void ms_delay(unsigned int x)        // 1 msec time delay program
    {
    unsigned int i,j;
    for (i=0;i<x;i++)
            {
            for (j=0;j<496;j++);
            }
    }
```

```
void main()
{
ADCON1=0x0F;
TRISA=0x00;
TRISB=0x00;                     // Set PORTB as output PORT
TRISC=0x00;
TRISD=0x00;
TRISE=0x00;

LATA=0x7F;                      // RA7 is not available
LATB=0xFF;                      // Set all 8 PORTB pins
LATC=0xC7;                      // RC3 is Not available and RC4 & RC5
                                are only input ports
LATD=0xFF;                      // Set all 8 PORTD pins
LATE=0x07;                      // only RE0 to RE2 in PORTE (3 PORTS)

 while(1)
 {
     ms_delay(500);             // Delay
                                // Toggle the all ports
     LATA = ~LATA;              // PORT A = 0x7F
     LATB = ~LATB;              // PORT B = 0xFF
     LATC = ~LATC;              // PORT C = 0xC7
     LATD = ~LATD;              // PORT D = 0xFF
     LATE = ~LATE;              // PORT E = 0x07
 }
}
```

x. ***Build Main Project***

Go to Production menu → Build Main Project / Click on Build Project icon 

The result of build process will be available on output window.

like **BUILD SUCCESSFUL**

xi. Simulation

Go to Debug menu → Debug Main Project /

Click on the Debug icon appearing on the Toolbar.

Pause and Reset

To view the output: Go to Window → Debugging →

Variables. Choose the respective registers to see the program output or Choose the SFRs in memory view.

xii. Single Step Execution and verification of variables

Press F7 for single step execution and watch the Variables/SFRs to verify the program sequence.

5. ADDITION OF TWO 8-BIT NUMBERS

Aim:

Write an assembly language program to add two 8-bit numbers using the PIC18F4550 microcontroller, and verify the result using the simulator.

Software Used:

- IDE: MPLAB X IDE v5.45
- PIC Assembler: pic-as (v2.31)

Algorithm:

1. Define the PIC18 configuration bits using the config directive, include xc.inc, set the processor, define the vector for reset and interrupts, and set the starting address for the main program.
2. Initialize the first operand at X1 and the second operand at X2.
3. Set PORTB and PORTD as output ports using the TRIS registers for storing the sum and the carry from the addition.
4. Move the first operand X1 to the 'temp' register via the WREG register.
5. Load the second operand into WREG.
6. Add WREG to the 'temp' register and store the sum in WREG.
7. Move the contents of WREG to LATB.
8. (Simulation result: window->debugging->watches->LATB)
9. Clear WREG.
10. Check the STATUS register for a carry; skip the next step if the carry flag is clear.
11. Increment WREG.
12. Move the contents of WREG to LATD.
13. (Simulation result: window->debugging->watches->LATD)
14. Halt the program.

Program:

```
; PIC18 Configuration Bits Setting
config PLLDIV = 5, CPUDIV = OSC1_PLL2, USBDIV = 2, FOSC = HS
config FCMEN = OFF, IESO = OFF, PWRT = OFF, BOR = OFF, BORV = 3, VREGEN = OFF
```

```
config WDT = OFF, WDTPS = 32768, CCP2MX = ON, PBADEN = OFF, LPT1OSC = OFF
config MCLRE = ON, STVREN = ON, LVP = OFF, XINST = OFF
config CP0 = OFF, CP1 = OFF, CP2 = OFF, CP3 = OFF, CPB = OFF, CPD = OFF
config WRT0 = OFF, WRT1 = OFF, WRT2 = OFF, WRT3 = OFF, WRTC = OFF, WRTB = OFF,
WRTD = OFF
config EBTR0 = OFF, EBTR1 = OFF, EBTR2 = OFF, EBTR3 = OFF, EBTRB = OFF
#include <xc.inc>

PROCESSOR   18F4550
pagewidth   132
radix       dec

; Reset Vector of Processor 18F4550
psect   resetVec, global, reloc=2, class=CODE, delta=1
resetVec:
   goto    main

; High Priority Vector is at 000008h
psect   hi_int_vec, global, reloc=2, class=CODE, delta=1
goto    HighISR
psect   HighIsr_code, global, reloc=2, class=CODE, delta=1
HighISR:
   return 0

; Low Priority Vector is at 000018h
psect   lo_int_vec, global, reloc=2, class=CODE, delta=1
goto    LowISR
psect   LowIsr_code, global, reloc=2, class=CODE, delta=1
LowISR:
   return 0

; Main Program
psect   main, global, reloc=2, class=CODE, delta=1
org 0x100
```

```
main:
    X1 EQU 0x64                 ; X1 = 0x64 (Operand 1)
    X2 EQU 0xB2                 ; X2 = 0xB2 (Operand 2)
    temp EQU 0x20               ; temp = 0x20 (File Register)
    MOVLW       0x00            ; Clear WREG
    MOVWF       TRISB, c        ; Initialize PORTB as output (sum)
    MOVWF       TRISD, c        ; Initialize PORTD as output (carry)
    MOVLW       X1              ; Move data1 (@X1 reg.) to WREG
    MOVWF       temp, c         ; Move WREG to temp reg.
    MOVLW       X2              ; Move data2 (@X2 reg.) to WREG
    ADDWF       temp, W, c      ; Add WREG with temp and move the sum to WREG
    MOVWF       LATB, A         ; Move the sum to LATB
    MOVLW       0x00            ; Clear WREG
    BTFSC       STATUS, 0, c    ; Test the carry at bit 0, skip the next instruction if it is clear
    INCF        WREG, W, c      ; Increment WREG
    MOVWF       LATD, c         ; Move carry to LATD
hlt: GOTO       hlt             ; Halt
    END resetVec
```

Experimental Result:

Input Data		**Output**	
Operands		**File Register**	**Operand**
X1	64 H	LATB	16 H (sum)
X2	B2 H	LATD	01 H (carry)

Calculation:

I/O	**in HEX**		**in Binary**		
Operand 1	64 H			**0110**	**0100**
Operand 2	B2 H			**1011**	**0010**
Result (carry & sum)	1 16 H		**1**	**0001**	**0110**

Conclusion:

The experiment demonstrating the addition of two 8-bit numbers using a PIC18F4550 microcontroller has been successfully carried out.

6. SUBTRACTION OF TWO 8-BIT NUMBERS

Aim:

Write an assembly language program to subtract two 8-bit numbers using the PIC18F4550 microcontroller and verify the result using the simulator.

Software Used:

- IDE: MPLAB X IDE v5.45
- PIC Assembler: pic-as (v2.31)

Algorithm:

1. Define the PIC18 configuration bits using the config directive, include xc.inc, set the processor, configure the reset and interrupt vectors, and establish the starting address for the main program.
2. Initialize the first operand as X1 and the second operand as X2.
3. Set PORTB and PORTD as output ports using the TRIS registers to display the difference and borrow from the subtraction result.
4. Move the first operand, X1, into the 'temp' register via WREG.
5. Load the second operand into WREG.
6. Subtract WREG from the 'temp' register and store the result in WREG.
7. Transfer the contents of WREG to LATB.
8. (Simulation result: window->debugging->watches->LATB)
9. Clear WREG.
10. Check the STATUS register for a carry; skip the next step if the carry flag is not set.
11. Increment WREG.
12. Transfer the contents of WREG to LATD.
13. (Simulation result: window->debugging->watches->LATD)
14. Halt the program.

Program:

```
; PIC18 Configuration Bits Setting
config PLLDIV = 5, CPUDIV = OSC1_PLL2, USBDIV = 2, FOSC = HS
config FCMEN = OFF, IESO = OFF, PWRT = OFF, BOR = OFF, BORV = 3, VREGEN = OFF
```

```
config WDT = OFF, WDTPS = 32768, CCP2MX = ON, PBADEN = OFF, LPT1OSC = OFF
config MCLRE = ON, STVREN = ON, LVP = OFF, XINST = OFF
config CP0 = OFF, CP1 = OFF, CP2 = OFF, CP3 = OFF, CPB = OFF, CPD = OFF
config WRT0 = OFF, WRT1 = OFF, WRT2 = OFF, WRT3 = OFF, WRTC = OFF, WRTB = OFF,
WRTD = OFF
config EBTR0 = OFF, EBTR1 = OFF, EBTR2 = OFF, EBTR3 = OFF, EBTRB = OFF
#include <xc.inc>

PROCESSOR  18F4550
pagewidth  132
radix      dec

; Reset Vector of Processor 18F4550
psect  resetVec, global, reloc=2, class=CODE, delta=1
resetVec:
   goto  main
; High Priority Vector is at 000008h
psect  hi_int_vec, global, reloc=2, class=CODE, delta=1
goto  HighISR
psect  HighIsr_code, global, reloc=2, class=CODE, delta=1
HighISR:
   return 0
; Low Priority Vector is at 000018h
psect  lo_int_vec, global, reloc=2, class=CODE, delta=1
goto  LowISR
psect  LowIsr_code, global, reloc=2, class=CODE, delta=1
LowISR:
   return 0

; Main Program
psect  main, global, reloc=2, class=CODE, delta=1
org 0x100
main:
   X1 EQU 0x42                ; X1 = 0x42 (Operand 1)
   X2 EQU 0x86                ; X2 = 0x86 (Operand 2)
```

```
temp EQU 0x20              ; temp = 0x20 (File register)
MOVLW      0x00            ; Clear WREG
MOVWF      TRISB, c        ; Initialize PORTB as output (Difference)
MOVWF      TRISD, c        ; Initialize PORTD as output (Borrow)
MOVLW      X1              ; Move data1 (@X1 reg.) to WREG
MOVWF      temp, c         ; Move WREG to temp reg.
MOVLW      X2              ; Move data2 (@X2 reg.) to WREG
SUBWF      temp, W, c      ; Subtract WREG from temp and move the
                           ; difference to WREG
MOVWF      LATB, c         ; Move the difference (WREG) to LATB
MOVLW      0x00            ; Move 0x00 to WREG
BTFSS      STATUS, 0, c    ; Test the carry at bit 0, skip the next
                           ; instruction if it is set
INCF       WREG, W, c      ; Increment WREG
MOVWF      LATD, c         ; Move borrow to LATD
hlt: GOTO  hlt             ; Halt
END resetVec
```

Experimental Result:

Input Data		Output	
Operands		File register	Operand
X1	42 H	LATB	BC H (Difference)
X2	86 H	LATD	01 H (Borrow)

Calculation:

I/O	in HEX		in Binary		
Operand 1	42 H			**0100**	**0010**
Operand 2	86 H			**1000**	**0110**
Result (Brw & Diff)	1 BC H		**1**	**1011**	**1100**

Conclusion:

The experiment demonstrating the subtraction of two 8-bit numbers using the PIC18F4550 microcontroller has been successfully completed.

7. ADDITION OF 'N' 8-BIT NUMBERS IN AN ARRAY

Aim:

Write an assembly language program to add N 8-bit numbers from an array using the PIC18F4550 microcontroller and verify the result with the simulator.

Software Used:

- IDE: MPLAB X IDE v5.45
- PIC Assembler: pic-as (v2.31)

Algorithm:

1. Define the PIC18 configuration bits using the config directive, include xc.inc, configure the processor, set the vectors for reset and interrupts, and specify the starting address for the main program.
2. Clear the Output and Carry registers.
3. Initialize the memory location for input data in FSR, setting FSR to point to address 30H.
4. Load the number of array elements into the Count register.
5. Clear WREG, which will be used to hold the sum of the addition.
6. Increment FSR.
7. Add the value in WREG to the content pointed to by FSR and store the result in WREG.
8. Check the STATUS register for a carry; skip the next step if the carry flag is not set.
9. Increment the Carry register.
10. Decrement the Count register; skip the next step if the Count register is zero.
11. Return to step 6.
12. Move the value in WREG (the sum) to LATB.
13. Move the value in the Carry register to LATD.
14. Halt the program.

Program:

```
; PIC18 Configuration Bits Setting
config PLLDIV = 5, CPUDIV = OSC1_PLL2, USBDIV = 2, FOSC = HS
config FCMEN = OFF, IESO = OFF, PWRT = OFF, BOR = OFF, BORV = 3, VREGEN = OFF
config WDT = OFF, WDTPS = 32768, CCP2MX = ON, PBADEN = OFF, LPT1OSC = OFF
config MCLRE = ON, STVREN = ON, LVP = OFF, XINST = OFF
config CP0 = OFF, CP1 = OFF, CP2 = OFF, CP3 = OFF, CPB = OFF, CPD = OFF
config WRT0 = OFF, WRT1 = OFF, WRT2 = OFF, WRT3 = OFF, WRTC = OFF, WRTB = OFF,
WRTD = OFF
config EBTR0 = OFF, EBTR1 = OFF, EBTR2 = OFF, EBTR3 = OFF, EBTRB = OFF
#include <xc.inc>

PROCESSOR   18F4550
pagewidth   132
radix       dec

; Reset Vector of Processor 18F4550
psect   resetVec, global, reloc=2, class=CODE, delta=1
resetVec:
   goto    main

; High Priority Vector is at 000008h
psect   hi_int_vec, global, reloc=2, class=CODE, delta=1
goto    HighISR
psect   HighIsr_code, global, reloc=2, class=CODE, delta=1
HighISR:
   return 0

; Low Priority Vector is at 000018h
psect   lo_int_vec, global, reloc=2, class=CODE, delta=1
goto    LowISR
psect   LowIsr_code, global, reloc=2, class=CODE, delta=1
LowISR:
   return 0
```

```
; Main Program
psect  main, global, reloc=2, class=CODE, delta=1
org 0x100
main:
  IP equ 0x30                    ; Address of operands (0x30 holds Array
                                 ; count, followed by array elements)
  Carry equ 0x40                 ; Temp registers for carry & count
  Count equ 0x41

  CLRF     TRISB, c              ; Initialize PORTB as output
  CLRF     TRISD, c              ; Initialize PORTD as output
  CLRF     Carry, c              ; Clear Carry register
  MOVLW    IP                    ; 1st address of input data to FSR0
  MOVWF    FSR0, c
  MOVF     IP, W, c              ; Move array count to WREG
  MOVWF    Count, c              ; Move count value to Count register
  MOVLW    0x00                  ; Clear WREG
 Again:
  INCF     FSR0, F, c            ; Increment the data pointer
  ADDWF    INDF0, W, c           ; Add WREG with the value of data pointer
                                 ; and hold the sum in WREG
  BTFSC    STATUS, 0, c          ; Check the carry, skip the next
                                 ; instruction if it is clear
  INCF     Carry, F, c           ; Increment carry register
  DECFSZ   Count, F, c           ; Decrement Count register, skip the next
                                 ; instruction if it is zero
  GOTO     Again
  MOVWF    LATB, c               ; Move the sum to PORTB
  MOVF     Carry, W, c           ; Move the carry to PORTD
  MOVWF    LATD, c
  hlt: GOTO  hlt                 ; Halt
  END resetVec
```

Experimental Result:

Input Data		Output	
File Register	**Operand**	**File Register**	**Operand**
30	04 H*	LATB	03 H (sum)
31	16 H	LATD	01 H (carry)
32	42 H		
33	73 H		
34	38 H		

* *Number of array elements*

Calculation:

I/O	in HEX
Count	04 H
Operand 1	16 H
Operand 2	42 H
Operand 3	73 H
Operand 4	38 H
Result	103 H

Conclusion:

The experiment demonstrating the addition of 'N' 8-bit numbers in an array using the PIC18F4550 microcontroller has been successfully completed.

8. ADDITION OF TWO 16-BIT NUMBERS

Aim:

Write an assembly language program to add two 16-bit binary numbers using the PIC18F4550 microcontroller and verify the result with the simulator.

Software Used:

- IDE: MPLAB X IDE v5.45
- PIC Assembler: pic-as (v2.31)

Algorithm:

1. Define the PIC18 configuration bits using the config directive, include xc.inc, configure the processor, set the vectors for reset and interrupts, and specify the starting address for the main program.
2. Load the first operand (X1 and X2) and the second operand (Y1 and Y2), and configure PORTB, PORTD, and PORTC as output ports.
3. Clear the Carry register.
4. Move the least significant byte (LSB) of the first operand (X1) into WREG.
5. Add the LSB of the second operand (Y1) to WREG and store the result in WREG.
6. Transfer the value in WREG to LATB.
7. Check the Carry flag in the STATUS register; skip the next step if the Carry flag is not set.
8. Increment the most significant byte (MSB) of the first operand (X2).
9. Move the MSB of the first operand (X2) into WREG.
10. Add the MSB of the second operand (Y2) to WREG and store the result in WREG.
11. Transfer the value in WREG to LATD.
12. Check the Carry flag in the STATUS register; skip the next step if the Carry flag is not set.
13. Increment the Carry register.
14. Transfer the value of the Carry register to LATC.
15. Halt the program.

Program:

```
; PIC18 Configuration Bits Setting
config PLLDIV = 5, CPUDIV = OSC1_PLL2, USBDIV = 2, FOSC = HS
config FCMEN = OFF, IESO = OFF, PWRT = OFF, BOR = OFF, BORV = 3, VREGEN = OFF
config WDT = OFF, WDTPS = 32768, CCP2MX = ON, PBADEN = OFF, LPT1OSC = OFF
config MCLRE = ON, STVREN = ON, LVP = OFF, XINST = OFF
```

```
config CP0 = OFF, CP1 = OFF, CP2 = OFF, CP3 = OFF, CPB = OFF, CPD = OFF
config WRT0 = OFF, WRT1 = OFF, WRT2 = OFF, WRT3 = OFF, WRTC = OFF, WRTB = OFF,
WRTD = OFF
config EBTR0 = OFF, EBTR1 = OFF, EBTR2 = OFF, EBTR3 = OFF, EBTRB = OFF
#include <xc.inc>
PROCESSOR  18F4550
pagewidth  132
radix      dec

; Reset Vector of Processor 18F4550
psect  resetVec, global, reloc=2, class=CODE, delta=1
resetVec:
   goto   main

; High Priority Vector is at 000008h
psect  hi_int_vec, global, reloc=2, class=CODE, delta=1
goto   HighISR
psect  HighIsr_code, global, reloc=2, class=CODE, delta=1
HighISR:
   return 0

; Low Priority Vector is at 000018h
psect  lo_int_vec, global, reloc=2, class=CODE, delta=1
goto   LowISR
psect  LowIsr_code, global, reloc=2, class=CODE, delta=1
LowISR:
   return 0

; Main Program
psect  main, global, reloc=2, class=CODE, delta=1
org 0x100
main:
   X1    equ    0xA3          ; Operand 1 – X1 (LSB) & X2 (MSB)
   X2    equ    0x81
   Y1    equ    0x61          ; Operand 2 – Y1 (LSB) & Y2 (MSB)
```

```
Y2      equ     0x92
Carry equu      0x30            ; temp register for Carry
temp equ        0x31
CLRF            TRISB, c        ; Initialize PORTB as output
CLRF            TRISD, c        ; Initialize PORTD as output
CLRF            TRISC, c        ; Initialize PORTD as output

CLRF            Carry, c        ; Clear Carry register
MOVLW           X1              ; Move LSB of operand 1 to temp
MOVWF           temp, c
MOVLW           Y1              ; Move LSB of operand 2 to WREG
ADDWF           temp, W, c      ; Add WREG with temp
                                ; and hold the sum in WREG
MOVWF           LATB, c         ; Move the LSBs of result to LATB
MOVLW           X2              ; Move the MSB of operand 1 to temp
MOVWF           temp, c
BTFSC           STATUS, 0, c    ; Check the carry, skip the next
                                ; instruction if the carry is clear
INCF            temp, F, c      ; Increment temp
MOVLW           Y2              ; Move MSB of operand 2 to WREG
ADDWF           temp, W, c      ; Add the WREG with temp
                                ; and hold the sum in WREG
MOVWF           LATD, c         ; Move the WREG to LATD
BTFSC           STATUS, 0, c    ; Check the carry, skip the next
                                ; instruction if the carry is clear
INCF Carry, c                   ; Increment Carry register
MOVF            Carry, W, c     ; Move the carry to LATC
MOVWF           LATC, c
 hlt:
 GOTO           hlt             ; Halt
 END resetVec
```

Experimental Result:

Input Data		Output	
Operands		File Register	Operand
X1	A3 H (LSB)	LATB	DF H (LSB)
X2	81 H (MSB)	LATD	13 H (MSB)
Y1	3C H (LSB)	LATC	01 H (carry)
Y2	92 H (MSB)		

Calculation:

I/O	in HEX		in Binary				
Operand 1	81A3 H			**1000**	**0001**	**1010**	**0011**
Operand 2	923C H			**1001**	**0010**	**0011**	**1100**
Result (C & S)	113DF H		**1**	**0001**	**0011**	**1101**	**1111**

Conclusion:

The experiment demonstrating the addition of two 16-bit numbers using the PIC18F4550 microcontroller has been successfully completed.

9. SUBTRACTION OF TWO 16-BIT NUMBERS

Aim:

Write an assembly language program to subtract two 16-bit binary numbers using the PIC18F4550 microcontroller and verify the result with the simulator.

Software Used:

- IDE: MPLAB X IDE v5.45
- PIC Assembler: pic-as (v2.31)

Algorithm:

1. Define the PIC18 configuration bits using the config directive, include xc.inc, configure the processor, set the vectors for reset and interrupts,

and specify the starting address for the main program.

2. Load the first operand (X1 and X2) and the second operand (Y1 and Y2), and configure PORTB, PORTD, and PORTC as output ports.
3. Clear the borrow registers (B1 and B2).
4. Move the least significant byte (LSB) of the second operand (Y1) into WREG.
5. Subtract the value in WREG from the LSB of the first operand (X1) and store the result in WREG.
6. Transfer the value in WREG to LATB.
7. Check the Carry flag in the STATUS register; skip the next step if the Carry flag is set.
8. Increment the first borrow register (B1).
9. Move the most significant byte (MSB) of the second operand (Y2) into WREG.
10. Subtract the value in WREG from the MSB of the first operand (X2) and store the result in WREG.
11. Transfer the value in WREG to the Temp register.
12. Move the value of the second borrow register into WREG.
13. Subtract the value in WREG from the Temp register and store the result in WREG.
14. Transfer the value in WREG to LATD.
15. Check the Carry flag in the STATUS register; skip the next step if the Carry flag is set.
16. Increment the second borrow register.
17. Move the value of the second borrow register into WREG.
18. Transfer the value in WREG to LATC.
19. Halt the program.

Program:

```
; PIC18 Configuration Bits Setting
config PLLDIV = 5, CPUDIV = OSC1_PLL2, USBDIV = 2, FOSC = HS
config FCMEN = OFF, IESO = OFF, PWRT = OFF, BOR = OFF, BORV = 3, VREGEN = OFF
config WDT = OFF, WDTPS = 32768, CCP2MX = ON, PBADEN = OFF, LPT1OSC = OFF
config MCLRE = ON, STVREN = ON, LVP = OFF, XINST = OFF
config CP0 = OFF, CP1 = OFF, CP2 = OFF, CP3 = OFF, CPB = OFF, CPD = OFF
```

```
config WRT0 = OFF, WRT1 = OFF, WRT2 = OFF, WRT3 = OFF, WRTC = OFF, WRTB = OFF,
WRTD = OFF
config EBTR0 = OFF, EBTR1 = OFF, EBTR2 = OFF, EBTR3 = OFF, EBTRB = OFF
#include <xc.inc>

PROCESSOR  18F4550
pagewidth  132
radix      dec

; Reset Vector of Processor 18F4550
psect  resetVec, global, reloc=2, class=CODE, delta=1
resetVec:
   goto   main

; High Priority Vector is at 000008h
psect  hi_int_vec, global, reloc=2, class=CODE, delta=1
goto   HighISR
psect  HighIsr_code, global, reloc=2, class=CODE, delta=1
HighISR:
   return 0

; Low Priority Vector is at 000018h
psect  lo_int_vec, global, reloc=2, class=CODE, delta=1
goto   LowISR
psect  LowIsr_code, global, reloc=2, class=CODE, delta=1
LowISR:
   return 0

; Main Program
psect  main, global, reloc=2, class=CODE, delta=1
org 0x100
main:
   X1 equ 0xA5                  ; Operand 1 – X1 (LSB) & X2 (MSB)
   X2 equ 0x87
   Y1 equ 0x32                  ; Operand 1 – Y1 (LSB) & Y2 (MSB)
```

```
Y2 equ 0x63
B1 equ 0x30                      ; temp registers for borrow 1 and borrow 2
B2 equ 0x31
temp equ 0x32
CLRF      TRISB, c               ; Initialize PORTB as output
CLRF      TRISD, c               ; Initialize PORTD as output
CLRF      TRISC, c               ; Initialize PORTD as output
CLRF      B1, c                  ; Clear borrow 1 register
CLRF      B2, c                  ; Clear borrow 2 register
MOVLW     X1                     ; Move X1 to WREG
MOVWF     temp, c                ; Move WREG to temp
MOVLW     Y1                     ; Move Y1 to WREG
SUBWF     temp, W, c             ; Subtract WREG from temp
                                 ; and hold the Diff. in WREG
MOVWF     LATB, c                ; Move the LSB (8-bits) of result to LATB
BTFSS     STATUS, 0, c           ; Check the carry, skip the next
                                 ; instruction if the carry is set
INCF      B1, F, c               ; Increment borrow register 1
MOVLW     X2                     ; Move X2 to WREG
MOVWF     temp, c                ; Move WREG to temp
MOVLW     Y2                     ; Move Y2 to WREG
SUBWF     temp, F, c             ; Subtract WREG from temp
                                 ; and hold the Diff. in temp
BTFSS     STATUS, 0, c           ; Check the carry, skip the next
                                 ; instruction if the carry is set
INCF      B2, c                  ; Increment borrow register 2
MOVF      B1, W, c               ; Move borrow 1 value to WREG
SUBWF     temp, W, c             ; Subtract WREG from temp
MOVWF     LATD, c                ; Move the MSB (8-bits) of result to LATD
MOVF      B2, W, c               ; Move the borrow to PORTC
```

```
MOVWF      LATC, c
hlt: GOTO  hlt          ; Halt
END resetVec
```

Experimental Result:

Input Data		Output	
Operands		File Register	Operand
X1	A5 H (LSB)	LATB	73 H (LSB)
X2	87 H (MSB)	LATD	24 H (MSB)
Y1	32 H (LSB)	LATC	00 H
Y2	63 H (MSB)		

Calculation:

I/O	in HEX		in Binary			
Minuend	87A5 H		1000	0111	1010	0101
Subtrahend	6332 H		0110	0011	0011	0010
Result(Difference)	2473 H		0010	0100	0111	0011

Conclusion:

The experiment demonstrating the subtraction of two 16-bit numbers using the PIC18F4550 microcontroller has been successfully completed.

10. MULTIPLICATION OF TWO 8-BIT NUMBERS

Aim:

Write an assembly language program to multiply two 8-bit binary numbers using the PIC18F4550 microcontroller and verify the result with the simulator.

Software Used:

- IDE: MPLAB X IDE v5.45
- PIC Assembler: pic-as (v2.31)

Algorithm:

1. Define the PIC18 configuration bits using the config directive, include xc.inc, configure the processor, set the vectors for reset and interrupts, and specify the starting address for the main program.
2. Initialize the Multiplicand and Multiplier variables with any values and configure PORTB and PORTD as output ports.
3. Clear the Carry register.
4. Move the Multiplicand to Temp register 1.
5. Move the Multiplier to Temp register 2.
6. Clear WREG.
7. Add the value in Temp register 1 to WREG and store the result in WREG.
8. Check the STATUS register for a carry; skip the next step if the carry flag is not set.
9. Increment the Carry register.
10. Decrement Temp register 2; skip the next step if it is zero.
11. Return to step 7.
12. Move the value in WREG (Least Significant Byte of the product) to LATB.
13. Move the value in the Carry register (Most Significant Byte of the product) to LATD.
14. Halt the program.

Program:

```
; PIC18 Configuration Bits Setting
config PLLDIV = 5, CPUDIV = OSC1_PLL2, USBDIV = 2, FOSC = HS
config FCMEN = OFF, IESO = OFF, PWRT = OFF, BOR = OFF, BORV = 3, VREGEN = OFF
config WDT = OFF, WDTPS = 32768, CCP2MX = ON, PBADEN = OFF, LPT1OSC = OFF
config MCLRE = ON, STVREN = ON, LVP = OFF, XINST = OFF
config CP0 = OFF, CP1 = OFF, CP2 = OFF, CP3 = OFF, CPB = OFF, CPD = OFF
config WRT0 = OFF, WRT1 = OFF, WRT2 = OFF, WRT3 = OFF, WRTC = OFF, WRTB = OFF,
WRTD = OFF
config EBTR0 = OFF, EBTR1 = OFF, EBTR2 = OFF, EBTR3 = OFF, EBTRB = OFF
#include <xc.inc>
```

```
PROCESSOR   18F4550
pagewidth   132
radix       dec

; Reset Vector of Processor 18F4550
psect   resetVec, global, reloc=2, class=CODE, delta=1
resetVec:
   goto    main

; High Priority Vector is at 000008h
psect   hi_int_vec, global, reloc=2, class=CODE, delta=1
goto    HighISR
psect   HighIsr_code, global, reloc=2, class=CODE, delta=1
HighISR:
   return 0

; Low Priority Vector is at 000018h
psect   lo_int_vec, global, reloc=2, class=CODE, delta=1
goto    LowISR
psect   LowIsr_code, global, reloc=2, class=CODE, delta=1
LowISR:
   return 0

; Main Program
psect   main, global, reloc=2, class=CODE, delta=1
org 0x100
main:
Multiplicand    equ 0x06        ; Operands
Multiplier      equ 0x04

Carry           equ 0x40        ; temp registers
temp1           equ 0x41
temp2           equ 0x42
```

```
    CLRF      TRISB, c          ; Initialize PORTB as output
    CLRF      TRISD, c          ; Initialize PORTD as output
    CLRF      Carry, c          ; Clear Carry register
    MOVLW     Multiplicand      ; Move Multiplicand to temp1
    MOVWF     temp1, c
    MOVLW     Multiplier        ; Move Multiplier to temp2
    MOVWF     temp2, c
    MOVLW     0x00              ; Clear WREG
Again:
    ADDWF     temp1, W, c       ; Add WREG with temp1 and store
                                ; the sum in WREG
    BTFSC     STATUS, 0, c      ; Check the carry, skip the next
                                ; instruction if it is clear
    INCF      Carry, F, c       ; Increment carry register
    DECFSZ    temp2, F, c       ; Decrement temp2 value; skip
                                ; the next instruction if it is zero
    GOTO      Again             ; Go to Again
    MOVWF     LATB, c           ; Move the Product-LSB to LATB
    MOVF      Carry, W, c       ; Move the Product-MSB to LATD
    MOVWF     LATD, c
    hlt: GOTO hlt               ; Halt
    END resetVec
```

Experimental Result:

Input Data		Output	
Operands		**File Register**	**Operand**
Multiplicand	06 H	LATB	18 H (Product-LSB)
Multiplier	04 H	LATD	00 H (Product-MSB)

Calculation:

I/O	in HEX
Multiplicand	06 H
Multiplier	04 H
Product	Multiplicand x Multiplier = 06H x 04H

Product (LSB)	18 H
Product (MSB)	00 H

Conclusion:

The experiment demonstrating the multiplication of two 8-bit numbers using the PIC18F4550 microcontroller has been successfully completed.

11. DIVISION OF TWO 8-BIT NUMBERS

Aim:

Write an assembly language program to divide two 8-bit binary numbers using the PIC18F4550 microcontroller and verify the result with the simulator.

Software Used:

- IDE: MPLAB X IDE v5.45
- PIC Assembler: pic-as (v2.31)

Algorithm:

1. Define the PIC18 configuration bits using the config directive, include xc.inc, configure the processor, set the vectors for reset and interrupts, and specify the starting address for the main program.
2. Assign values to the Dividend and Divisor variables, and configure PORTB and PORTD as output ports.
3. Clear the Quotient register.
4. Move the Dividend to the Temp register.
5. Load the Divisor into WREG.
6. Increment the Quotient register.
7. Subtract the value in WREG from the Temp register and store the result back in the Temp register.
8. Check the STATUS register for the negative flag; skip the next step if it is set.
9. Return to step 6.

10. Decrement the Quotient register.
11. Add the value in WREG to the Temp register and store the result in WREG.
12. Move the value in WREG (the Remainder) to LATD.
13. Move the Quotient value to LATB.
14. Halt the program.

Program:

```
; PIC18 Configuration Bits Setting
config PLLDIV = 5, CPUDIV = OSC1_PLL2, USBDIV = 2, FOSC = HS
config FCMEN = OFF, IESO = OFF, PWRT = OFF, BOR = OFF, BORV = 3, VREGEN = OFF
config WDT = OFF, WDTPS = 32768, CCP2MX = ON, PBADEN = OFF, LPT1OSC = OFF
config MCLRE = ON, STVREN = ON, LVP = OFF, XINST = OFF
config CP0 = OFF, CP1 = OFF, CP2 = OFF, CP3 = OFF, CPB = OFF, CPD = OFF
config WRT0 = OFF, WRT1 = OFF, WRT2 = OFF, WRT3 = OFF, WRTC = OFF, WRTB = OFF,
WRTD = OFF
config EBTR0 = OFF, EBTR1 = OFF, EBTR2 = OFF, EBTR3 = OFF, EBTRB = OFF
#include <xc.inc>

PROCESSOR  18F4550
pagewidth  132
radix      dec

; Reset Vector of Processor 18F4550
psect  resetVec, global, reloc=2, class=CODE, delta=1
resetVec:
   goto   main

; High Priority Vector is at 000008h
psect  hi_int_vec, global, reloc=2, class=CODE, delta=1
goto   HighISR
psect  HighIsr_code, global, reloc=2, class=CODE, delta=1
HighISR:
   return 0

; Low Priority Vector is at 000018h
```

```
psect  lo_int_vec, global, reloc=2, class=CODE, delta=1
goto   LowISR
psect  LowIsr_code, global, reloc=2, class=CODE, delta=1
LowISR:
   return 0

; Main Program
psect  main, global, reloc=2, class=CODE, delta=1
org 0x100
main:
Dividend equ 0x19               ; Operands
Divisor equ 0x03
Quotient equ 0x40               ; temp registers
temp equu 0x41

   CLRF      TRISB, c           ; Initialize PORTB as output
   CLRF      TRISD, c           ; Initialize PORTD as output
   CLRF      Quotient, c        ; Clear Quotient file register
   MOVLW     Dividend           ; Move Dividend to WREG
   MOVWF     temp, c            ; Move WREG to temp reg.
   MOVLW     Divisor            ; Move Divisor to WREG
Again:
   INCF      Quotient, F, c     ; Increment Quotient
   SUBWF     temp, F, c         ; Subtract WREG from temp and move the
                                ; difference to temp
   BTFSS     STATUS, 4, c       ; Check the negative flag, skip the next
                                ; instruction if it is set
   GOTO      Again              ; Go to Again
   DECF      Quotient, F, c     ; Decrement Quotient
   ADDWF     temp, W, c         ; Add WREG with dividend and hold
                                ; the result in WREG
   MOVWF     LATD, c            ; Move the remainder to PORTD
   MOVF      Quotient, W, c     ; Move the Quotient to PORTB
   MOVWF     LATB, c
```

```
hlt:
GOTO        hlt             ; Halt
END resetVec
```

Experimental Result:

Input Data		Output	
Operands		**File Register**	**Operand**
Dividend	19 H	LATB	08 H (Quotient)
Divisor	03 H	LATD	01 H (Remainder)

Calculation:

I/O	in HEX
Dividend	19 H
Divisor	03 H
Division	Dividend / Divisor = 19H / 03H
Remainder	01 H
Quotient	08 H

Conclusion:

The experiment demonstrating the division of two 8-bit numbers using the PIC18F4550 microcontroller has been successfully completed.

12. 1'S COMPLIMENT OF AN 8-BIT NUMBER

Aim:

Write an assembly language program to compute the 1's complement of an 8-bit number using the PIC18F4550 microcontroller and verify the result using the simulator.

Software Used:

- IDE: MPLAB X IDE v5.45
- PIC Assembler: pic-as (v2.31)

Algorithm:

1. Define the PIC18 configuration bits using the config directive, include xc.inc, configure the processor, set the vectors for reset and interrupts, and specify the starting address for the main program.
2. Set PORTB as an output port.
3. Complement the input data and move the result to WREG.
4. Store the value in WREG to LATB.
5. Halt the program.

Program:

```
; PIC18 Configuration Bits Setting
config PLLDIV = 5, CPUDIV = OSC1_PLL2, USBDIV = 2, FOSC = HS
config FCMEN = OFF, IESO = OFF, PWRT = OFF, BOR = OFF, BORV = 3, VREGEN = OFF
config WDT = OFF, WDTPS = 32768, CCP2MX = ON, PBADEN = OFF, LPT1OSC = OFF
config MCLRE = ON, STVREN = ON, LVP = OFF, XINST = OFF
config CP0 = OFF, CP1 = OFF, CP2 = OFF, CP3 = OFF, CPB = OFF, CPD = OFF
config WRT0 = OFF, WRT1 = OFF, WRT2 = OFF, WRT3 = OFF, WRTC = OFF, WRTB = OFF,
WRTD = OFF
config EBTR0 = OFF, EBTR1 = OFF, EBTR2 = OFF, EBTR3 = OFF, EBTRB = OFF
#include <xc.inc>

PROCESSOR  18F4550
pagewidth  132
radix      dec

; Reset Vector of Processor 18F4550
psect  resetVec, global, reloc=2, class=CODE, delta=1
resetVec:
   goto   main

; High Priority Vector is at 000008h
psect  hi_int_vec, global, reloc=2, class=CODE, delta=1
goto   HighISR
psect  HighIsr_code, global, reloc=2, class=CODE, delta=1
HighISR:
   return 0
```

```
; Low Priority Vector is at 000018h
psect  lo_int_vec, global, reloc=2, class=CODE, delta=1
goto   LowISR
psect  LowIsr_code, global, reloc=2, class=CODE, delta=1
LowISR:
   return 0

; Main Program
psect  main, global, reloc=2, class=CODE, delta=1
org 0x100
main:
X equ 0x75
temp equ 0x30

   CLRF        TRISB, c        ; Initialize PORTB as output
   CLRF        LATB, c         ; Clear LATB
   MOVLW       X               ; Move the input data to WREG
   MOVWF       temp, c         ; Move WREG to temp register
   COMF        temp, W, c      ; Complement the value of temp register
                               ; and hold the result in WREG.
   MOVWF       LATB, c         ; Move the WREG to LATB
   hlt: GOTO   hlt             ; Halt
   END resetVec
```

Experimental Result:

Input Data		Output	
Operand		File Register	Operand
X	75 H	LATB	8A H

Calculation:

I/O	in HEX		in Binary	
Operand	75 H		**0111**	**0101**
Result	8A H		**1000**	**1010**

Conclusion:

The experiment demonstrating the 1's complement of an 8-bit number using the PIC18F4550 microcontroller has been successfully completed.

13. 2'S COMPLIMENT OF AN 8-BIT NUMBER

Aim:

Write an assembly language program to calculate the 2's complement of an 8-bit number using the PIC18F4550 microcontroller and verify the result with the simulator.

Software Used:

- IDE: MPLAB X IDE v5.45
- PIC Assembler: pic-as (v2.31)

Algorithm:

1. Define the PIC18 configuration bits using the config directive, include xc.inc, configure the processor, set the vectors for reset and interrupts, and specify the starting address for the main program.
2. Set PORTB as an output port.
3. Complement the input data and store the result in the Temp register.
4. Load the literal value 0x01 into WREG.
5. Add the value in WREG to the Temp register and store the result in WREG.
6. Store the value in WREG to LATB.
7. Halt the program.

Program:

```
; PIC18 Configuration Bits Setting
config PLLDIV = 5, CPUDIV = OSC1_PLL2, USBDIV = 2, FOSC = HS
config FCMEN = OFF, IESO = OFF, PWRT = OFF, BOR = OFF, BORV = 3, VREGEN = OFF
config WDT = OFF, WDTPS = 32768, CCP2MX = ON, PBADEN = OFF, LPT1OSC = OFF
config MCLRE = ON, STVREN = ON, LVP = OFF, XINST = OFF
config CP0 = OFF, CP1 = OFF, CP2 = OFF, CP3 = OFF, CPB = OFF, CPD = OFF
```

```
config WRT0 = OFF, WRT1 = OFF, WRT2 = OFF, WRT3 = OFF, WRTC = OFF, WRTB = OFF,
WRTD = OFF
config EBTR0 = OFF, EBTR1 = OFF, EBTR2 = OFF, EBTR3 = OFF, EBTRB = OFF
#include <xc.inc>

PROCESSOR  18F4550
pagewidth  132
radix      dec

; Reset Vector of Processor 18F4550
psect  resetVec, global, reloc=2, class=CODE, delta=1
resetVec:
   goto  main

; High Priority Vector is at 000008h
psect  hi_int_vec, global, reloc=2, class=CODE, delta=1
goto  HighISR
psect  HighIsr_code, global, reloc=2, class=CODE, delta=1
HighISR:
   return 0

; Low Priority Vector is at 000018h
psect  lo_int_vec, global, reloc=2, class=CODE, delta=1
goto  LowISR
psect  LowIsr_code, global, reloc=2, class=CODE, delta=1
LowISR:
   return 0

; Main Program
psect  main, global, reloc=2, class=CODE, delta=1
org 0x100
main:
X equ 0x75
temp equ 0x30
```

```
CLRF        TRISB, c      ; Initialize PORTB as output
CLRF        LATB, c       ; Clear LATB
MOVLW       X             ; Move the input data to WREG
MOVWF       temp, c       ; Move WREG to the temp register
COMF        temp, F, c    ; Complement the value of temp register
                          ; and hold the result in temp register.
MOVLW       0x01          ; Move literal value 0x01 to WREG
ADDWF       temp, W, c    ; Add WREG with temp register and hold
                          ; the result in WREG
MOVWF       LATB, c       ; Move the WREG to LATB/PORTB
hlt: GOTO   hlt           ; Halt
END resetVec
```

Experimental Result:

Input Data		Output	
Operand		File Register	Operand
X	75 H	LATB	8B H

Calculation:

I/O	in HEX		in Binary	
Operand	75 H		**0111**	**0101**
1's complement			**1000**	**1010**
Add 01H			**0000**	**0001**
Result	8B H		**1000**	**1011**

Conclusion:

The experiment demonstrating the 2's complement of an 8-bit number using the PIC18F4550 microcontroller has been successfully completed.

14. LARGEST NUMBER IN AN ARRAY

Aim:

Write an assembly language program to find the largest number in an array of N 8-bit numbers using the PIC18F4550 microcontroller and verify the result with the simulator.

Software Used:

- IDE: MPLAB X IDE v5.45
- PIC Assembler: pic-as (v2.31)

Algorithm:

1. Define the PIC18 configuration bits using the config directive, include xc.inc, configure the processor, set the vectors for reset and interrupts, and specify the starting address for the main program.
2. Set PORTB as an output port.
3. Initialize the memory pointer to access the array elements using FSR.
4. Load the content pointed to by FSR into WREG.
5. Set the WREG value as the array count in the Count register.
6. Increment FSR to point to the next memory location.
7. Load the content pointed to by FSR into WREG.
8. Decrement the Count register.
9. Move the WREG value to the Temp register.
10. Increment FSR to point to the next memory location.
11. Subtract the WREG value from the content at the memory location pointed to by FSR and store the result in WREG.
12. Check the STATUS register for the carry flag; skip the next step if the carry flag is not set.
13. Jump to step 18.
14. Move the Temp register value to WREG.
15. Decrement the Count register; skip the next step if it is zero.
16. Jump to step 9.
17. Jump to step 21.

18. Load the content pointed to by FSR into WREG.
19. Decrement the Count register; skip the next step if it is zero.
20. Jump to step 9.
21. Move the WREG value to LATB.
22. Halt the program.

Program:

```
; PIC18 Configuration Bits Setting
config PLLDIV = 5, CPUDIV = OSC1_PLL2, USBDIV = 2, FOSC = HS
config FCMEN = OFF, IESO = OFF, PWRT = OFF, BOR = OFF, BORV = 3, VREGEN = OFF
config WDT = OFF, WDTPS = 32768, CCP2MX = ON, PBADEN = OFF, LPT1OSC = OFF
config MCLRE = ON, STVREN = ON, LVP = OFF, XINST = OFF
config CP0 = OFF, CP1 = OFF, CP2 = OFF, CP3 = OFF, CPB = OFF, CPD = OFF
config WRT0 = OFF, WRT1 = OFF, WRT2 = OFF, WRT3 = OFF, WRTC = OFF, WRTB = OFF,
WRTD = OFF
config EBTR0 = OFF, EBTR1 = OFF, EBTR2 = OFF, EBTR3 = OFF, EBTRB = OFF
#include <xc.inc>

PROCESSOR  18F4550
pagewidth  132
radix      dec

; Reset Vector of Processor 18F4550
psect  resetVec, global, reloc=2, class=CODE, delta=1
resetVec:
   goto   main

; High Priority Vector is at 000008h
psect  hi_int_vec, global, reloc=2, class=CODE, delta=1
goto   HighISR
psect  HighIsr_code, global, reloc=2, class=CODE, delta=1
HighISR:
   return 0

; Low Priority Vector is at 000018h
psect  lo_int_vec, global, reloc=2, class=CODE, delta=1
```

```
goto   LowISR
psect  LowIsr_code, global, reloc=2, class=CODE, delta=1
LowISR:
   return 0

; Main Program
psect  main, global, reloc=2, class=CODE, delta=1
org 0x100
main:
Array equ 0x30
Count equ 0x40
Temp equ 0x41
   CLRF      TRISB, c        ; Initialize PORTB as output
   CLRF      LATB, c         ; Clear PORTB
   MOVLW     Array           ; Move 0x30 to WREG
   MOVWF     FSR0, c         ; Load memory pointer by 0x30
   MOVF      INDF0, W, c     ; Move content of 0x30 to WREG
   MOVWF     Count, c        ; Move WREG to Count Register
   INCF      FSR0, c         ; Increment memory pointer
   MOVF      INDF0, W, c     ; Move the content of memory to WREG
   DECF      Count, c        ; Decrement Count register

Again:
   MOVWF     Temp, c         ; Move WREG to Temp register
   INCF      FSR0, c         ; Increment memory pointer
   SUBWF     INDF0, W, c     ; Subtract WREG from the memory and
                             ; hold the result in WREG
   BTFSC     STATUS, 0, c    ; Test the STATUS register for Carry;
                             ; skip the next instruction if it is clear
   GOTO      Next            ; Go to next
   MOVF      Temp, W, c      ; Move Temp value to WREG
   DECFSZ    Count, c        ; Decrement Count register; skip the
                             ; next instruction if it is zero
   GOTO      Again           ; Go to Again
```

```
    GOTO        Result          ; Go to Result
Next:
    MOVF        INDF0, W, c     ; Move memory to WREG
    DECFSZ      Count, c        ; Decrement Count register; skip the
                                ; next instruction if it is zero
    GOTO        Again           ; Go to Again
Result:
    MOVWF       LATB, c         ; Move WREG to LATB
    GOTO        $               ; Halt
    END resetVec
```

Experimental Result:

Input Data		Output	
Operands		File Register	Operand
30	04 H*	LATB	CD H
31	56 H		
32	92 H		
33	13 H		
34	CD H		

* *Number of array elements*

Conclusion:

The experiment demonstrating how to find the largest element in an array of N 8-bit numbers using the PIC18F4550 microcontroller has been successfully completed.

15. SMALLEST NUMBER IN AN ARRAY

Aim:

Write an assembly language program to find the smallest number in an array of N 8-bit numbers using the PIC18F4550 microcontroller and verify the result with the simulator.

Software Used:

- IDE: MPLAB X IDE v5.45
- PIC Assembler: pic-as (v2.31)

Algorithm:

1. Define the PIC18 configuration bits using the config directive, include xc.inc, configure the processor, set the vectors for reset and interrupts, and specify the starting address for the main program.
2. Set PORTB as an output port.
3. Initialize the memory pointer to access the array elements using FSR.
4. Load the content pointed to by FSR into WREG.
5. Set the WREG value as the array count in the Count register.
6. Increment FSR to point to the next memory location.
7. Load the content pointed to by FSR into WREG.
8. Decrement the Count register.
9. Move the WREG value to the Temp register.
10. Increment FSR to point to the next memory location.
11. Subtract the WREG value from the content at the memory location pointed to by FSR and store the result in WREG.
12. Check the STATUS register for the carry flag; skip the next step if the carry flag is set.
13. Jump to step 18.
14. Move the Temp register value to WREG.
15. Decrement the Count register; skip the next step if it is zero.
16. Jump to step 9.
17. Jump to step 21.
18. Load the content pointed to by FSR into WREG.
19. Decrement the Count register; skip the next step if it is zero.
20. Jump to step 9.
21. Move the WREG value to LATB.
22. Halt the program.

Program:

```
; PIC18 Configuration Bits Setting
```

```
config PLLDIV = 5, CPUDIV = OSC1_PLL2, USBDIV = 2, FOSC = HS
config FCMEN = OFF, IESO = OFF, PWRT = OFF, BOR = OFF, BORV = 3, VREGEN = OFF
config WDT = OFF, WDTPS = 32768, CCP2MX = ON, PBADEN = OFF, LPT1OSC = OFF
config MCLRE = ON, STVREN = ON, LVP = OFF, XINST = OFF
config CP0 = OFF, CP1 = OFF, CP2 = OFF, CP3 = OFF, CPB = OFF, CPD = OFF
config WRT0 = OFF, WRT1 = OFF, WRT2 = OFF, WRT3 = OFF, WRTC = OFF, WRTB = OFF,
WRTD = OFF
config EBTR0 = OFF, EBTR1 = OFF, EBTR2 = OFF, EBTR3 = OFF, EBTRB = OFF
#include <xc.inc>

PROCESSOR  18F4550
pagewidth  132
radix      dec

; Reset Vector of Processor 18F4550
psect  resetVec, global, reloc=2, class=CODE, delta=1
resetVec:
  goto   main

; High Priority Vector is at 000008h
psect  hi_int_vec, global, reloc=2, class=CODE, delta=1
goto   HighISR
psect  HighIsr_code, global, reloc=2, class=CODE, delta=1
HighISR:
  return 0

; Low Priority Vector is at 000018h
psect  lo_int_vec, global, reloc=2, class=CODE, delta=1
goto   LowISR
psect  LowIsr_code, global, reloc=2, class=CODE, delta=1
LowISR:
  return 0

; Main Program
psect  main, global, reloc=2, class=CODE, delta=1
org 0x100
```

```
main:
Array equ 0x30
Count equ 0x40
Temp equ 0x41
    CLRF      TRISB, c        ; Initialize PORTB as output
    CLRF      LATB, c         ; Clear PORTB
    MOVLW     Array           ; Move 0x30 to WREG
    MOVWF     FSR0, c         ; Load memory pointer by 0x30
    MOVF      INDF0, W, c     ; Move content of 0x30 to WREG
    MOVWF     Count, c        ; Move WREG to Count Register
    INCF      FSR0, c         ; Increment memory pointer
    MOVF      INDF0, W, c     ; Move the content of memory to WREG
    DECF      Count, c        ; Decrement Count register

Again:
    MOVWF     Temp, c         ; Move WREG to Temp register
    INCF      FSR0, c         ; Increment memory pointer
    SUBWF     INDF0, W, c     ; Subtract WREG from the memory and
                              ; hold the result in WREG
    BTFSS     STATUS, 0, c    ; Test the STATUS register for Carry;
                              ; skip the next instruction if it is set
    GOTO      Next            ; Go to next
    MOVF      Temp, W, c      ; Move Temp value to WREG
    DECFSZ    Count, c        ; Decrement Count register; skip the
                              ; next instruction if it is zero
    GOTO      Again           ; Go to Again
    GOTO      Result          ; Go to Result
Next:
    MOVF      INDF0, W, c     ; Move memory to WREG
    DECFSZ    Count, c        ; Decrement Count register; skip the
                              ; next instruction if it is zero
    GOTO      Again           ; Go to Again
Result:
    MOVWF     LATB, c         ; Move WREG to LATB
```

```
GOTO        $                   ; Halt
END resetVec
```

Experimental Result:

Input Data		Output	
Operands		File Register	Operand
30	04 H*	LATB	13 H
31	56 H		
32	92 H		
33	13 H		
34	CD H		

* *Number of array elements*

Conclusion:

The experiment demonstrating how to find the smallest element in an array of N 8-bit numbers using the PIC18F4550 microcontroller has been successfully completed.

16. DESCENDING ORDER OF AN ARRAY

Aim:

Develop an assembly language program to sort an array of 8-bit binary numbers in descending order using the PIC18F4550 microcontroller and verify the output using the simulator.

Software Used:

- IDE: MPLAB X IDE v5.45
- PIC Assembler: pic-as (v2.31)

Algorithm:

1. Set the PIC18 configuration bits using the config directive, include xc.inc, configure the processor, set the vectors for reset and interrupts, and specify the starting address for the main program.

2. Initialize the memory pointer to the starting address of the array using FSR.
3. Load the first value of the array into the Count 1 (outer loop) and Count 2 (inner loop) registers.
4. Decrement both Count 1 and Count 2 registers by 1.
5. Load the value pointed to by FSR into WREG.
6. Increment the memory pointer (FSR).
7. Subtract the WREG value from the content at the memory location pointed to by FSR and store the result in WREG.
8. Check the STATUS register for the carry flag; if set, skip the next step.
9. Jump to step 23.
10. Load the value pointed to by FSR into WREG.
11. Store the WREG value in the Temp 1 register.
12. Decrement the memory pointer (FSR).
13. Load the value pointed to by FSR into WREG.
14. Store the WREG value in the Temp 2 register.
15. Load the content of the Temp 1 register into WREG.
16. Store the WREG value at the memory location pointed to by FSR.
17. Increment the memory pointer (FSR).
18. Load the content of the Temp 2 register into WREG.
19. Store the WREG value at the memory location pointed to by FSR.
20. Decrement the Count 2 register; if it reaches zero, skip the next step.
21. Jump to step 5.
22. Jump to step 25.
23. Decrement the Count 2 register; if it reaches zero, skip the next step.
24. Jump to step 5.
25. Load the first value of the array into the Count 2 register.
26. Decrement the Count 2 register.
27. Increment the memory pointer (FSR).
28. Decrement the Count 1 register; if it reaches zero, skip the next step.
29. Jump to step 5.
30. Halt the program.

Program:

```
; PIC18 Configuration Bits Setting
config PLLDIV = 5, CPUDIV = OSC1_PLL2, USBDIV = 2, FOSC = HS
config FCMEN = OFF, IESO = OFF, PWRT = OFF, BOR = OFF, BORV = 3, VREGEN = OFF
config WDT = OFF, WDTPS = 32768, CCP2MX = ON, PBADEN = OFF, LPT1OSC = OFF
config MCLRE = ON, STVREN = ON, LVP = OFF, XINST = OFF
config CP0 = OFF, CP1 = OFF, CP2 = OFF, CP3 = OFF, CPB = OFF, CPD = OFF
config WRT0 = OFF, WRT1 = OFF, WRT2 = OFF, WRT3 = OFF, WRTC = OFF, WRTB = OFF,
WRTD = OFF
config EBTR0 = OFF, EBTR1 = OFF, EBTR2 = OFF, EBTR3 = OFF, EBTRB = OFF
#include <xc.inc>

PROCESSOR  18F4550
pagewidth  132
radix      dec

; Reset Vector of Processor 18F4550
psect  resetVec, global, reloc=2, class=CODE, delta=1
resetVec:
   goto  main

; High Priority Vector is at 000008h
psect  hi_int_vec, global, reloc=2, class=CODE, delta=1
goto   HighISR
psect  HighIsr_code, global, reloc=2, class=CODE, delta=1
HighISR:
   return 0

; Low Priority Vector is at 000018h
psect  lo_int_vec, global, reloc=2, class=CODE, delta=1
goto   LowISR
psect  LowIsr_code, global, reloc=2, class=CODE, delta=1
LowISR:
   return 0

; Main Program
```

```
psect   main, global, reloc=2, class=CODE, delta=1
org 0x100
main:
Array equ 0x30
Count1 equ 0x40
Count2 equ 0x41
Temp1 equ 0x42
Temp2 equ 0x43
   MOVLW     Array            ; Move 0x30 to WREG
   MOVWF     FSR0, c          ; Load memory pointer by 0x30
   MOVF      INDF0, W, c      ; Move the content of 0x30 to WREG
   MOVWF     Count1, c        ; Move WREG to Count1 Register
   DECF      Count1, c        ; Decrement Count1 register
   MOVWF     Count2, c        ; Move WREG to Count2 Register
   DECF      Count2, c        ; Decrement Count2 register
   INCF      FSR0, c          ; Increment memory pointer
Again:
   MOVF      INDF0, W, c      ; Move the content of memory to WREG
   INCF      FSR0, c          ; Increment memory pointer
   SUBWF     INDF0, W, c      ; Subtract WREG from the memory and
                              ; hold the result in WREG
   BTFSS     STATUS, 0, c     ; Test the STATUS register for Carry;
                              ; skip the next instruction if it is set
   GOTO      Next             ; Go to next
   MOVF      INDF0, W, c      ; Move the content of memory to WREG
   MOVWF     Temp1, c         ; Move the WREG to Temp1 register
   DECF      FSR0, c          ; Decrement memory pointer
   MOVF      INDF0, W, c      ; Move the content of memory to WREG
   MOVWF     Temp2, c         ; Move the WREG to Temp2 register
   MOVF      Temp1, W, c      ; Move Temp1 register to the WREG
   MOVWF     INDF0, c         ; Move the WREG to the location
                              ; pointed by FSR
   INCF      FSR0, c          ; Increment memory pointer
   MOVF      Temp2, W, c      ; Move Temp2 register to the WREG
```

```
    MOVWF     INDF0, c        ; Move the WREG to the location
                              ; pointed by FSR
    DECFSZ    Count2, c       ; Decrement Count Register; skip the
                              ; next instruction if it is zero
    GOTO      Again           ; Go to Again
    GOTO      Outer           ; Go to Outer
Next:
    DECFSZ    Count2, c       ; Decrement Count Register; skip the
                              ; next instruction if it is zero
    GOTO      Again           ; Go to Again
Outer:
    MOVLW     Array           ; Move 0x30 to WREG
    MOVWF     FSR0, c         ; Move the WREG to the FSR
    MOVF      INDF0, W, c     ; Move the content of 0x30 to WREG
    MOVWF     Count2, c       ; Move WREG to Count Register
    DECF      Count2, c       ; Decrement Count Register
    INCF      FSR0, c         ; Increment memory pointer
    DECFSZ    Count1, c       ; Decrement Count Register; skip the
                              ; next instruction if it is zero
    GOTO      Again           ; Go to Again
    GOTO      $               ; Halt
    END resetVec
```

Experimental Result:

Before Execution		After Execution	
Memory location	**Operand**	**Memory location**	**Operand**
30	04 H*	30	04 H*
31	56 H	31	CD H
32	92 H	32	92 H
33	13 H	33	56 H
34	CD H	34	13 H

* *Number of array elements*

Conclusion:

The experiment demonstrating the sorting of an array of numbers in descending order using a PIC18F4550 Microcontroller has been successfully conducted.

17. ASCENDING ORDER OF AN ARRAY

Aim:

Write an assembly language program to sort an array of 8-bit binary numbers in ascending order using the PIC18F4550 microcontroller and verify the output with the simulator.

Software Used:

- IDE: MPLAB X IDE v5.45
- PIC Assembler: pic-as (v2.31)

Algorithm:

1. Define the PIC18 configuration bits using the config directive, include xc.inc, configure the processor, set the vectors for reset and interrupts, and specify the starting address for the main program.
2. Set the memory pointer to the starting address of the array using FSR.
3. Load the first value of the array into the Count 1 (outer loop) and Count 2 (inner loop) registers.
4. Decrement both the Count 1 and Count 2 registers by 1.
5. Load the value pointed to by FSR into WREG.
6. Increment the memory pointer (FSR).
7. Subtract the WREG value from the value at the memory location pointed to by FSR and store the result in WREG.
8. Check the STATUS register for the carry flag; skip the next step if the carry flag is clear.
9. Jump to step 23.
10. Load the value pointed to by FSR into WREG.

11. Move the WREG value into the Temp 1 register.
12. Decrement the memory pointer (FSR).
13. Load the value pointed to by FSR into WREG.
14. Move the WREG value into the Temp 2 register.
15. Transfer the value from the Temp 1 register into WREG.
16. Store the WREG value at the memory location pointed to by FSR.
17. Increment the memory pointer (FSR).
18. Transfer the value from the Temp 2 register into WREG.
19. Store the WREG value at the memory location pointed to by FSR.
20. Decrement the Count 2 register; skip the next step if it is zero.
21. Jump to step 5.
22. Jump to step 25.
23. Decrement the Count 2 register; skip the next step if it is zero.
24. Jump to step 5.
25. Load the first value of the array into the Count 2 register.
26. Decrement the Count 2 register.
27. Increment the memory pointer (FSR).
28. Decrement the Count 1 register; skip the next step if it is zero.
29. Jump to step 5.
30. Halt.

Program:

```
; PIC18 Configuration Bits Setting
config PLLDIV = 5, CPUDIV = OSC1_PLL2, USBDIV = 2, FOSC = HS
config FCMEN = OFF, IESO = OFF, PWRT = OFF, BOR = OFF, BORV = 3, VREGEN = OFF
config WDT = OFF, WDTPS = 32768, CCP2MX = ON, PBADEN = OFF, LPT1OSC = OFF
config MCLRE = ON, STVREN = ON, LVP = OFF, XINST = OFF
config CP0 = OFF, CP1 = OFF, CP2 = OFF, CP3 = OFF, CPB = OFF, CPD = OFF
config WRT0 = OFF, WRT1 = OFF, WRT2 = OFF, WRT3 = OFF, WRTC = OFF, WRTB = OFF,
WRTD = OFF
config EBTR0 = OFF, EBTR1 = OFF, EBTR2 = OFF, EBTR3 = OFF, EBTRB = OFF
#include <xc.inc>

PROCESSOR  18F4550
pagewidth  132
```

```
radix    dec

; Reset Vector of Processor 18F4550
psect  resetVec, global, reloc=2, class=CODE, delta=1
resetVec:
  goto   main
; High Priority Vector is at 000008h
psect  hi_int_vec, global, reloc=2, class=CODE, delta=1
goto   HighISR
psect  HighIsr_code, global, reloc=2, class=CODE, delta=1
HighISR:
  return 0
; Low Priority Vector is at 000018h
psect  lo_int_vec, global, reloc=2, class=CODE, delta=1
goto   LowISR
psect  LowIsr_code, global, reloc=2, class=CODE, delta=1
LowISR:
  return 0

; Main Program
psect  main, global, reloc=2, class=CODE, delta=1
org 0x100
main:
Array equ 0x30
Count1 equ 0x40
Count2 equ 0x41
Temp1 equ 0x42
Temp2 equ 0x43

  MOVLW     Array        ; Move 0x30 to WREG
  MOVWF     FSR0, c      ; Load memory pointer by 0x30
  MOVF      INDF0, W, c  ; Move the content of 0x30 to WREG
  MOVWF     Count1, c    ; Move WREG to Count1 Register
  DECF      Count1, c    ; Decrement Count1 register
```

```
    MOVWF     Count2, c       ; Move WREG to Count2 Register
    DECF      Count2, c       ; Decrement Count2 register
    INCF      FSR0, c         ; Increment memory pointer
Again:
    MOVF      INDF0, W, c     ; Move the content of memory to WREG
    INCF      FSR0, c         ; Increment memory pointer
    SUBWF     INDF0, W, c     ; Subtract WREG from the memory and
                              ; hold the result in WREG
    BTFSC     STATUS, 0, c    ; Test the STATUS register for Carry;
                              ; skip the next instruction if it is clear
    GOTO      Next            ; Go to next
    MOVF      INDF0, W, c     ; Move the content of memory to WREG
    MOVWF     Temp1, c        ; Move the WREG to Temp1 register
    DECF      FSR0, c         ; Decrement memory pointer
    MOVF      INDF0, W, c     ; Move the content of memory to WREG
    MOVWF     Temp2, c        ; Move the WREG to Temp2 register
    MOVF      Temp1, W, c     ; Move Temp1 register to the WREG
    MOVWF     INDF0, c        ; Move the WREG to the location
                              ; pointed by FSR
    INCF      FSR0, c         ; Increment memory pointer
    MOVF      Temp2, W, c     ; Move Temp2 register to the WREG
    MOVWF     INDF0, c        ; Move the WREG to the location
                              ; pointed by FSR
    DECFSZ    Count2, c       ; Decrement Count Register; skip the
                              ; next instruction if it is zero
    GOTO      Again           ; Go to Again
    GOTO      Outer           ; Go to Outer
Next:
    DECFSZ    Count2, c       ; Decrement Count Register; skip the
                              ; next instruction if it is zero
    GOTO      Again           ; Go to Again
Outer:
    MOVLW     Array           ; Move 0x30 to WREG
    MOVWF     FSR0, c         ; Move the WREG to the FSR
```

```
MOVF      INDF0, W, c    ; Move the content of 0x30 to WREG
MOVWF     Count2, c      ; Move WREG to Count Register
DECF      Count2, c      ; Decrement Count Register
INCF      FSR0, c        ; Increment memory pointer
DECFSZ    Count1, c      ; Decrement Count Register; skip the
                         ; next instruction if it is zero
GOTO      Again          ; Go to Again
GOTO      $              ; Halt
END resetVec
```

Experimental Result:

Before Execution		After Execution	
Memory location	**Operand**	**Memory location**	**Operand**
30	04 H*	30	04 H*
31	56 H	31	13 H
32	92 H	32	56 H
33	13 H	33	92 H
34	CD H	34	CD H

* *Number of array elements*

Conclusion:

The experiment demonstrating the sorting of numbers in an array in ascending order using a PIC18F4550 Microcontroller has been successfully conducted.

18. BLOCK DATA TRANSFER

Aim:

Write an assembly language program to transfer N bytes of data from one memory to another memory block using the PIC18F4550 Microcontroller and verify the output using the simulator.

Software Used:

- IDE: MPLAB X IDE v5.45
- PIC Assembler: pic-as (v2.31)

Algorithm:

1. Define the PIC18 configuration bits using the config directive, include xc.inc, set the processor, set the vector for reset and interrupts, and set the starting address for the main program.
2. Load the starting address of the source block (0x30) into WREG.
3. Transfer the WREG value to the Temp1 register.
4. Load the starting address of the destination block (0x40) into WREG.
5. Transfer the WREG value to the Temp2 register.
6. Copy the Temp1 register value to WREG.
7. Transfer the WREG value to the FSR.
8. Load the data pointed to by the FSR into WREG.
9. Store the WREG value in the Data1 register.
10. Increment the memory pointer (FSR).
11. Copy the FSR value to WREG.
12. Store the WREG value in the Temp1 register.
13. Copy the Temp2 register value to WREG.
14. Transfer the WREG value to the FSR.
15. Move the Data1 register value to WREG.
16. Store the WREG value at the memory location pointed to by the FSR.
17. Increment the memory pointer (FSR).
18. Copy the FSR value to WREG.
19. Store the WREG value in the Temp2 register.
20. Decrement the Count register; skip the next instruction if it is zero.
21. Return to step 6.
22. Halt the program.

Program:

```
; PIC18 Configuration Bits Setting
config PLLDIV = 5, CPUDIV = OSC1_PLL2, USBDIV = 2, FOSC = HS
config FCMEN = OFF, IESO = OFF, PWRT = OFF, BOR = OFF, BORV = 3, VREGEN = OFF
```

```
config WDT = OFF, WDTPS = 32768, CCP2MX = ON, PBADEN = OFF, LPT1OSC = OFF
config MCLRE = ON, STVREN = ON, LVP = OFF, XINST = OFF
config CP0 = OFF, CP1 = OFF, CP2 = OFF, CP3 = OFF, CPB = OFF, CPD = OFF
config WRT0 = OFF, WRT1 = OFF, WRT2 = OFF, WRT3 = OFF, WRTC = OFF, WRTB = OFF,
WRTD = OFF
config EBTR0 = OFF, EBTR1 = OFF, EBTR2 = OFF, EBTR3 = OFF, EBTRB = OFF
#include <xc.inc>

PROCESSOR  18F4550
pagewidth  132
radix      dec

; Reset Vector of Processor 18F4550
psect  resetVec, global, reloc=2, class=CODE, delta=1
resetVec:
   goto  main

; High Priority Vector is at 000008h
psect  hi_int_vec, global, reloc=2, class=CODE, delta=1
goto  HighISR
psect  HighIsr_code, global, reloc=2, class=CODE, delta=1
HighISR:
   return 0

; Low Priority Vector is at 000018h
psect  lo_int_vec, global, reloc=2, class=CODE, delta=1
goto  LowISR
psect  LowIsr_code, global, reloc=2, class=CODE, delta=1
LowISR:
   return 0

; Main Program
psect  main, global, reloc=2, class=CODE, delta=1
org 0x100
main:
Count equ 0x20
```

```
Block1 equ 0x30
Block2 equ 0x40
Temp1 equ 0x21
Temp2 equ 0x22
Data1 equ 0x23

    MOVLW     Block1         ; Move 0x30 to WREG
    MOVWF     Temp1, c       ; Move the WREG to the Temp1 register
    MOVLW     Block2         ; Move 0x30 to WREG
    MOVWF     Temp2, c       ; Move the WREG to the Temp2 register
Again:
    MOVF      Temp1, W, c    ; Move the Temp1 register to the WREG
    MOVWF     FSR0, c        ; Move the WREG to the FSR
    MOVF      INDF0, W, c    ; Move content of 0x30 to WREG
    MOVWF     Data1, c       ; Move the WREG to the Data1 register
    INCF      FSR0, c        ; Increment FSR
    MOVF      FSR0, W, c     ; Move the FSR to the WREG
    MOVWF     Temp1, c       ; Move the WREG to the Temp1 register
    MOVF      Temp2, W, c    ; Move the Temp2 register to the WREG
    MOVWF     FSR0, c        ; Move the WREG to the FSR
    MOVF      Data1, W, c    ; Move the Data1 register to the WREG
    MOVWF     INDF0, c       ; Move the WREG to the memory
                             ; location pointed by FSR
    INCF      FSR0, c        ; Increment FSR
    MOVF      FSR0, W, c     ; Move the FSR to the WREG
    MOVWF     Temp2, c       ; Move the WREG to the Temp2 register
    DECFSZ    Count, c       ; Decrement Count Register, skip the
                             ; next instruction if it is zero
    GOTO      Again          ; Go to Again
    GOTO      $              ; Halt
    END resetVec
```

Experimental Result:

Before Execution		After Execution	
Memory location	**Operand**	**Memory location**	**Operand**
20	05 H*	20	00 H
30	54 H	40	54 H
31	23 H	41	23 H
32	A4 H	42	A4 H
33	49 H	43	49 H
34	B7 H	44	B7 H

** Number of elements in Source block to be transferred*

Conclusion:

The experiment demonstrating the transfer of N bytes of data from one memory block to another using the PIC18F4550 Microcontroller has been successfully completed.

19. FIBONACCI SERIES

Aim:

Write an assembly language program to generate N elements of the Fibonacci series in 8-bit binary format using the PIC18F4550 Microcontroller. Verify the results using a simulator.

Software Used:

- IDE: MPLAB X IDE v5.45
- PIC Assembler: pic-as (v2.31)

Algorithm:

1. Define the PIC18 configuration bits using the config directive. Include xc.inc, configure the processor, set the vectors for reset and interrupts, and specify the starting address for the main program.

2. Clear the WREG register.
3. Copy the value of WREG to the Temp1 register (this represents the first value of the series).
4. Load the literal value 0x01 into WREG.
5. Copy the value of WREG to the Temp2 register (this represents the second value of the series).
6. Set the starting address for output in FSR by moving it through WREG.
7. Store the value from Temp1 in the memory location pointed to by FSR.
8. Decrement the Count register.
9. Increment the FSR.
10. Store the value from Temp2 in the memory location pointed to by FSR.
11. Decrement the Count register.
12. Increment the FSR.
13. Add the value of Temp1 to WREG and store the result in WREG.
14. Store the value from WREG in the memory location pointed to by FSR.
15. Move the value from Temp2 to WREG.
16. Copy the value from WREG to Temp1.
17. Load the value from the memory location pointed to by FSR into WREG.
18. Move the value from WREG to Temp2.
19. Increment the FSR.
20. Decrement the Count register; skip the next instruction if it is zero.
21. Jump to step 13.
22. Halt the program.

Program:

```
; PIC18 Configuration Bits Setting
config PLLDIV = 5, CPUDIV = OSC1_PLL2, USBDIV = 2, FOSC = HS
config FCMEN = OFF, IESO = OFF, PWRT = OFF, BOR = OFF, BORV = 3, VREGEN = OFF
config WDT = OFF, WDTPS = 32768, CCP2MX = ON, PBADEN = OFF, LPT1OSC = OFF
config MCLRE = ON, STVREN = ON, LVP = OFF, XINST = OFF
config CP0 = OFF, CP1 = OFF, CP2 = OFF, CP3 = OFF, CPB = OFF, CPD = OFF
config WRT0 = OFF, WRT1 = OFF, WRT2 = OFF, WRT3 = OFF, WRTC = OFF, WRTB = OFF,
WRTD = OFF
```

```
config EBTR0 = OFF, EBTR1 = OFF, EBTR2 = OFF, EBTR3 = OFF, EBTRB = OFF
#include <xc.inc>

PROCESSOR  18F4550
pagewidth  132
radix      dec

; Reset Vector of Processor 18F4550
psect  resetVec, global, reloc=2, class=CODE, delta=1
resetVec:
   goto   main

; High Priority Vector is at 000008h
psect  hi_int_vec, global, reloc=2, class=CODE, delta=1
goto   HighISR
psect  HighIsr_code, global, reloc=2, class=CODE, delta=1
HighISR:
   return 0

; Low Priority Vector is at 000018h
psect  lo_int_vec, global, reloc=2, class=CODE, delta=1
goto   LowISR
psect  LowIsr_code, global, reloc=2, class=CODE, delta=1
LowISR:
   return 0

; Main Program
psect  main, global, reloc=2, class=CODE, delta=1
org 0x100
main:
Count equ 0x30
Series equ 0x40
Temp1 equ 0x31
Temp2 equ 0x32
```

```
    MOVLW     0x00            ; Move 0x30 to WREG
    MOVWF     Temp1, c        ; Move the WREG to the Temp1 register
    MOVLW     0x01            ; Move 0x30 to WREG
    MOVWF     Temp2, c        ; Move the WREG to the Temp1 register
    MOVLW     Series          ; Move the starting address of output to
                              ; the WREG
    MOVWF     FSR0, c         ; Move the WREG to FSR
    MOVF      Temp1, W, c     ; Move the Temp1 register to the WREG
    MOVWF     INDF0, c        ; Move the WREG to the location
                              ; pointed by the FSR
    DECF      Count, c        ; Decrement the Count register
    INCF      FSR0, c         ; Increment the memory pointer
    MOVF      Temp2, W, c     ; Move the Temp2 register to the WREG
    MOVWF     INDF0, c        ; Move the WREG to the location
                              ; pointed by the FSR
    DECF      Count, c        ; Decrement the Count register
    INCF      FSR0, c         ; Increment the memory pointer
Again:
    ADDWF     Temp1, W, c     ; Add the WREG with Temp1 register
                              ; and hold the result in the WREG
    MOVWF     INDF0, c        ; Move the WREG to the location
                              ; pointed by the FSR
    MOVF      Temp2, W, c     ; Move the Temp2 register to the WREG
    MOVWF     Temp1, c        ; Move the WREG to the Temp1 register
    MOVF      INDF0, W, c     ; Move the content pointed by FSR to
                              ; the WREG
    MOVWF     Temp2, c        ; Move the WREG to the Temp2 register
    INCF      FSR0, c         ; Increment memory pointer
    DECFSZ    Count, c        ; Decrement the Count register; skip the
                              ; next instruction if it is zero
    GOTO      Again           ; Go to Again
    GOTO      $               ; Halt
    END resetVec
```

Experimental Result:

Before Execution		After Execution	
Memory location	Operand	Memory location	Operand
30	0A H	40	00 H
		41	01 H
		42	01 H
		43	02 H
		44	03 H
		45	05 H
		46	08 H
		47	0D H
		48	15 H
		49	22 H

Conclusion:

The experiment to generate the Fibonacci series using the PIC18F4550 Microcontroller has been successfully demonstrated.

20. BINARY TO ASCII CONVERSION

Aim:

Write an assembly language program to convert a binary number to its ASCII representation using the PIC18F4550 Microcontroller and verify the result with the simulator.

Software Used:

- IDE: MPLAB X IDE v5.45
- PIC Assembler: pic-as (v2.31)

Algorithm:

1. Define the PIC18 configuration bits using the config directive, include

xc.inc, configure the processor, set the vectors for reset and interrupts, and specify the starting address for the main program.

2. Define file registers to hold the values of the binary number and its ASCII equivalent.
3. Load the literal value 0x0A into WREG.
4. Subtract this value from the Binary register and store the result in WREG.
5. Transfer the WREG value to the Temp register.
6. Check the STATUS register for the carry flag; skip the next step if the carry flag is set.
7. Jump to step 12.
8. Load the literal value 0x41 into WREG.
9. Add this value to the Temp register and store the result in WREG.
10. Move the WREG value to the ASCII register.
11. Halt the program.
12. Load the literal value 0x30 into WREG.
13. Add this value to the Binary register and store the result in WREG.
14. Move the WREG value to the ASCII register.
15. Halt the program.

Program:

```
; PIC18 Configuration Bits Setting
config PLLDIV = 5, CPUDIV = OSC1_PLL2, USBDIV = 2, FOSC = HS
config FCMEN = OFF, IESO = OFF, PWRT = OFF, BOR = OFF, BORV = 3, VREGEN = OFF
config WDT = OFF, WDTPS = 32768, CCP2MX = ON, PBADEN = OFF, LPT1OSC = OFF
config MCLRE = ON, STVREN = ON, LVP = OFF, XINST = OFF
config CP0 = OFF, CP1 = OFF, CP2 = OFF, CP3 = OFF, CPB = OFF, CPD = OFF
config WRT0 = OFF, WRT1 = OFF, WRT2 = OFF, WRT3 = OFF, WRTC = OFF, WRTB = OFF, WRTD =
OFF
config EBTR0 = OFF, EBTR1 = OFF, EBTR2 = OFF, EBTR3 = OFF, EBTRB = OFF
#include <xc.inc>

PROCESSOR  18F4550
pagewidth  132
radix      dec
```

```
; Reset Vector of Processor 18F4550
psect  resetVec, global, reloc=2, class=CODE, delta=1
resetVec:
   goto   main

; High Priority Vector is at 000008h
psect  hi_int_vec, global, reloc=2, class=CODE, delta=1
goto   HighISR
psect  HighIsr_code, global, reloc=2, class=CODE, delta=1
HighISR:
   return 0

; Low Priority Vector is at 000018h
psect  lo_int_vec, global, reloc=2, class=CODE, delta=1
goto   LowISR
psect  LowIsr_code, global, reloc=2, class=CODE, delta=1
LowISR:
   return 0

; Main Program
psect  main, global, reloc=2, class=CODE, delta=1
org 0x100
main:
Binary equ 0x30
ASCII equ 0x31
Temp equ 0x32

   MOVLW     0x0A            ; Move 0x30 to WREG
   SUBWF     Binary, 0       ; Subtract the WREG from the binary
                             ; value and hold the result in the WREG.
   MOVWF     Temp            ; Move the WREG to the Temp register
   BTFSS     STATUS, 0, c    ; Test the carry in STATUS register; skip
                             ; the next instruction if the carry is clear
   GOTO      Next            ; Go to Next
```

```
    MOVLW    0x41          ; Move the literal value 0x41 to WREG
    ADDWF    Temp, 0       ; Add the WREG with the Temp register
                           ; and hold the result in the WREG.
    MOVWF    ASCII         ; Move the WREG to the ASCII register
    GOTO     $             ; Halt
Next:
    MOVLW    0x30          ; Move the literal value 0x30 to WREG
    ADDWF    Binary, 0     ; Add the WREG with the Binary
                           ; register and hold the result in WREG.
    MOVWF    ASCII         ; Move the WREG to the ASCII register
    GOTO     $             ; Halt
END resetVec
```

Experimental Result:

Before Execution		After Execution	
Memory location	**Operand**	**Memory location**	**Operand**
30	05 H (Binary)	30	05 H (Binary)
31	-	31	35 H (ASCII)

Before Execution		After Execution	
Memory location	**Operand**	**Memory location**	**Operand**
30	0E H (Binary)	30	0E H (Binary)
31	-	31	45 H (ASCII)

Calculation:

Step	Binary Number	ASCII Number
1	05 H	05 – 0A (Carry will set) 05 + 30 = 35 H
2	0E H	0E – 0A = 04 H (No carry) 04 + 41 = 45 H

Conclusion:

The experiment to convert a binary number to its ASCII equivalent using the PIC18F4550 Microcontroller has been successfully demonstrated.

21. ASCII TO BINARY CONVERSION

Aim:

Write an assembly language program to convert an ASCII number into its equivalent binary number using the PIC18F4550 microcontroller and verify the result using the simulator.

Software Used:

- IDE: MPLAB X IDE v5.45
- PIC Assembler: pic-as (v2.31)

Algorithm:

1. Define the PIC18 configuration bits using the config directive, include xc.inc, configure the processor, set the vectors for reset and interrupts, and specify the starting address for the main program.
2. Define file registers to store the values of ASCII and Binary.
3. Load the literal value 0x30 into WREG.
4. Subtract WREG from the ASCII register and store the result in WREG.
5. Move the value from WREG to the Temp register.
6. Load WREG with 0x30 again.
7. Subtract WREG from the Temp register and store the result in WREG.
8. Check the carry flag in the STATUS register; skip the next step if the carry flag is set.
9. Jump to step 13.
10. Load WREG with 0x07.
11. Subtract WREG from the Temp register and store the result in WREG.
12. Move the value from WREG to the Binary register.
13. Halt.
14. Move the value from the Temp register to WREG.

15. Move WREG to the Binary register.
16. Halt.

Program:

```
; PIC18 Configuration Bits Setting
config PLLDIV = 5, CPUDIV = OSC1_PLL2, USBDIV = 2, FOSC = HS
config FCMEN = OFF, IESO = OFF, PWRT = OFF, BOR = OFF, BORV = 3, VREGEN = OFF
config WDT = OFF, WDTPS = 32768, CCP2MX = ON, PBADEN = OFF, LPT1OSC = OFF
config MCLRE = ON, STVREN = ON, LVP = OFF, XINST = OFF
config CP0 = OFF, CP1 = OFF, CP2 = OFF, CP3 = OFF, CPB = OFF, CPD = OFF
config WRT0 = OFF, WRT1 = OFF, WRT2 = OFF, WRT3 = OFF, WRTC = OFF, WRTB = OFF,
WRTD = OFF
config EBTR0 = OFF, EBTR1 = OFF, EBTR2 = OFF, EBTR3 = OFF, EBTRB = OFF
#include <xc.inc>

PROCESSOR   18F4550
pagewidth   132
radix       dec

; Reset Vector of Processor 18F4550
psect   resetVec, global, reloc=2, class=CODE, delta=1
resetVec:
    goto    main

; High Priority Vector is at 000008h
psect   hi_int_vec, global, reloc=2, class=CODE, delta=1
goto    HighISR
psect   HighIsr_code, global, reloc=2, class=CODE, delta=1
HighISR:
    return 0

; Low Priority Vector is at 000018h
psect   lo_int_vec, global, reloc=2, class=CODE, delta=1
goto    LowISR
psect   LowIsr_code, global, reloc=2, class=CODE, delta=1
```

```
LowISR:
   return 0

; Main Program
psect   main, global, reloc=2, class=CODE, delta=1
org 0x100
main:
ASCII equ 0x40
Binary equ 0x41
Temp equ 0x50

   MOVLW     0x30           ; Move the literal value 0x30 to WREG.
   SUBWF     ASCII, 0       ; Subtract the WREG from the ASCII
                            ; register and hold the result in WREG.
   MOVWF     Temp           ; Move the WREG to the Temp register
   MOVLW     0x0A           ; Move 0x30 to WREG
   SUBWF     Temp, 0        ; Subtract the WREG from the Temp
                            ; register and hold the result in WREG
   BTFSS     STATUS, 0, c   ; Test the Carry flag; skip the next
                            ; instruction if the carry flag is set
   GOTO      Next           ; Go to Next
   MOVLW     0x07           ; Move the literal value 0x07 to WREG
   SUBWF     Temp, 0        ; Subtract the WREG from the Temp
                            ; register and hold the result in WREG
   MOVWF     Binary         ; Move the WREG to the Binary register
   GOTO      $              ; Halt
Next:
   MOVF      Temp, W, c     ; Move the Temp register to the WREG
   MOVWF     Binary         ; Move the WREG to the Binary register
   GOTO      $              ; Halt
END resetVec
```

Experimental Result:

Before Execution		After Execution	
Memory location	Operand	Memory location	Operand
40	37 H	40	37 H
41	-	41	07 H

Before Execution		After Execution	
Memory location	Operand	Memory location	Operand
40	44 H	40	44 H
41	-	41	0D H

Calculation:

Step	Binary Number	ASCII Number
1	37 H	37H – 30H = 07H 07H – 0AH (Carry will set) = 07H is ASC37II number
2	44 H	44H – 30H = 14 H 14H – 0AH (No carry) 14H – 07H = 0D H

Conclusion:

The experiment to convert an ASCII number to its equivalent binary number using the PIC18F4550 Microcontroller has been successfully demonstrated.

22. BINARY TO GRAY CODE CONVERSION

Aim:

Write an assembly language program to convert binary code into Gray code using the PIC18F4550 Microcontroller and verify the result with a simulator.

Software Used:

- IDE: MPLAB X IDE v5.45
- PIC Assembler: pic-as (v2.31)

Algorithm:

1. Define the PIC18 configuration bits using the config directive, include xc.inc, configure the processor, set the vectors for reset and interrupts, and specify the starting address for the main program.
2. Define file registers to store the values of Binary and Gray.
3. Load the input binary value into the WREG.
4. Copy the WREG value to the Temp register.
5. Clear the carry flag in the STATUS register.
6. Rotate the Temp register right through the carry and store the result in the WREG.
7. XOR the WREG value with the content of the Binary register and store the result in the WREG.
8. Copy the WREG value to the Gray register.
9. Halt the program.

Program:

```
; PIC18 Configuration Bits Setting
config PLLDIV = 5, CPUDIV = OSC1_PLL2, USBDIV = 2, FOSC = HS
config FCMEN = OFF, IESO = OFF, PWRT = OFF, BOR = OFF, BORV = 3, VREGEN = OFF
config WDT = OFF, WDTPS = 32768, CCP2MX = ON, PBADEN = OFF, LPT1OSC = OFF
config MCLRE = ON, STVREN = ON, LVP = OFF, XINST = OFF
config CP0 = OFF, CP1 = OFF, CP2 = OFF, CP3 = OFF, CPB = OFF, CPD = OFF
config WRT0 = OFF, WRT1 = OFF, WRT2 = OFF, WRT3 = OFF, WRTC = OFF, WRTB = OFF,
WRTD = OFF
config EBTR0 = OFF, EBTR1 = OFF, EBTR2 = OFF, EBTR3 = OFF, EBTRB = OFF
#include <xc.inc>

PROCESSOR  18F4550
pagewidth  132
radix      dec

; Reset Vector of Processor 18F4550
```

```
psect  resetVec, global, reloc=2, class=CODE, delta=1
resetVec:
   goto   main

; High Priority Vector is at 000008h
psect  hi_int_vec, global, reloc=2, class=CODE, delta=1
goto   HighISR
psect  HighIsr_code, global, reloc=2, class=CODE, delta=1
HighISR:
   return 0

; Low Priority Vector is at 000018h
psect  lo_int_vec, global, reloc=2, class=CODE, delta=1
goto   LowISR
psect  LowIsr_code, global, reloc=2, class=CODE, delta=1
LowISR:
   return 0
; Main Program
psect  main, global, reloc=2, class=CODE, delta=1
org 0x100
main:
Binary equ 0x30
Gray equ 0x31
Temp equ 0x40
   MOVF        Binary, W, c     ; Move the Binary register to the WREG
   MOVWF       Temp             ; Move the WREG to the Temp register
   BCF         STATUS, 0, c     ; Clear carry flag
   RRCF        Temp, 0          ; Rotate right the Temp register with
                                ; carry and hold the result in the WREG
   XORWF       Binary, 0        ; XOR the WREG with the Binary
                                ; register and hold the result in WREG
   MOVWF       Gray             ; Move the WREG to the Gray register
   GOTO        $                ; Halt
END resetVec
```

Calculation:

1D H

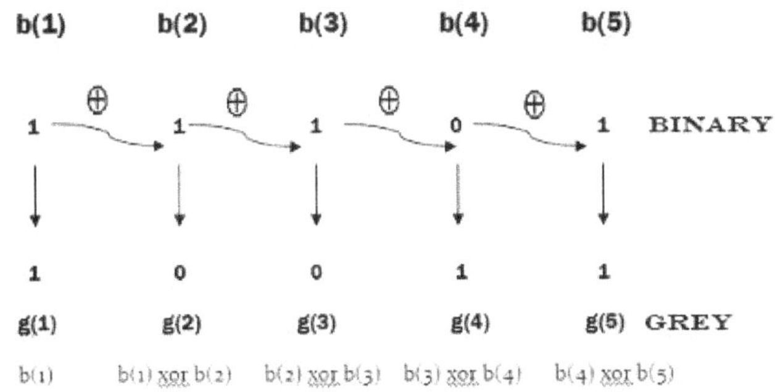

13 H

Experimental Result:

Before Execution		After Execution	
Memory location	**Operand**	**Memory location**	**Operand**
30	1D H	30	1D H
31	-	31	13 H

Conclusion:

The experiment to convert binary code to Gray code using the PIC18F4550 microcontroller has been successfully completed.

23. GRAY CODE TO BINARY CONVERSION

Aim:

Write an assembly language program to convert Gray code to a binary number using the PIC18F4550 microcontroller and verify the result with a simulator.

Software Used:

- IDE: MPLAB X IDE v5.45
- PIC Assembler: pic-as (v2.31)

Algorithm:

1. Define the PIC18 configuration bits using the config directive. Include xc.inc, configure the processor, set the reset and interrupt vectors, and specify the starting address for the main program.
2. Define file registers to hold the values for Gray and Binary codes.
3. Load the input Gray code value into the WREG.
4. Transfer the WREG value to the Temp register.
5. Load the literal value 0x07 into the WREG.
6. Transfer the WREG value to the Count register.
7. Clear the carry flag in the STATUS register.
8. Rotate the Temp register right with carry, and store the result in the WREG.
9. XOR the WREG with the value in the Gray register, and store the result back in the WREG.
10. Transfer the WREG value to the Temp register.
11. Decrement the Count register; skip the next step if it is zero.
12. Return to step 7.
13. Transfer the WREG value to the Binary register.
14. Halt the program.

Program:

```
; PIC18 Configuration Bits Setting
config PLLDIV = 5, CPUDIV = OSC1_PLL2, USBDIV = 2, FOSC = HS
config FCMEN = OFF, IESO = OFF, PWRT = OFF, BOR = OFF, BORV = 3, VREGEN = OFF
config WDT = OFF, WDTPS = 32768, CCP2MX = ON, PBADEN = OFF, LPT1OSC = OFF
config MCLRE = ON, STVREN = ON, LVP = OFF, XINST = OFF
config CP0 = OFF, CP1 = OFF, CP2 = OFF, CP3 = OFF, CPB = OFF, CPD = OFF
config WRT0 = OFF, WRT1 = OFF, WRT2 = OFF, WRT3 = OFF, WRTC = OFF, WRTB = OFF,
WRTD = OFF
config EBTR0 = OFF, EBTR1 = OFF, EBTR2 = OFF, EBTR3 = OFF, EBTRB = OFF
#include <xc.inc>

PROCESSOR  18F4550
pagewidth  132
radix      dec
```

```
; Reset Vector of Processor 18F4550
psect   resetVec, global, reloc=2, class=CODE, delta=1
resetVec:
   goto    main
; High Priority Vector is at 000008h
psect   hi_int_vec, global, reloc=2, class=CODE, delta=1
goto    HighISR
psect   HighIsr_code, global, reloc=2, class=CODE, delta=1
HighISR:
   return 0
; Low Priority Vector is at 000018h
psect   lo_int_vec, global, reloc=2, class=CODE, delta=1
goto    LowISR
psect   LowIsr_code, global, reloc=2, class=CODE, delta=1
LowISR:
   return 0

; Main Program
psect   main, global, reloc=2, class=CODE, delta=1
org 0x100
main:
Gray equ 0x30
Binary equ 0x31
Temp equ 0x40
Count equ 0x41
   MOVF       Gray, W, c       ; Move Gray register to the WREG
   MOVWF      Temp             ; Move the WREG to the Temp register
   MOVLW      0x07             ; Move literal value 0x07 to the WREG
   MOVWF      Count            ; Move the WREG to the Count register
Again:
   BCF        STATUS, 0, c     ; Clear Carry flag
   RRCF       Temp, 0          ; Rotate Temp register right with carry
                               ; and hold the result in the WREG
   XORWF      Gray, 0          ; XOR the WREG with the Gray register
```

```
                                ; and hold the result in the WREG
    MOVWF       Temp            ; Move the WREG to the Temp register
    DECFSZ      Count           ; Decrement the Count register; skip the
                                ; next instruction if it is zero
    GOTO        Again           ; Go to Again
    MOVWF       Binary          ; Move the WREG to the Binary register
    GOTO        $               ; Halt
END resetVec
```

Experimental Result:

Before Execution		After Execution	
Memory location	**Operand**	**Memory location**	**Operand**
30	13 H	30	13 H
31	-	31	1D H

Calculation:

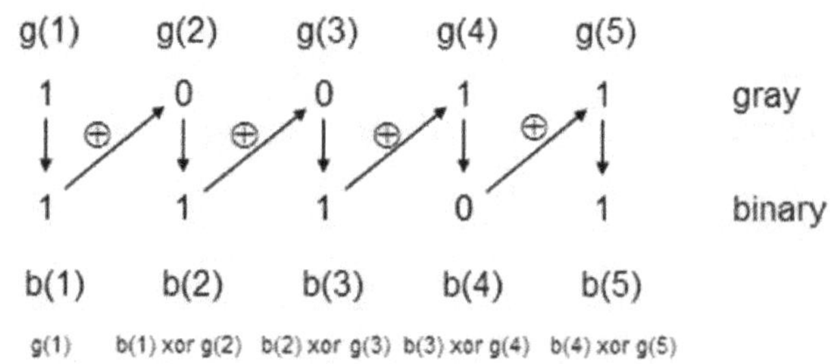

Conclusion:

The experiment for the gray code to binary number conversion using the PIC18F4550 Microcontroller has been demonstrated.

24. LOGICAL OPERATION - DEMORGAN's LAW

Aim:

Write an assembly language program to implement De Morgan's Laws using the PIC18F4550 Microcontroller and verify the results using the simulator.

Software Used:

- IDE: MPLAB X IDE v5.45
- PIC Assembler: pic-as (v2.31)

Theory:

De Morgan's laws are commonly written as:

$$\overline{A+B} = \overline{A} \cdot \overline{B},$$

and

$$\overline{A \cdot B} = \overline{A} + \overline{B}$$

where,

- . is a logical AND
- \+ is a logical OR

Algorithm:

Verification of Demorgan's First Law

1. Define the PIC18 configuration bits using the config directive, include xc.inc, configure the processor, set the vectors for reset and interrupts, and specify the starting address for the main program.
2. Declare the necessary variables.
3. Call the Fun_LHS function.
4. Call the Fun_RHS function.
5. Halt the program execution.

Fun_LHS subroutine:

1. Load the value of A1 into the WREG.
2. Perform a logical OR operation between WREG and the B1 register, and store the result back in WREG.
3. Transfer the value from WREG to the Temp register.
4. Complement the value in the Temp register.
5. Move the value from the Temp register to the LHS register.
6. Return from the function.

Fun_LHS subroutine:

1. Complement the value in A1 and load it into WREG.
2. Transfer the value from WREG to the Temp register.
3. Complement the value in B1 and load it into WREG.
4. Perform a logical AND operation between WREG and the Temp register, and store the result in WREG.
5. Transfer the value from WREG to the RHS register.
6. Return from the function.

Program:

```
; PIC18 Configuration Bits Setting
config PLLDIV = 5, CPUDIV = OSC1_PLL2, USBDIV = 2, FOSC = HS
config FCMEN = OFF, IESO = OFF, PWRT = OFF, BOR = OFF, BORV = 3, VREGEN = OFF
config WDT = OFF, WDTPS = 32768, CCP2MX = ON, PBADEN = OFF, LPT1OSC = OFF
config MCLRE = ON, STVREN = ON, LVP = OFF, XINST = OFF
config CP0 = OFF, CP1 = OFF, CP2 = OFF, CP3 = OFF, CPB = OFF, CPD = OFF
config WRT0 = OFF, WRT1 = OFF, WRT2 = OFF, WRT3 = OFF, WRTC = OFF, WRTB = OFF,
WRTD = OFF
config EBTR0 = OFF, EBTR1 = OFF, EBTR2 = OFF, EBTR3 = OFF, EBTRB = OFF
#include <xc.inc>

PROCESSOR  18F4550
pagewidth  132
radix      dec

; Reset Vector of Processor 18F4550
psect  resetVec, global, reloc=2, class=CODE, delta=1
resetVec:
   goto   main

; High Priority Vector is at 000008h
psect  hi_int_vec, global, reloc=2, class=CODE, delta=1
goto   HighISR
psect  HighIsr_code, global, reloc=2, class=CODE, delta=1
HighISR:
   return 0
```

```
; Low Priority Vector is at 000018h
psect  lo_int_vec, global, reloc=2, class=CODE, delta=1
goto   LowISR
psect  LowIsr_code, global, reloc=2, class=CODE, delta=1
LowISR:
   return 0

; Main Program
psect  main, global, reloc=2, class=CODE, delta=1
org 0x100
main:
   A1    equ 0x30
   B1    equ 0x31
   LHS  equ 0x32
   RHS  equ 0x33
   Temp equ 0x40
   CALL        Fun_LHS        ; Call the Fun_LHS subroutine
   CALL        Fun_RHS        ; Call the Fun_LHS subroutine
   GOTO        $              ; Halt

Fun_LHS:
   MOVF        A1, W, c       ; Move A1 Register to the WREG
   IORWF       B1, W          ; OR the WREG with B1 register and
                              ; hold the result in WREG
   MOVWF       Temp           ; Move the WREG to the Temp register
   COMF        Temp, W        ; Compliment the Temp register and
                              ; hold the result in WREG
   MOVWF       LHS            ; Move the WREG to the LHS register
   RETURN                     ; Return to the main function

Fun_RHS:
   COMF        A1, W          ; Complement A1 register and move the
                              ; result to the WREG
```

```
    MOVWF     Temp          ; Move the WREG to the Temp register
    COMF      B1, W         ; Complement B1 register and move the
                            ; result to the WREG
    ANDWF     Temp, W       ; AND the WREG with the Temp
                            ; register and hold the result in WREG
    MOVWF     RHS           ; Move the WREG to the RHS register
    RETURN                  ; Return to the main function
END resetVec
```

Experimental Result:

Before Execution		After Execution	
Memory location	**Operand**	**Memory location**	**Operand**
A1	24 H	LHS	93 H
B1	68 H	RHS	93 H

Calculation:

Step	Formula Elements	Output Value
LHS	$A + B$ $\overline{A + B}$	24H OR 68H = 6CH Complement of 6CH = 93H
RHS	$\overline{A}$ $\overline{B}$ $\overline{A} . \overline{B}$	Complement of 24H = DBH Complement of 68H = 97H DBH **AND** 93H = 93H

Conclusion:

The experiment to verify De Morgan's Law using the PIC18F4550 Microcontroller has been successfully completed.

25. 4-BIT BINARY COUNTER

Aim:

Design and implement a 4-bit binary counter system using the PIC18F4550 Microcontroller and an assembly language program. Verify the system's output.

Hardware Requirements:

- PIC18F4550 Microcontroller, 20 MHz Crystal (1), 15 pF Disc Capacitors (2), 220 nF Disc Capacitor (1), 100 nF Disc Capacitor (1), Resistor 10K (1), and Push Button (1)
- LEDs (4), Resistors 120 ohm (4)

Software Used:

- IDE: MPLAB X IDE v5.45
- PIC Assembler: pic-as (v2.31)

Algorithm:

1. Define the PIC18 configuration bits using the config directive. Include xc.inc, configure the processor, set the vectors for reset and interrupts, and specify the starting address for the main program.
2. Configure PORTD as an output port and clear LATD.
3. Clear the Digit Carry flag.
4. Call the delay function.
5. Add 0x01 to the LATD register.
6. Check the Digit Carry flag; skip the next step if the flag is set.
7. Go back to step 4.
8. Return to step 2.

Delay Subroutine:

1. Initialize the value of counter1.
2. Initialize the value of counter2.
3. Initialize the value of counter3.
4. Decrement counter3; skip the next step if counter3 is zero.
5. Return to step 4.
6. Decrement counter2; skip the next step if counter2 is zero.
7. Return to step 3.
8. Decrement counter1; skip the next step if counter1 is zero.
9. Return to step 2.
10. Return to the main program.

Program:

```
; PIC18 Configuration Bits Setting
```

```
config PLLDIV = 5, CPUDIV = OSC1_PLL2, USBDIV = 2, FOSC = HS
config FCMEN = OFF, IESO = OFF, PWRT = OFF, BOR = OFF, BORV = 3, VREGEN = OFF
config WDT = OFF, WDTPS = 32768, CCP2MX = ON, PBADEN = OFF, LPT1OSC = OFF
config MCLRE = ON, STVREN = ON, LVP = OFF, XINST = OFF
config CP0 = OFF, CP1 = OFF, CP2 = OFF, CP3 = OFF, CPB = OFF, CPD = OFF
config WRT0 = OFF, WRT1 = OFF, WRT2 = OFF, WRT3 = OFF, WRTC = OFF, WRTB = OFF,
WRTD = OFF
config EBTR0 = OFF, EBTR1 = OFF, EBTR2 = OFF, EBTR3 = OFF, EBTRB = OFF
#include <xc.inc>

PROCESSOR   18F4550
pagewidth   132
radix       dec

; Reset Vector of Processor 18F4550
psect   resetVec, global, reloc=2, class=CODE, delta=1
resetVec:
   goto    main

; High Priority Vector is at 000008h
psect   hi_int_vec, global, reloc=2, class=CODE, delta=1
goto    HighISR
psect   HighIsr_code, global, reloc=2, class=CODE, delta=1
HighISR:
   return 0

; Low Priority Vector is at 000018h
psect   lo_int_vec, global, reloc=2, class=CODE, delta=1
goto    LowISR
psect   LowIsr_code, global, reloc=2, class=CODE, delta=1
LowISR:
   return 0

; Main Program
psect   main, global, reloc=2, class=CODE, delta=1
org 0x100
```

```
main:
  d1 equ 0x30                        ; Declaration of files d1, d2 & d3
  d2 equ 0x31
  d3 equ 0x32
  MOVLW     0x00
  MOVWF     TRISD                    ; All bits in PORTD are output
  MOVWF     LATD                     ; Count Value set to 00h
  BCF       STATUS, 1, c             ; Clear Digit Carry (DC)
Next:
  CALL      Delay                    ; Call time delay
  MOVLW     0x01                     ; Setting increment
  ADDWF     LATD, F                  ; Increment counter
  BTFSS     STATUS, 1, c             ; if DC is set, skip the next instruction
  GOTO      Next                     ; Go to Next label
  GOTO      main                     ; Go to main label

Delay:
  MOVLW     0x02                     ; Count1 = 02h
  MOVWF     d1
  MOVLW     0xFF                     ; Count2 = ffh
  MOVWF     d2
  MOVLW     0xFF                     ; Count3 = ffh
  MOVWF     d3
  DECFSZ    d3, F                    ; Decrement d3 register; skip the next
                                     ; instruction if it is zero
  GOTO      $-1
  DECFSZ    d2, F                    ; Decrement d2 register; skip the next
                                     ; instruction if it is zero
  GOTO      $-5
  DECFSZ    d1, F                    ; Decrement d1 register; skip the next
                                     ; instruction if it is zero
  GOTO      $-9
  RETURN                             ; Return to the main function
END resetVec
```

Experimental Result:

Counting means incrementing or decrementing the values of an operator, with respect to its previous state value. This particular counter is implemented with PIC18F4550 Microcontroller. It can start counts from 0000 to 1111.

RD3	RD2	RD1	RD0
0	0	0	0
0	0	0	1
0	0	1	0
0	0	1	1
0	1	0	0
0	1	0	1
0	1	1	0
0	1	1	1
1	0	0	0
1	0	0	1
1	0	1	0
1	0	1	1
1	1	0	0
1	1	0	1
1	1	1	0
1	1	1	1

Circuit Diagram:

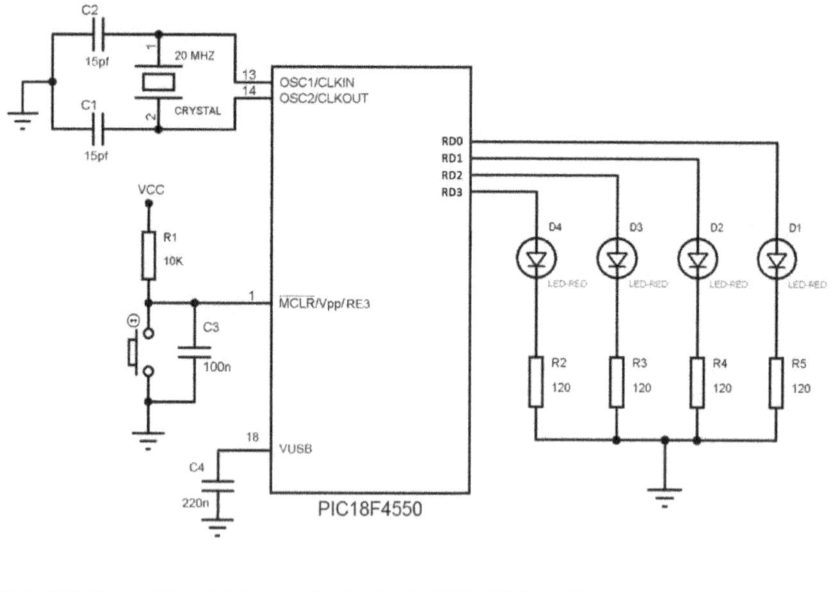

Conclusion:

The embedded system for implementing a 4-bit binary counter using a PIC18F4550 Microcontroller and assembly language has been successfully demonstrated.

26. SQUARE WAVEFORM GENERATION USING SOFTWARE DELAY

Aim:

Develop an embedded system using the PIC18F4550 Microcontroller to generate a 500 Hz square wave signal through software delay and verify its output using an assembly language program.

Hardware Requirements:

- PIC18F4550 Microcontroller, 20 MHz Crystal (1), 15 pF Disc Capacitors (2), 220 nF Disc Capacitor (1), 100 nF Disc Capacitor (1), Resistor 10K (1), and Push Button (1)
- Oscilloscope

Software Used:

- IDE: MPLAB X IDE v5.45
- PIC Assembler: pic-as (v2.31)

Theory:

Time delay generation is a crucial aspect of microcontroller applications, and it can be implemented in two primary ways:

- Software-based time delay
- On-chip timer-based time delay

When calculating time delays using software, consider the following factors:

- External Crystal Oscillator: The frequency of the crystal connected to the PIC18F4550 can range from 4 MHz to 20 MHz.

- Instruction Cycle Calculation: The time taken for the CPU to execute an instruction depends on the instruction cycle. In the PIC18F series, one instruction cycle comprises four oscillator periods. The clock input (from OSC1) is divided internally by four to produce four non-overlapping Quadrature clocks (Q1, Q2, Q3, and Q4). The program counter (PC) increments every Q1, and the instruction is fetched from program memory and latched into the instruction register in Q4. The instruction is decoded and executed during the next cycle. Due to pipeline operation, most instructions are executed in a single cycle, except for program branches.

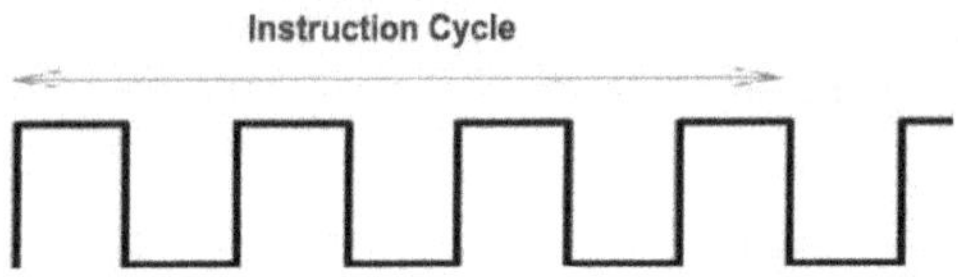

Calculating the instruction cycle of PIC18F for the following crystals:

4 MHz: 4 MHz/4 = 1 MHz

Instruction cycle = 1/1 MHz = 1 us [us=microsecond]

20 MHz: 20 MHz/4 = 5 MHz

Instruction cycle = 1/5 MHz = 0.2 us

Instructions – Execution time for 20 MHz:

Label	**Instructions**	**Instruction Cycle**	**No. of times to be executed**	**Total Execution Time**
Delay:	MOVLW D'07'	1	1	= **1*1***0.2μS = 0.2 μS
	MOVWF A1	1	1	= **1*1***0.2μS = 0.2 μS
back2:	MOVLW D'237'	1	7	= **1*7***0.2μS =1.4 μS
	MOVWF A2	1	7	= **1*7***0.2μS =1.4 μS
Back1:	DECFSZ B1, 1	1 / 2	236 x **7** 1 x **7**	=**1*236*7***0.2μS =330.4 μS = **1*7***0.2μS =1.4 μS
	GOTO Back1	2	236 x **7**	= **2*236*7***0.2μS =660.8μS
	DECFSZ A1, 1	1 / 2	6 1	= **1*6***0.2μS = 1.2 μS =**2*1***0.2μS = 0.4 μS

	GOTO Back2	2	6	= **2*6***0.2μS	= 2.4 μS
	RETURN	2	1	= **2*1***0.2μS	= 0.4 μS

Time delay = (0.2 + 0.2 + 1.4 + 1.4 + 330.4 + 1.4 + 660.8 + 1.2 + 0.4 + 2.4 + 0.4) μS
= 1000.2 μS = ~ 1 mS

Algorithm:

Main Program:

1. Define the PIC18 configuration bits using the config directive, include xc.inc, set the processor type, configure the vectors for reset and interrupts, and specify the starting address for the main program.
2. Configure PORTD0 as an output port.
3. Clear LATD0.
4. Call the Delay subroutine.
5. Set LATD0.
6. Call the Delay subroutine.
7. Return to step 3.

Delay Subroutine:

1. Load the outer loop count value into the A1 register.
2. Load the inner loop count value into the B1 register.
3. Decrement the B1 register; skip the next step if it is zero.
4. Return to step 3.
5. Decrement the A1 register; skip the next step if it is zero.
6. Return to step 2.
7. Return to the main program.

Program:

```
; PIC18 Configuration Bits Setting
config PLLDIV = 5, CPUDIV = OSC1_PLL2, USBDIV = 2, FOSC = HS
config FCMEN = OFF, IESO = OFF, PWRT = OFF, BOR = OFF, BORV = 3, VREGEN = OFF
config WDT = OFF, WDTPS = 32768, CCP2MX = ON, PBADEN = OFF, LPT1OSC = OFF
config MCLRE = ON, STVREN = ON, LVP = OFF, XINST = OFF
config CP0 = OFF, CP1 = OFF, CP2 = OFF, CP3 = OFF, CPB = OFF, CPD = OFF
config WRT0 = OFF, WRT1 = OFF, WRT2 = OFF, WRT3 = OFF, WRTC = OFF, WRTB = OFF,
WRTD = OFF
```

```
config EBTR0 = OFF, EBTR1 = OFF, EBTR2 = OFF, EBTR3 = OFF, EBTRB = OFF
#include <xc.inc>

PROCESSOR  18F4550
pagewidth  132
radix      dec
; Reset Vector of Processor 18F4550
psect  resetVec, global, reloc=2, class=CODE, delta=1
resetVec:
   goto   main
; High Priority Vector is at 000008h
psect  hi_int_vec, global, reloc=2, class=CODE, delta=1
goto   HighISR
psect  HighIsr_code, global, reloc=2, class=CODE, delta=1
HighISR:
   return 0
; Low Priority Vector is at 000018h
psect  lo_int_vec, global, reloc=2, class=CODE, delta=1
goto   LowISR
psect  LowIsr_code, global, reloc=2, class=CODE, delta=1
LowISR:
   return 0
; Main Program
psect  main, global, reloc=2, class=CODE, delta=1
org 0x100
main:
   A1    equ 0x30
   B1    equ 0x31

   BCF          TRISD, 0          ; RD0 in PORTD is output
repeat:
   BCF          LATD, 0           ; Clear RD0
   call         Delay             ; Call delay subroutine
   BSF          LATD, 0           ; Set RD1
```

```
    call          Delay          ; Call delay subroutine
    GOTO          repeat         ; Goto repeat

Delay:
    MOVLW         7              ; Outer loop count D'7' at WREG
    MOVWF         A1             ; Move the WREG to A1 register
Back2:
    MOVLW         237            ; Inner loop count D'237' at WREG
    MOVWF         B1             ; Move the WREG to B1 register
Back1:
    DECFSZ B1, 1                 ; Decrement B1 register; skip the next
                                 ; instruction if it is zero
    GOTO Back1                   ; Go to Back1
    DECFSZ A1, 1                 ; Decrement B1 register; skip the next
                                 ; instruction if it is zero
    GOTO Back2                   ; Go to Back2
    RETURN                       ; Return from subroutine
END resetVec
```

Circuit Diagram:

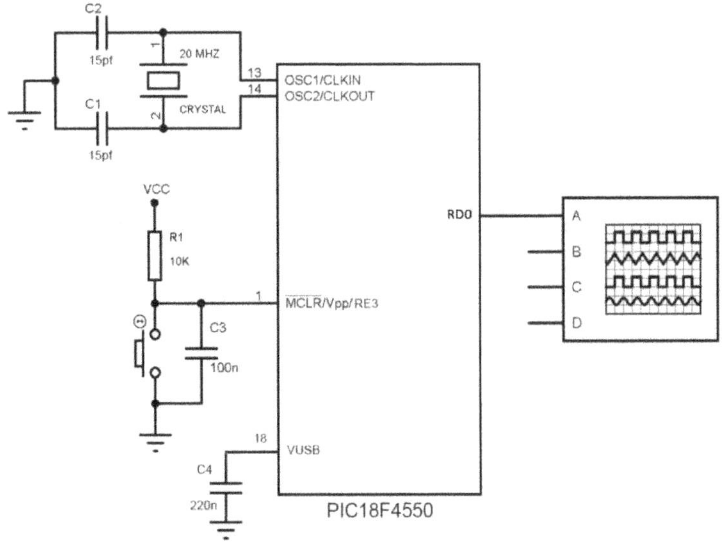

Calculation:

Frequency of square wave:

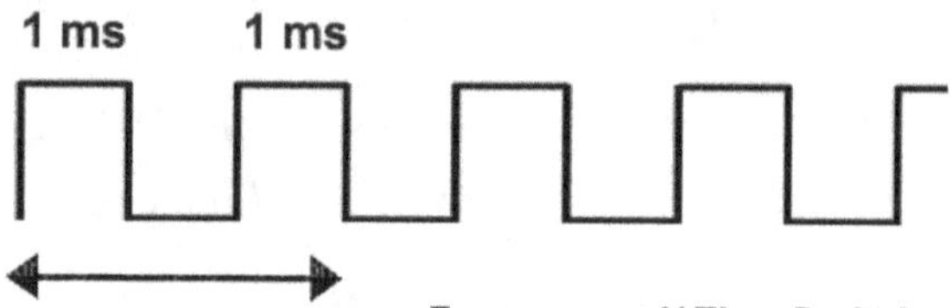

Time Period = 1 ms + 1 ms = 2 ms

Frequency = 1/ Time Period = 1 / 2 ms = 500 Hz

Experimental Result:

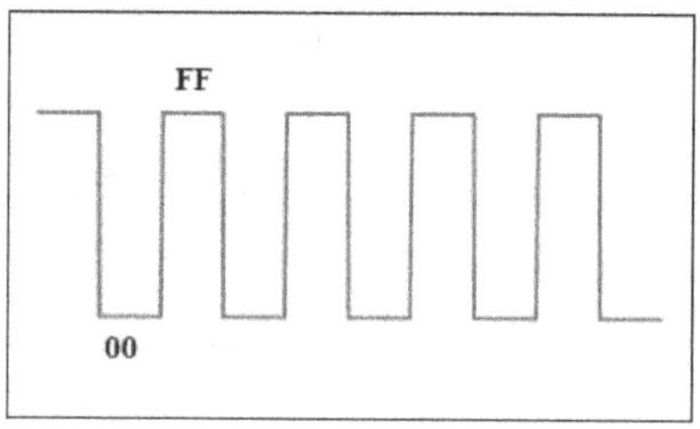

Conclusion:

The embedded system for generating a 50 Hz square wave using the PIC18F4550 Microcontroller and an assembly language program has been successfully demonstrated.

27. FLASHING OF LED

Aim:

Develop an embedded system to blink an LED using the PIC18F4550 Microcontroller with an Embedded C program, and verify the output.

Hardware Requirements:

- PIC18F4550 Microcontroller, 20 MHz Crystal (1), 15 pF Disc Capacitors (2), 220 nF Disc Capacitor (1), 100 nF Disc Capacitor (1), Resistor 10K (1), and Push Button (1)

- LED (1), Resistor 220 (1)

Software Used:

- IDE: MPLAB X IDE v5.45
- Compiler: XC8 - v2.31

Algorithm:

1. Define the PIC18 configuration bits using the pragma directive, include xc.h, and set the crystal frequency for _XTAL_FREQ to utilize the built-in delay function.
2. Configure PORTD0 (RD0) as an output port using the TRISD register (set to '1' for input and '0' for output).
3. Clear RD0 to turn off the LED.
4. Call the delay function to wait for 500 milliseconds.
5. Set RD0 to turn on the LED.
6. Call the delay function again to wait for 500 milliseconds.
7. Repeat the steps from step 3.

Program:

```
#pragma config PLLDIV = 5, CPUDIV = OSC1_PLL2, USBDIV = 2, FOSC = HS, FCMEN =
OFF, IESO = OFF
#pragma config PWRT = OFF, BOR = OFF, BORV = 3, VREGEN = OFF, WDT = OFF,
WDTPS = 32768
#pragma config CCP2MX = ON, PBADEN = OFF, LPT1OSC = OFF, MCLRE = ON
#pragma config STVREN = ON, LVP = OFF, ICPRT = OFF, XINST = OFF
#pragma config CP0 = OFF, CP1 = OFF, CP2 = OFF, CP3 = OFF, CPB = OFF, CPD = OFF
#pragma config WRT0 = OFF, WRT1 = OFF, WRT2 = OFF, WRT3 = OFF, WRTC = OFF,
WRTB = OFF, WRTD = OFF
#pragma config EBTR0 = OFF, EBTR1 = OFF, EBTR2 = OFF, EBTR3 = OFF, EBTRB = OFF

#include <xc.h>
#define _XTAL_FREQ   20000000
void main()
{
   TRISD0 = 0;                    // Set PORTD0 (RD0) as output port
   while (1)
```

```
    {
        LATD0 = 0;               // Clear LATD0
        __delay_ms(500);         // 500 ms delay using built-in function
        LATD0 = 1;               // Set LATD0
        __delay_ms(500);         // 500 ms delay using built-in function
    }
}
```

Circuit Diagram:

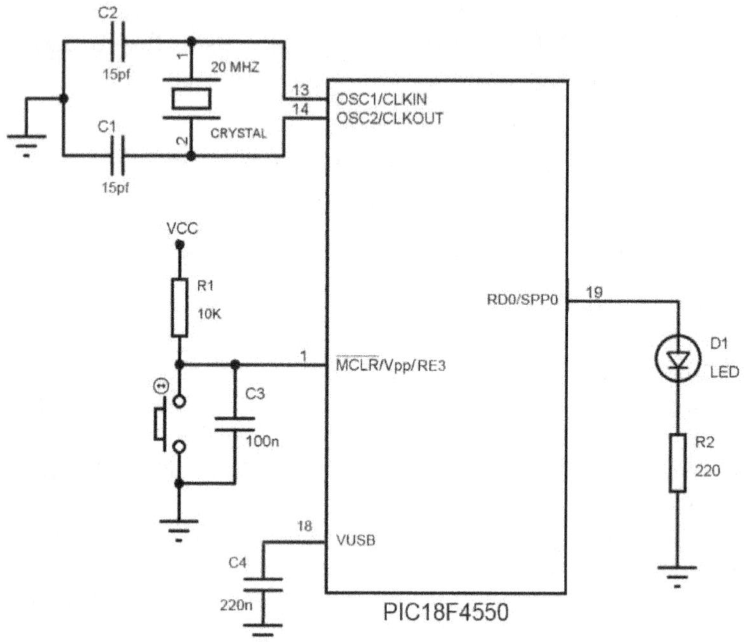

Experimental Result:

The LED connected to RD0 is flashing at regular time interval (500 ms + 500 ms).

Conclusion:

The embedded system for flashing an LED using the PIC18F4550 Microcontroller and an embedded C program has been successfully demonstrated.

28. READ KEY

Aim:

Design an embedded system to read a key press and toggle an LED using the PIC18F4550 Microcontroller and an Embedded C program. Verify the system's functionality.

Hardware Requirements:

- PIC18F4550 Microcontroller, 20 MHz Crystal (1), 15 pF Disc Capacitors (2), 220 nF Disc Capacitor (1), 100 nF Disc Capacitor (1), Resistor 10K (1), and Push Button (1)
- Key/ Push Button (1), Disc Capacitor 100 nF (1), Resistor 2.2 K (1), Resistor 220 (1), LED (1)

Software Used:

- IDE: MPLAB X IDE v5.45
- Compiler: XC8 - v2.31

Theory:

The pushbutton is a type of switch used to turn a circuit on or off. In this setup, the pushbutton is connected to the input port PORTC0 (RC0) and is paired with a pull-up resistor. When the switch is not pressed, RC0 receives the VCC potential. When the switch is pressed, RC0 is grounded. An LED is connected to PORTD0 (RD0) and will toggle its state with each key press.

Algorithm:

1. Define the PIC18 configuration bits using the pragma directive, include xc.h, and set the crystal frequency for _XTAL_FREQ to utilize the built-in delay function.
2. Initialize PORTC0 as an input port and PORTD0 as an output port using the TRISC and TRISD registers.
3. Clear RD0 (LED port).
4. If the key connected to RC0 is pressed:

4.1 Introduce a 50 ms delay to debounce the key.

4.2 Proceed with the following steps if the key remains pressed; otherwise, skip steps 4.3 and 4.4.

4.3 Toggle the state of RD0.

4.4 Wait for the key to be released.

5. Repeat the sequence starting from step 4.

Program:

```
#pragma config PLLDIV = 5, CPUDIV = OSC1_PLL2, USBDIV = 2, FOSC = HS, FCMEN = OFF, IESO = OFF
#pragma config PWRT = OFF, BOR = OFF, BORV = 3, VREGEN = OFF, WDT = OFF, WDTPS = 32768
#pragma config CCP2MX = ON, PBADEN = OFF, LPT1OSC = OFF, MCLRE = ON
#pragma config STVREN = ON, LVP = OFF, ICPRT = OFF, XINST = OFF
#pragma config CP0 = OFF, CP1 = OFF, CP2 = OFF, CP3 = OFF, CPB = OFF, CPD = OFF
#pragma config WRT0 = OFF, WRT1 = OFF, WRT2 = OFF, WRT3 = OFF, WRTC = OFF, WRTB = OFF, WRTD = OFF
#pragma config EBTR0 = OFF, EBTR1 = OFF, EBTR2 = OFF, EBTR3 = OFF, EBTRB = OFF
#include <xc.h>
#define _XTAL_FREQ 20000000
#define LED LATD0
#define KEY PORTCbits.RC0
void main()  {                    // Main Function
  TRISC0 = 1;                     // PORTC0 is configured as input port
  TRISD0 = 0;                     // PORTD0 is configured as output port
  LED = 0;                        // Clear PORTD0
  while (1)                       // Forever loop
  {
  if(KEY == 0)                    // If the switch is pressed
  {
  __delay_ms(50);                 // Debounce Delay
  if(KEY == 0)                    // If the switch is still pressed
    {
     LED = ~ LED;                 // Toggle LED
     while(KEY == 0);             // Wait for release
    }
```

```
    }
  }
}
```

Circuit Diagram:

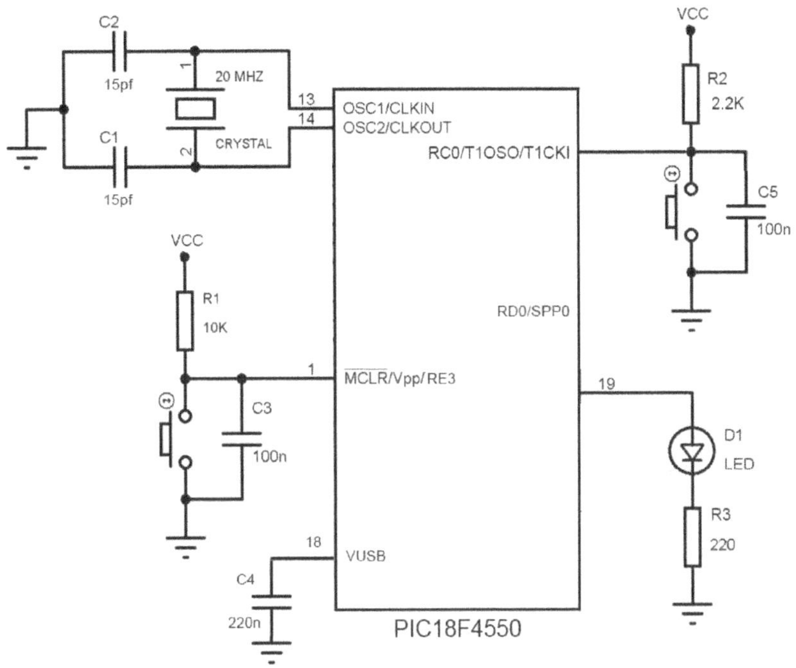

Conclusion:

The experiment to read the status of a key and toggle an LED using a PIC18F4550 Microcontroller and an embedded C program has been successfully demonstrated.

29. TRAFFIC LIGHT CONTROLLER

Aim:

Develop an embedded system for a traffic light controller using the PIC18F4550 Microcontroller and an Embedded C program, and verify its functionality.

Hardware Requirements:

- PIC18F4550 Microcontroller, 20 MHz Crystal (1), 15 pF Disc Capacitors (2), 220 nF Disc Capacitor (1), 100 nF Disc Capacitor (1), Resistor 10K (1), and Push Button (1)
- LEDs Red (4), LEDs Yellow (4), LEDs Green (4), and Resistor 120 (12)

Software Used:

- IDE: MPLAB X IDE v5.45
- Compiler: XC8 - v2.31

Theory:

The traffic light arrangement of the proposed traffic light system is shown in the below figure.

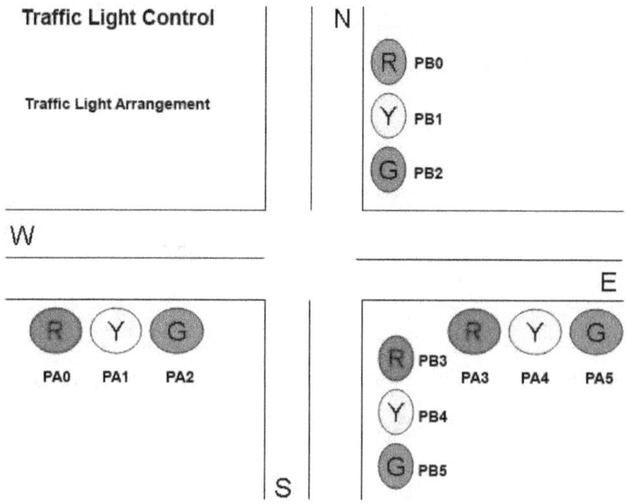

The traffic light sequence for the controller is described as follows:

1. Allow traffic to flow from West to East and East to West for 20 seconds.
2. Provide a transition period of 4 seconds with yellow lights on.
3. Allow traffic to flow from North to South and South to North for 20 seconds.
4. Provide a transition period of 4 seconds with yellow lights on.

5. Repeat the sequence.

South			North			East			West			HEX RD/RB
Green	Yellow	Red	Green	Yellow	Red	Green	Yellow	Red	Green	Yellow	Red	
RD5	RD4	RD3	RD2	RD1	RD0	RB5	RB4	RB3	RB2	RB1	RB0	
0	0	1	0	0	1	1	0	0	1	0	0	09/24
Delay for 6 seconds												
0	1	0	0	1	0	0	1	0	0	1	0	12/12
Delay for 2 seconds												
1	0	0	1	0	0	0	0	1	0	0	1	24/09
Delay for 6 seconds												
0	1	0	0	1	0	0	1	0	0	1	0	12/12
Delay for 2 seconds												

Algorithm:

1. Define the PIC18 configuration bits using the pragma directive, include xc.h, and set the crystal frequency for _XTAL_FREQ to utilize the built-in delay function.
2. Initialize the digital values for the traffic light sequence as array elements for PORTB and PORTD.
3. Configure PORTB and PORTD as output ports.
4. Output the PB_Val[0] element to LATB.
5. Output the PD_Val[0] element to LATD.
6. Introduce a delay of 5000 ms.
7. Output the PB_Val[1] element to LATB.
8. Output the PD_Val[1] element to LATD.
9. Introduce a delay of 1000 ms.
10. Output the PB_Val[2] element to LATB.
11. Output the PD_Val[2] element to LATD.
12. Introduce a delay of 5000 ms.
13. Output the PB_Val[3] element to LATB.
14. Output the PD_Val[3] element to LATD.

15. Introduce a delay of 1000 ms.
16. Repeat from step 4.

Program:

```
#pragma config PLLDIV = 5, CPUDIV = OSC1_PLL2, USBDIV = 2, FOSC = HS, FCMEN =
OFF, IESO = OFF
#pragma config PWRT = OFF, BOR = OFF, BORV = 3, VREGEN = OFF, WDT = OFF,
WDTPS = 32768
#pragma config CCP2MX = ON, PBADEN = OFF, LPT1OSC = OFF, MCLRE = ON
#pragma config STVREN = ON, LVP = OFF, ICPRT = OFF, XINST = OFF
#pragma config CP0 = OFF, CP1 = OFF, CP2 = OFF, CP3 = OFF, CPB = OFF, CPD = OFF
#pragma config WRT0 = OFF, WRT1 = OFF, WRT2 = OFF, WRT3 = OFF, WRTC = OFF,
WRTB = OFF, WRTD = OFF
#pragma config EBTR0 = OFF, EBTR1 = OFF, EBTR2 = OFF, EBTR3 = OFF, EBTRB = OFF

#include <xc.h>
#define _XTAL_FREQ 20000000

void main()
{
   unsigned char PB_Val[4] = {0x24,0x12,0x09,0x12};
   unsigned char PD_Val[4] = {0x09,0x12,0x24,0x12};
   TRISB = 0x00;              // set PORTB as output
   TRISD = 0x00;              // set PORTD as output
   LATB = 0x00;               // Clear LATB
   LATD = 0x00;               // Clear LATD
while (1)
   {
      LATB = PB_Val[0];       // 0x24 to LATB
      LATD = PD_Val[0];       // 0x09 to LATD
      __delay_ms(5000);       // Delay for 5 sec
      LATB = PB_Val[1];       // 0x12 to LATB
      LATD = PD_Val[1];       // 0x12 to LATD
      __delay_ms(1000);       // Delay for 1 sec
      LATB = PB_Val[2];       // 0x09 to LATB
      LATD = PD_Val[2];       // 0x24 to LATD
```

```
        __delay_ms(5000);          // Delay for 5 sec
        LATB = PB_Val[3];          // 0x12 to LATB
        LATD = PD_Val[3];          // 0x12 to LATD
        __delay_ms(1000);          // Delay for 1 sec
    }
}
```

Experimental - Output:

Sequence	PORTD	PORTB
1	09H	24H
2	12H	12H
3	24H	09H
4	12H	12H

Circuit Diagram:

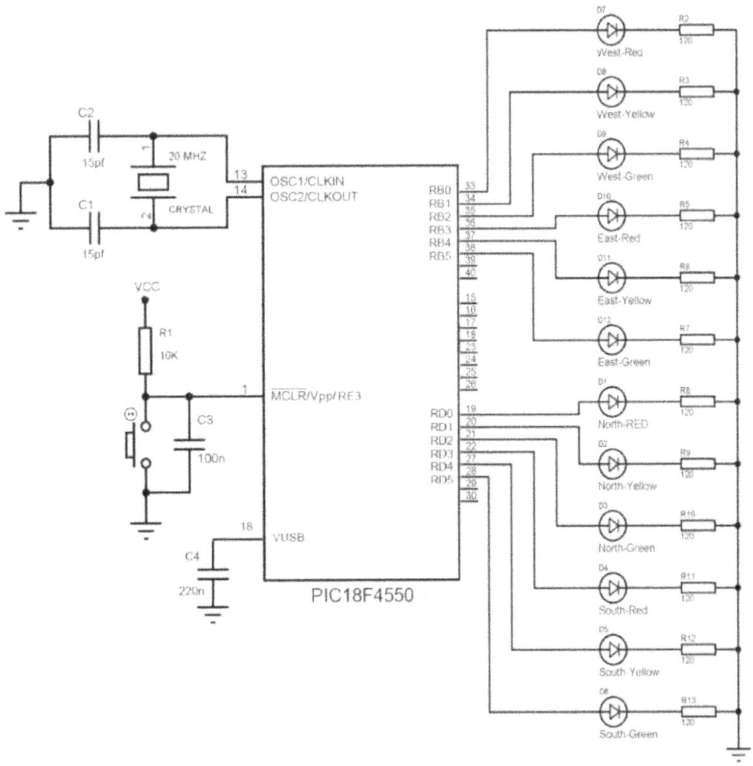

Conclusion:

The embedded system for controlling traffic lights using the PIC18F4550 Microcontroller and an embedded C program has been successfully demonstrated.

30. SEVEN SEGMENT DISPLAY INTERFACE

Aim:

Develop an embedded system to count seconds using a 2-digit seven-segment LED display, employing a PIC18F4550 Microcontroller and an embedded C program. Verify the output of the system.

Hardware Requirements:

- PIC18F4550 Microcontroller, 20 MHz Crystal (1), 15 pF Disc Capacitors (2), 220 nF Disc Capacitor (1), 100 nF Disc Capacitor (1), Resistor 10K (1), and Push Button (1)
- CA Seven Segment Display (2), NPN Transistor BC547 (2), Resistor 1K (2)

Software Used:

- IDE: MPLAB X IDE v5.45
- Compiler: XC8 - v2.31

Theory:

A seven-segment display is an electronic component used to show numbers and some letters. It features seven LED segments that can be lit in various combinations to form different characters. Seven-segment displays come in two main types: common anode and common cathode.

Common Cathode (CC) Display: In this configuration, the cathode terminals of all seven segments are connected to a common ground. When operating the display, this common cathode should be connected to the ground of the power source.

Common Anode (CA) Display: Here, the anode terminals of all seven segments are linked to a common terminal. For proper operation, this common anode should be connected to the positive terminal of the power source.

Each segment of the display is activated by sending specific hexadecimal codes to the appropriate pins. Below is a table showing the display codes for digits 0 through 9 for a common anode display:

Number To display	H	G	F	E	D	C	B	A	HEX
0	1	1	0	0	0	0	0	0	0xC0
1	1	1	1	1	1	0	0	1	0xF9
2	1	0	1	0	0	1	0	0	0xA4
3	1	0	1	1	0	0	0	0	0xB0
4	1	0	0	1	1	0	0	1	0x99
5	1	0	0	1	0	0	1	0	0x92
6	1	0	0	0	0	0	1	0	0x82
7	1	1	1	1	1	0	0	0	0xF8
8	1	0	0	0	0	0	0	0	0x80
9	1	0	0	1	0	0	0	0	0x90

The multiplexing technique is used to control multiple seven-segment displays with a limited number of microcontroller pins. By rapidly switching between displays, it creates the illusion that all segments are active at once, even though only one display is illuminated at any given moment. For a seconds' counter circuit using two seven-segment displays, multiplexing efficiently drives both displays. In this setup:

PORTD provides the segment code inputs to the displays, ensuring the correct segments light up for each digit.

PORTB manages which display is active, enabling the alternating display of the two units.

This rapid switching between the displays gives the appearance that both displays are on simultaneously, thereby showing the full time on both seven-segment displays.

Algorithm:

1. Define the PIC18 configuration bits using the pragma directive, include xc.h, and set the crystal frequency for _XTAL_FREQ to utilize the built-in delay function.
2. Initialize the seven-segment digit codes for a common anode display.
3. Configure PORTB and PORTD as output ports using the TRIS registers.
4. Clear the LATB and LATD registers.
5. Initialize the variables i, j, and k.
6. Create a for loop with a target value of 100 (covering 'a' to 'f'):
   a. Select digit 0 by setting RB1 = 1.
   b. Send the segment code to PORTD, indexed by i.
   c. Implement a 5 ms delay.
   d. Select digit 1 by setting RB0 = 1.
   e. Send the segment code to PORTD, indexed by j.
   f. Implement a 5 ms delay.
7. Increment the value of i.
8. If i equals 10, set i to 0 and increment j.
9. If j equals 6, set j to 0.
10. Repeat the steps from step 6.

Program:

```
#pragma config PLLDIV = 5, CPUDIV = OSC1_PLL2, USBDIV = 2, FOSC = HS, FCMEN =
OFF, IESO = OFF
#pragma config PWRT = OFF, BOR = OFF, BORV = 3, VREGEN = OFF, WDT = OFF,
WDTPS = 32768
#pragma config CCP2MX = ON, PBADEN = OFF, LPT1OSC = OFF, MCLRE = ON
#pragma config STVREN = ON, LVP = OFF, ICPRT = OFF, XINST = OFF
#pragma config CP0 = OFF, CP1 = OFF, CP2 = OFF, CP3 = OFF, CPB = OFF, CPD = OFF
#pragma config WRT0 = OFF, WRT1 = OFF, WRT2 = OFF, WRT3 = OFF, WRTC = OFF,
WRTB = OFF, WRTD = OFF
#pragma config EBTR0 = OFF, EBTR1 = OFF, EBTR2 = OFF, EBTR3 = OFF, EBTRB = OFF

#include <xc.h>
#define _XTAL_FREQ 20000000
#define DIGIT_MSB LATB0
```

```
#define DIGIT_LSB LATB1
#define SEGMENT LATD

void main()
{
   unsigned char Segment_Code[10] = {0xc0, 0xf9, 0xa4, 0xb0, 0x99, 0x92,
    0x83, 0xf8, 0x80, 0x98};          // seven-segment digit codes for CA
   TRISB = 0x00;                      // set PORTB as output
   TRISD = 0x00;                      // set PORTD as output
   LATB = 0x00;                       // Clear PORTB
   LATD = 0x00;                       // Clear PORTD
   int i=0,j=0,k;

  while (1)
   {
      for (k=0; k<100; k++)
      {
      DIGIT_MSB=0; DIGIT_LSB=1;         //select LSB digit
      SEGMENT = Segment_Code[i];        //Send the segment code
                                        // indexed by i to PORTD
      __delay_ms(5);                    //buffer delay time for 5 ms
      DIGIT_MSB=1; DIGIT_LSB=0;         //select LSB digit
      SEGMENT = Segment_Code[j];        //Send the segment code
                                        // indexed by j to PORTD
      __delay_ms(5);                    // buffer delay time for 5 ms
      }
      i++;                              // increment the digit0 value
      if (i==10)                        // if digit0 is >9
      {
      i=0;                              // digit0 index is cleared and digit1
                                        // index is increment by 1
      j++;
      }
      if(j==6)                          // if digit1 index is >5, clear digit1 index
```

```
        {
        j=0;
        }
    }
}
```

Circuit Diagram:

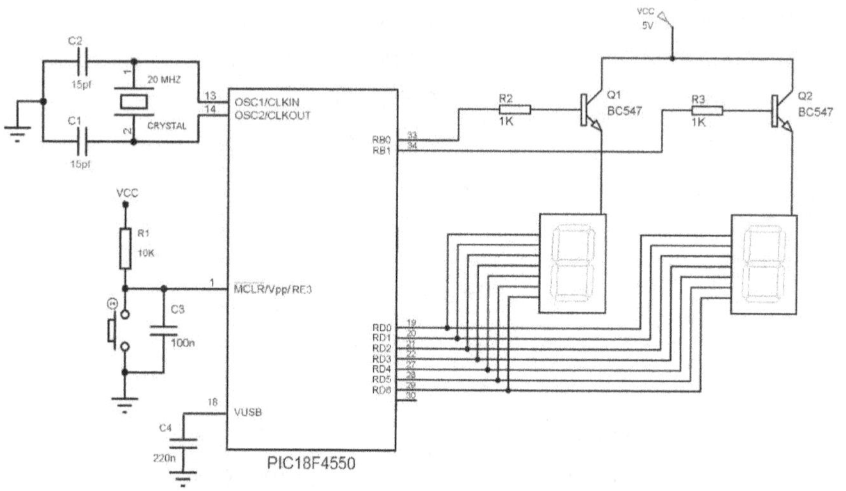

Conclusion:

The embedded system for a seconds' counter using a 2-digit seven-segment LED display, implemented with a PIC18F4550 Microcontroller and an embedded C program, has been successfully demonstrated.

31. LCD INTERFACE IN 4-BIT MODE

Aim:

Design and implement an embedded system to display characters on a 16x2 LCD screen using a PIC18F4550 Microcontroller and an Embedded C program. Verify the output of the system.

Hardware Requirements:

- PIC18F4550 Microcontroller, 20 MHz Crystal (1), 15 pF Disc Capacitors (2), 220 nF Disc Capacitor (1), 100 nF Disc Capacitor (1), Resistor 10K (1), and Push Button (1)
- 16x2 LCD

Software Used:

- IDE: MPLAB X IDE v5.45
- Compiler: XC8 - v2.31

Theory:

A 16×2 LCD is an output device used to display data or information. The term "16x2" refers to the LCD's ability to display 16 characters per line across two lines. This type of LCD can show numbers, characters, and special symbols. To display characters, you need to send the ASCII value of the character to the data register. Additionally, to configure the LCD, you must send command words to its command register.

LCD Pin description:

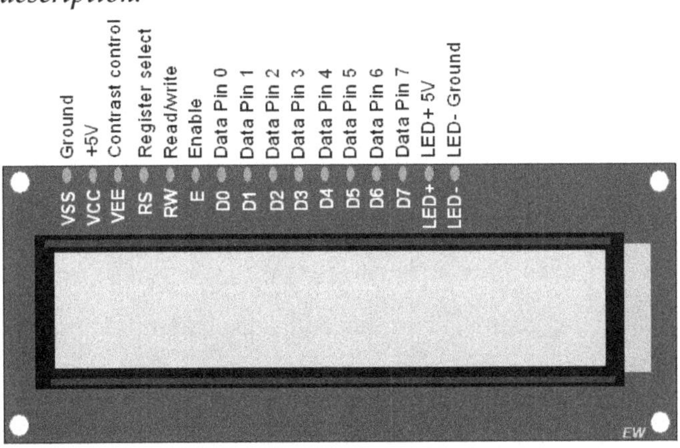

- **Vss/GND, Vdd, VE & +Ve**
  - Supply +5V to Vdd(pin2) and +Ve (pin15)
  - Connect Ground to Vss (pin1) and backlight cathode (pin16)
  - VE is used to control the contrast of the LCD screen.
- **RS, Register select**

- There are two important registers in the LCD. One is a data register and the other is the command register.
- If data is sent to data register the data is considered as data to be displayed on the LCD. If the command is sent to the command register which configures the LCD.
  * If RS=0, the command register is selected
  * If RS=1, the data register is selected

- **R/W, Read/Write**

  It is an input pin that allows the user to read data from the LCD or write data into the LCD.

  * To write data to LCD connect R/W pin to GND
  * To read data from LCD connect R/W pin to VCC

S. No	HEX Value	Command to LCD
1	0x01	Clear Display Screen
2	0x30	Function set: 8-bit, 1 Line, 5x7 Dots
3	0x38	Function set: 8-bit, 2 Line, 5x7 Dots
4	0x20	Function set: 4-bit, 1 Line, 5x7 Dots
5	0x28	Function set: 4-bit, 2 Line, 5x7 Dots
6	0x06	Entry Mode
7	0x08	Display off, Cursor off
8	0x0E	Display on, Cursor on
9	0x0C	Display on, Cursor off
10	0x0F	Display on, Cursor blinking
11	0x18	Shift entire display left
12	0x1C	Shift entire display right
13	0x10	Move cursor left by one character
14	0x14	Move cursor right by one character
15	0x80	Force cursor to beginning of first row
16	0xC0	Force cursor to beginning of second row

Algorithm:

Here the16x2 LCD is interfaced with PIC18F4550 in 4-bit mode.

Only RS, E, D4, D6, D7 and D8 pins of LCD will be used for the interfacing. (RW pin is grounded)

Main File:

1. Define the PIC18 configuration bits using the pragma directive, include xc.h, and set the crystal frequency for _XTAL_FREQ to use the built-in delay function.
2. Configure RD2 and RD3 as RS (Register Select) and EN (Enable), respectively.
3. Configure RD4, RD5, RD6, and RD7 as the data bus lines for the LCD.
4. Include the header file lcd4bit_head.h.
5. Set PORTD as output ports using the TRIS registers.
6. Call the lcd_init() function to initialize the LCD in 4-bit mode.
7. Use the lcd_cmd() function to send the command 0x80 to the LCD to position the cursor at the first row, first column.
8. Use the lcd_display() function to display the text "Interfacing LCD."
9. Use the lcd_cmd() function to send the command 0xC0 to the LCD to position the cursor at the second row, first column.
10. Use the lcd_display() function to display the text "With PIC18F MCU."
11. Add a 3000 ms delay to hold the displayed text on the screen.
12. Clear the LCD screen.
13. Repeat the steps from step 5.

Header file:

1. Lcd_WriteBit() function

   Write the LSB of argument value to RD4-RD7.
2. lcd_cmd () function
   1. Make RS pin low, RS=0.
   2. Send higher nibble of argument value to Lcd_WriteBit().
   3. Give High to Low pulse to Enable (E).

   iv. Make RS pin low, RS=0.
   v. Send lower nibble of argument value to Lcd_WriteBit().
   vi. Give High to Low pulse to Enable (E).
3. lcd_data () function
   i. Make RS pin high, RS=1.
   ii. Send higher nibble of argument to Lcd_WriteBit().
   iii. Give High to Low pulse to Enable (E).
   iv. Make RS pin high, RS=1.
   v. Send lower nibble of argument to Lcd_WriteBit().
   vi. Give High to Low pulse to Enable (E).
4. lcd_display () function
   i. Call lcd_data () function to write the character to LCD until the null characer received from argument variable.
   ii. Make 10 ms delay.
   iii. Increment argument variable.
5. lcd_init() function

   Call lcd_cmd() function to write the commands 0x02, 0x28, 0x0C, 0x06, and 0x01 to the LCD.

Program:

// Main file:

```
#pragma config PLLDIV = 5, CPUDIV = OSC1_PLL2, USBDIV = 2, FOSC = HS, FCMEN =
OFF, IESO = OFF
#pragma config PWRT = OFF, BOR = OFF, BORV = 3, VREGEN = OFF, WDT = OFF,
WDTPS = 32768
#pragma config CCP2MX = ON, PBADEN = OFF, LPT1OSC = OFF, MCLRE = ON
#pragma config STVREN = ON, LVP = OFF, ICPRT = OFF, XINST = OFF
#pragma config CP0 = OFF, CP1 = OFF, CP2 = OFF, CP3 = OFF, CPB = OFF, CPD = OFF
#pragma config WRT0 = OFF, WRT1 = OFF, WRT2 = OFF, WRT3 = OFF, WRTC = OFF,
WRTB = OFF, WRTD = OFF
#pragma config EBTR0 = OFF, EBTR1 = OFF, EBTR2 = OFF, EBTR3 = OFF, EBTRB = OFF

#include <xc.h>
#define _XTAL_FREQ 20000000
#define RS      LATD2                   // RD2 is named as RS
#define EN      LATD3                   // RD3 is named as EN
```

```
#define D4     LATD4                        // 4-bit mode (RD4-D4, RD5-D5
#define D5     LATD5                        // RD6-D6, RD7-D7)
#define D6     LATD6
#define D7     LATD7
#include "lcd4bit_head.h"                   // Include header file - lcd4bit_head.h

void main() {                               // Main function
  TRISD = 0x00;                             // set PORT D as output ports
  lcd_init ();                              // Call lcd_init() function
  while (1) {                               // Forever loop
    lcd_cmd(0x80);                          // cursor position at 0th addr of line1
    lcd_display("Interfacing LCD");         // Call lcd_display() function
    lcd_cmd(0xC0);                          // cursor position at 0th addr of line2
    lcd_display("With PIC18F MCU");         // Call lcd_display() function
    __delay_ms(3000);                       // Make 3000 ms delay time
    lcd_cmd(0x01);                          // clear the screen
  }
}
-----------------------------------------------------------------------------------------------
// Header file: lcd4bit_head.h
void Lcd_WriteBit(unsigned char bt) {       //write the nibble on 4-bit data bus of LCD
  if(bt & 1)
    D4 = 1;
  else
    D4 = 0;
  if(bt & 2)
    D5 = 1;
  else
    D5 = 0;
  if(bt & 4)
    D6 = 1;
  else
    D6 = 0;
  if(bt & 8)
```

```
        D7 = 1;
    else
        D7 = 0;
}

void lcd_cmd(unsigned char CMD) {          // Definition of lcd_cmd() function
    RS = 0;                                // Make RS pin low to select CMD reg.
    Lcd_WriteBit((CMD >> 4) & 0x0FU);      // Send Higher Nibble of CMD
    EN = 1;                                // Give High to Low pulse to Enable (E)
    __delay_ms(2);
    EN = 0;
    __delay_ms(5);
    RS = 0;
    Lcd_WriteBit(CMD & 0x0FU);             // Send Lower Nibble of CMD
    EN = 1;                                // Give High to Low pulse to Enable (E)
    __delay_ms(2);
    EN = 0;
    __delay_ms(5);
}

void lcd_data(unsigned char DAT) {         // Definition of lcd_data() function
    RS = 1;                                // Make RS pin high to select data reg.
    Lcd_WriteBit((DAT >> 4) & 0x0FU);      // Send Higher Nibble of data
    EN = 1;                                // Give High to Low pulse to Enable (E)
    __delay_ms(2);
    EN = 0;
    __delay_ms(5);
    RS = 1;
    Lcd_WriteBit(DAT & 0x0FU);             // Send Lower Nibble of data
    EN = 1;                                // Give High to Low pulse to Enable (E)
    __delay_ms(2);
    EN = 0;
    __delay_ms(5);
}
```

```
void lcd_display(char *x){              // Definition of lcd_display () function
  while(*x!=0x0) {                      // Condition is true until null character
  lcd_data(*x);                         // Send a character to LCD screen
  __delay_ms(10);                       // Make 10 ms delay
  x++;                                  // Increment pointer variable
  }
}
void lcd_init () {
  lcd_cmd(0x02); __delay_ms(12);        // 16X2 LCD in 4-bit mode
  lcd_cmd(0x28); __delay_ms(12);        // 2 lines, 5X7 dots in 4-bit mode
  lcd_cmd(0x0C); __delay_ms(12);        // Display ON Cursor OFF
  lcd_cmd(0x06); __delay_ms(12);        // Auto Increment cursor
  lcd_cmd(0x01); __delay_ms(12);        // Clear Display
}
```

Circuit Diagram:

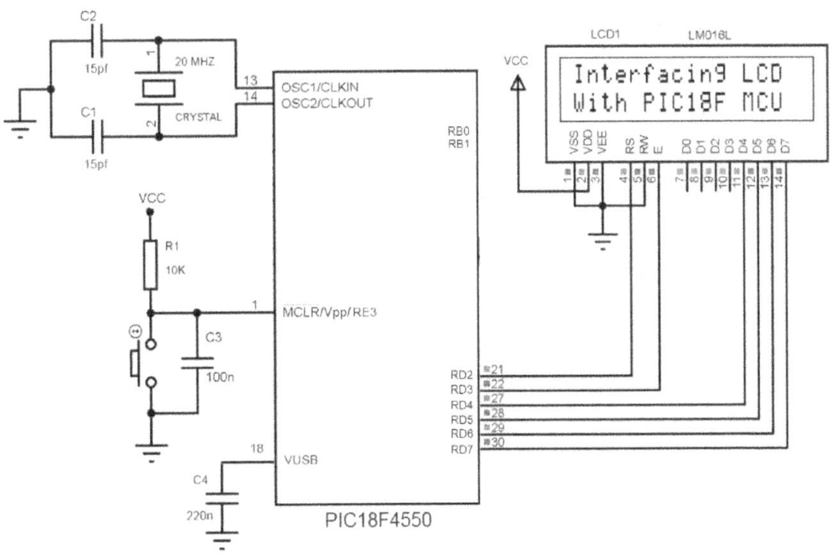

Experimental Output:

Display on LCD Screen	
Line 1	Interfacing LCD
Line 2	With PIC18F MCU

Conclusion:

An embedded system that displays characters on a 16x2 LCD using a PIC18F4550 Microcontroller and an embedded C program has been successfully demonstrated.

32. HEX KEYBOARD INTERFACE

Aim:

Develop an embedded system to interface a hex keyboard and display the pressed key number on a seven-segment display using a PIC18F4550 Microcontroller and an embedded C program, and verify its output.

Hardware Requirements:

- PIC18F4550 Microcontroller, 20 MHz Crystal (1), 15 pF Disc Capacitors (2), 220 nF Disc Capacitor (1), 100 nF Disc Capacitor (1), Resistor 10K (1), and Push Button (1)
- Hex key board and CA Seven Segment Display

Software Used:

- IDE: MPLAB X IDE v5.45
- Compiler: XC8 - v2.31

Theory:

A hex keyboard consists of 16 keys arranged in a 4×4 matrix. Typically, it includes keys representing numbers 0-9 and letters A, B, C, D, along with * and #. The keyboard has eight communication lines: R1, R2, R3, R4 (for the rows) and C1, C2, C3, C4 (for the columns). When a key is pressed, the corresponding row and column terminals connected to that key are shorted. The diagram of a typical hex keypad is shown in the figure below.

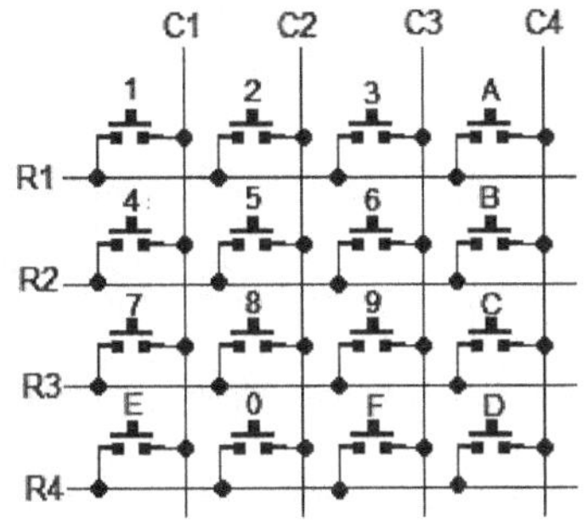

The column scanning method is used to identify the pressed key. In this method, one specific row is kept low while the other rows remain high. The logic status of each column line is then scanned. If a particular column is found to be low, it indicates that the key between that column and the low row has been pressed.

Algorithm:

Main Program:

1. Define the PIC18 configuration bits using the pragma directive, include xc.h, and define the crystal frequency for _XTAL_FREQ to use the built-in delay function.
2. Define PORTB for keyboard terminals and PORTD for the 7-segment display.
3. Configure the least significant 4 bits of PORTB as output ports and the most significant 4 bits of PORTB as input ports using the TRIS register.
4. Configure PORTD as an output port using the TRIS register.
5. Clear PORTD.
6. Set the key value to 0xFF.
7. Call the Read_Key() function and store the return value in the segment (PORTD) variable.
8. Introduce a 200 ms delay.
9. Repeat from step 7.

Subroutine: Read_Key()

1. Scan ROW1 of the keyboard by clearing r1 and setting r2, r3, and r4.
   If c1 is clear, return 0x8E to display F on 7 segment.
   If c2 is clear, return 0x86 to display E on 7 segment.
   If c3 is clear, return 0xA1 to display D on 7 segment.
   If c4 is clear, return 0xC6 to display C on 7 segment.
2. Scan ROW2 of the keyboard by clearing r2 and setting r1, r3, and r4.
   If c1 is clear, return 0x83 to display B on 7 segment.
   If c2 is clear, return 0x88 to display A on 7 segment.
   If c3 is clear, return 0x90 to display 9 on 7 segment.
   If c4 is clear, return 0x80 to display 8 on 7 segment.
3. Scan ROW3 of the keyboard by clearing r3 and setting r1, r2, and r4.
   If c1 is clear, return 0xF8 to display 7 on 7 segment.
   If c2 is clear, return 0x82 to display 6 on 7 segment.
   If c3 is clear, return 0x92 to display 5 on 7 segment.
   If c4 is clear, return 0x99 to display 4 on 7 segment.
4. Scan ROW4 of the keyboard by clearing r4 and setting r1, r2, and r3.
   If c1 is clear, return 0xB0 to display 3 on 7 segment.
   If c2 is clear, return 0xA4 to display 2 on 7 segment.
   If c3 is clear, return 0xF9 to display 1 on 7 segment.
   If c4 is clear, return 0xC0 to display 0 on 7 segment.

Program:

```
#pragma config PLLDIV = 5, CPUDIV = OSC1_PLL2, USBDIV = 2, FOSC = HS, FCMEN =
OFF, IESO = OFF
#pragma config PWRT = OFF, BOR = OFF, BORV = 3, VREGEN = OFF, WDT = OFF,
WDTPS = 32768
#pragma config CCP2MX = ON, PBADEN = OFF, LPT1OSC = OFF, MCLRE = ON
#pragma config STVREN = ON, LVP = OFF, ICPRT = OFF, XINST = OFF
#pragma config CP0 = OFF, CP1 = OFF, CP2 = OFF, CP3 = OFF, CPB = OFF, CPD = OFF
#pragma config WRT0 = OFF, WRT1 = OFF, WRT2 = OFF, WRT3 = OFF, WRTC = OFF,
WRTB = OFF, WRTD = OFF
#pragma config EBTR0 = OFF, EBTR1 = OFF, EBTR2 = OFF, EBTR3 = OFF, EBTRB = OFF

#include <xc.h>
#define _XTAL_FREQ 20000000
#define r1  LATB0                    // RB0-RB3 connected with r1 to r4
```

```
#define r2  LATB1
#define r3  LATB2
#define r4  LATB3
#define c1  PORTBbits.RB4          // RB4-RB7 connected with c1 to c4
#define c2  PORTBbits.RB5
#define c3  PORTBbits.RB6
#define c4  PORTBbits.RB7
#define segment LATD               // PORTD is connected with 7 segment
unsigned char key;                 // Global declaration
unsigned char Read_Key(void);              // Function declaration

// C    D    E    F                // Keys position at HEX keyboard
// 8    9    A    B
// 4    5    6    7
// 0    1    2    3

void main(void)                    // Main function
{
  TRISB = 0xF0;                    // RB7-RB4 are input ports and
                                   // PB3-RB0 are output ports

  TRISD = 0x00;                    // PORTD as output port
  LATD = 0x00;                     // Clear PORTD
  key = 0xff;                      // Assume no key pressed
 while(1)
  {
  segment = Read_Key();            // Read the pressed key and move it to
                                   // the seven segment display

  key = segment;
  __delay_ms(200);                 // Make 200 ms delay
  }
}

// Scan all the keys in the HEX keypad and detect the pressed key that
// will be return to the main function
```

```
unsigned char Read_Key(void)
{
r1=0; r2=1; r3=1; r4=1; __delay_ms(10);     // Scan r1 of keyboard
if (c1==0){__delay_ms(200); while(c1==0); return 0x8e;}          //f
if (c2==0){__delay_ms(200); while(c2==0); return 0x86;}          //e
if (c3==0){__delay_ms(200); while(c3==0); return 0xa1;}          //d
if (c4==0){__delay_ms(200); while(c4==0); return 0xc6;}          //c

r1=1; r2=0; r3=1; r4=1; __delay_ms(10);     // Scan r2 of keyboard
if (c1==0){__delay_ms(200); while(c1==0); return 0x83;}          //b
if (c2==0){__delay_ms(200); while(c2==0); return 0x88;}          //a
if (c3==0){__delay_ms(200); while(c3==0); return 0x90;}          //9
if (c4==0){__delay_ms(200); while(c4==0); return 0x80;}          //8

r1=1; r2=1; r3=0; r4=1; __delay_ms(10);     // Scan r3 of keyboard
if (c1==0){__delay_ms(200); while(c1==0); return 0xf8;}          //7
if (c2==0){__delay_ms(200); while(c2==0); return 0x82;}          //6
if (c3==0){__delay_ms(200); while(c3==0); return 0x92;}          //5
if (c4==0){__delay_ms(200); while(c4==0); return 0x99;}          //4

r1=1; r2=1; r3=1; r4=0; __delay_ms(10);     // Scan r4 of keyboard
if (c1==0){__delay_ms(200); while(c1==0); return 0xb0;}          //3
if (c2==0){__delay_ms(200); while(c2==0); return 0xa4;}          //2
if (c3==0){__delay_ms(200); while(c3==0); return 0xf9;}          //1
if (c4==0){__delay_ms(200); while(c4==0); return 0xc0;}          //0

return (key);
}
```

Circuit Diagram:

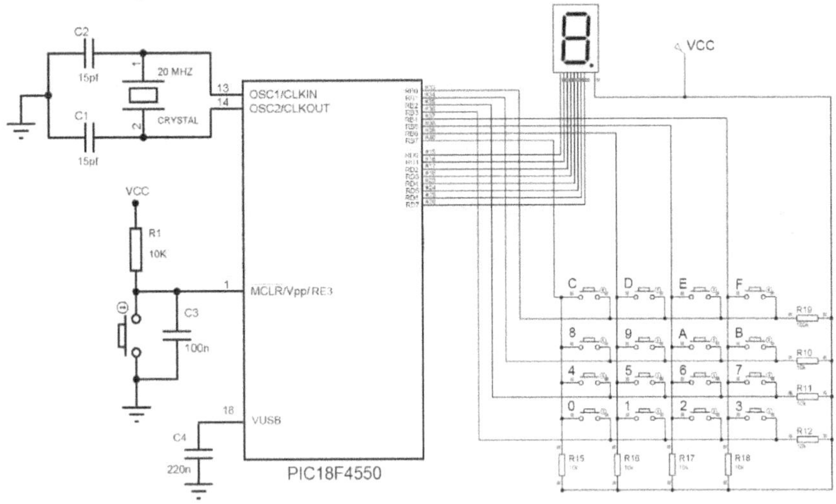

Experimental Output:

Name of the Key pressed	Character on the 7 segment display
0	0
1	1
2	2
3	3
4	4
5	5
6	6
7	7
8	8
9	9
A	A
B	B
C	C
D	D
E	E
F	F

Conclusion:

The experiment to interface a hex keyboard and display the pressed key number on a seven-segment display using a PIC18F4550 Microcontroller and an embedded C program has been successfully demonstrated.

33. SOLID STATE RELAY INTERFACE

Aim:

Develop an embedded system to control a solid-state relay using a PIC18F4550 Microcontroller and an embedded C program. Verify its output.

Hardware Requirements:

- PIC18F4550 Microcontroller, 20 MHz Crystal (1), 15 pF Disc Capacitors (2), 220 nF Disc Capacitor (1), 100 nF Disc Capacitor (1), Resistor 10K (1), and Push Button (1)
- IC MOC3021 (1), TRIAC BT136 (1), NPN Transistor BC548 (1), AC lamp (1), Resistor 220 (1), Resistor 470 (1), Resistor 1 K (1), Resistor 10 K (1), 100 nF Disc Capacitor (1), and Push Button (1)

Software Used:

- IDE: MPLAB X IDE v5.45
- Compiler: XC8 - v2.31

Theory:

A solid-state relay is a non-contact switch entirely composed of semiconductor elements. It serves as an equivalent to an electromechanical relay and can control electrical loads without using moving parts.

Solid-state relays can drive high-current loads with a small control signal. They offer several advantages over electromagnetic relays, including no contact points, no sparks, fast switching speed, high reliability, long lifespan, strong anti-interference capability, and a compact size.

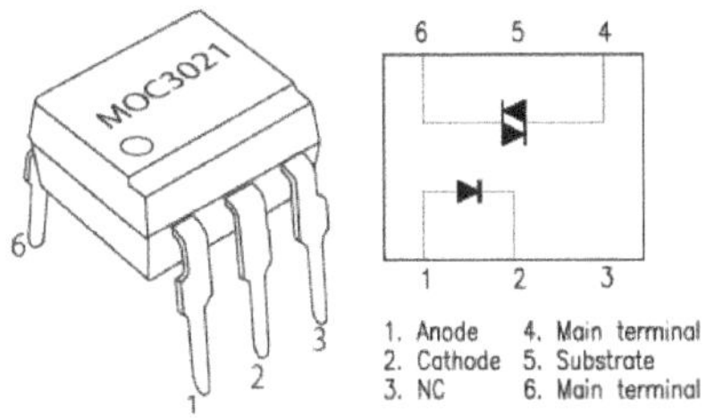

Algorithm:

1. Define the PIC18 configuration bits using the pragma directive, include xc.h, and define the crystal frequency for _XTAL_FREQ to utilize the built-in delay function.
2. Define a key for PORTD7 and a relay for LATC0.
3. Initialize PORTD7 as an input port and PORTC0 as an output port using the TRISD and TRISC registers (0 for output; 1 for input).
4. Clear LATC0.
5. If the key is pressed, execute the following block; otherwise, skip it. (IF block)
   5.1 Introduce a 50 ms delay for key debounce.
   5.2 Recheck the key; if it is still pressed, proceed to the next steps. If not, skip steps 5.3 and 5.4.
   5.3 Toggle the state of the relay.
   5.4 Wait for the key to be released.
6. Repeat the steps starting from step 5.

Program:

```
#pragma config PLLDIV = 5, CPUDIV = OSC1_PLL2, USBDIV = 2, FOSC = HS, FCMEN =
OFF, IESO = OFF
#pragma config PWRT = OFF, BOR = OFF, BORV = 3, VREGEN = OFF, WDT = OFF, WDTPS
= 32768
#pragma config CCP2MX = ON, PBADEN = OFF, LPT1OSC = OFF, MCLRE = ON
#pragma config STVREN = ON, LVP = OFF, ICPRT = OFF, XINST = OFF
#pragma config CP0 = OFF, CP1 = OFF, CP2 = OFF, CP3 = OFF, CPB = OFF, CPD = OFF
#pragma config WRT0 = OFF, WRT1 = OFF, WRT2 = OFF, WRT3 = OFF, WRTC = OFF, WRTB
= OFF, WRTD = OFF
#pragma config EBTR0 = OFF, EBTR1 = OFF, EBTR2 = OFF, EBTR3 = OFF, EBTRB = OFF
#include <xc.h>
```

```
#define _XTAL_FREQ 20000000
#define Key PORTDbits.RD7
#define Relay LATC0
void main() {                 // Main Function
   TRISD7 = 1;                // PORTD7 is configured as input port
   TRISC0 = 0;                // PORTC0 is configured as output port
   Relay = 0;                 // Clear RC0
while (1) {                   // Forever loop
   if(Key == 0)               // If the switch is pressed
   {
   __delay_ms(50);            // Debounce Delay
   if(Key == 0)               // If the switch is still pressed
     {
       Relay = ~ Relay;       // Toggle Solid state relay
       while(Key == 0);      // Wait for release
     } }
  }
}
```

Circuit Diagram:

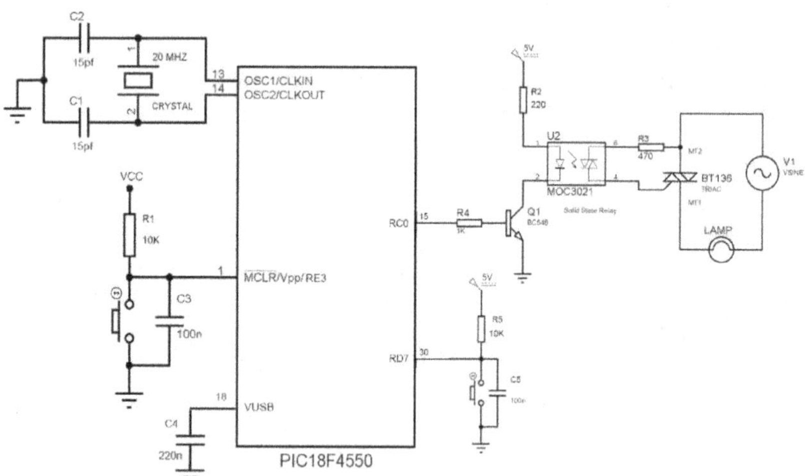

Conclusion:

The embedded system for controlling an AC lamp using a solid-state relay and a PIC18F4550 Microcontroller, along with an embedded C program, has been successfully demonstrated.

34. DC MOTOR DIRECTION CONTROLLER

Aim:

Develop an embedded system to control the direction of rotation of a DC motor using a PIC18F4550 Microcontroller and an embedded C program. Verify its output.

Hardware Requirements:

- PIC18F4550 Microcontroller, 20 MHz Crystal (1), 15 pF Disc Capacitors (2), 220 nF Disc Capacitor (1), 100 nF Disc Capacitor (1), Resistor 10K (1), and Push Button (1)
- NPN Transistors BC 548 (4), 12V DC Motor (1), Resistor 1 K (4), IN4007 Diode (4), Resistor 10 K (2), Disc Capacitor 100 nF, Push Button (2)

Software Used:

- IDE: MPLAB X IDE v5.45
- Compiler: XC8 - v2.31

Algorithm:

1. Define the PIC18 configuration bits using the pragma directive, include xc.h, and define the crystal frequency for _XTAL_FREQ to use the built-in delay function.
2. Initialize PORTB0 and PORTB1 as input ports for switches A and B, respectively.
3. Initialize PORTC0 and PORTC1 as output ports for OUT1 and OUT2. Clear OUT1 and OUT2.
4. If switch A is pressed, execute the following block; otherwise, skip

it. (If block)

a. Introduce a 50 ms delay for key debounce.

b. Recheck if switch A is still pressed. If it is, proceed to the next steps; otherwise, skip steps 4(c) and 4(d).

c. Set OUT1 and clear OUT2.

d. Wait for switch A to be released.

5. If switch B is pressed, execute the following block; otherwise, skip it. (If block)

   a. Introduce a 50 ms delay for key debounce.

   b. Recheck if switch B is still pressed. If it is, proceed to the next steps; otherwise, skip steps 5(c) and 5(d).

   c. Set OUT2 and clear OUT1.

   d. Wait for switch B to be released.

6. Repeat the steps starting from step 4.

Program:

```
#pragma config PLLDIV = 5, CPUDIV = OSC1_PLL2, USBDIV = 2, FOSC = HS, FCMEN =
OFF, IESO = OFF
#pragma config PWRT = OFF, BOR = OFF, BORV = 3, VREGEN = OFF, WDT = OFF,
WDTPS = 32768
#pragma config CCP2MX = ON, PBADEN = OFF, LPT1OSC = OFF, MCLRE = ON
#pragma config STVREN = ON, LVP = OFF, ICPRT = OFF, XINST = OFF
#pragma config CP0 = OFF, CP1 = OFF, CP2 = OFF, CP3 = OFF, CPB = OFF, CPD = OFF
#pragma config WRT0 = OFF, WRT1 = OFF, WRT2 = OFF, WRT3 = OFF, WRTC = OFF,
WRTB = OFF, WRTD = OFF
#pragma config EBTR0 = OFF, EBTR1 = OFF, EBTR2 = OFF, EBTR3 = OFF, EBTRB = OFF

#include <xc.h>
#define _XTAL_FREQ 20000000
#define SW_A PORTBbits.RB0
#define SW_B PORTBbits.RB1
#define OUT1 LATC0
#define OUT2 LATC1

void main()                    // Main Function
{
```

```
TRISB = 0x03;                    // PORTB 0&1 are configured as input ports
TRISC = 0x00;                    // PORTC is configured as output port
OUT1 = 0;                        // Clear output to stop motor
OUT2 = 0;
while (1)                        // Forever loop
{
if(SW_A == 0)                    // If the switch is pressed
{
__delay_ms(50);                  // Debounce Delay
if(SW_A == 0)                    // If the switch is still pressed
  {
  OUT1 = 1;                      // Motor rotates Anti-clock wise
  OUT2 = 0;
  while(SW_A == 0);              // Wait for release
  }
 }
if(SW_B == 0)  {                 // If the switch is pressed
__delay_ms(50);                  // Debounce Delay
if(SW_B == 0)  {                 // If the switch is still pressed
  OUT1 = 0;                      // Motor rotates Anti-clock wise
  OUT2 = 1;
  while(SW_B == 0);              // Wait for release
  }
 }
}
}
```

Circuit Diagram:

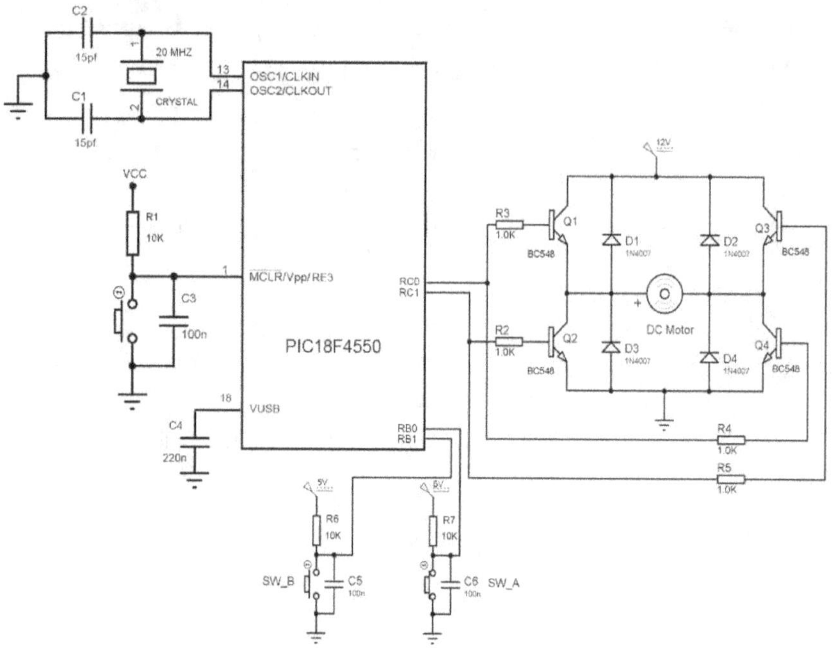

Conclusion:

The embedded system for controlling the direction of a DC motor using an H-bridge circuit, a PIC18F4550 Microcontroller, and an embedded C program has been successfully demonstrated.

35. STEPPER MOTOR INTERFACE

Aim:

Develop an embedded system to control the rotation of a stepper motor by 360 degrees clockwise and 360 degrees counterclockwise using a PIC18F4550 Microcontroller and an embedded C program. Verify its output.

Hardware Requirements:

- PIC18F4550 Microcontroller, 20 MHz Crystal (1), 15 pF Disc Capacitors (2), 220 nF Disc Capacitor (1), 100 nF Disc Capacitor (1),

Resistor 10K (1), and Push Button (1)

- Motor Driver ULN2003/ ULN2803, and Stepper Motor

Software Used:

- IDE: MPLAB X IDE v5.45
- Compiler: XC8 - v2.31

Theory:

A stepper motor is a brushless, synchronous DC electric motor that divides a full rotation into a number of equal steps. It is also known as a step motor. For instance, in a 200-step motor, one complete rotation (360°) is divided into 200 steps, making each step equal to 1.8°. There are two types of stepper motors: unipolar and bipolar. Unipolar stepper motors are more commonly used due to their ease of operation. A unipolar motor features center-tapped windings, where the center connection of the coils is tied together and used as the power terminal.

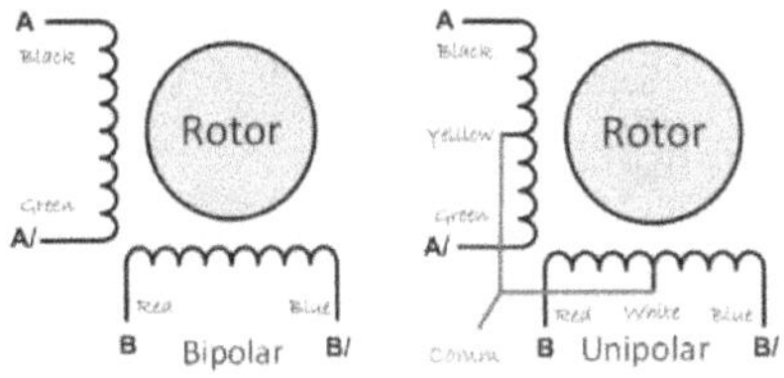

If a standard stepper motor has a step angle of 1.8 degrees, the number of steps required to complete one full revolution (360 degrees) can be calculated as follows:

$$\text{Steps per Revolution} = 360^0 / \text{Step Angle} = 360^0/1.8^0 = 200$$

Therefore, 200 steps are required to complete one full revolution.

Stepper motors can be driven using three different patterns or sequences:

Wave Drive Sequence:

- Only one phase (coil) is energized at a time.
- The sequence energizes the phases in a specific order (e.g., Coil A, then Coil B, then Coil C, then Coil D).
- This is a 4-step sequence where each phase is activated individually.

Full Step Drive Sequence:

- Two phases (coils) are energized simultaneously in a specific sequence.
- In a 4-step sequence, this typically involves energizing two adjacent coils at a time (e.g., Coils A and B, then B and C, then C and D, then D and A).
- This method provides greater torque and smoother operation compared to the wave drive sequence.

Half Step Drive Sequence:

- Alternates between the wave drive and full step drive patterns.
- In this method, one phase is energized (wave drive), followed by two adjacent phases energized together (full step drive), then the next phase, and so on.
- This results in an 8-step sequence, providing higher resolution and smoother motion by effectively doubling the number of steps per revolution compared to the full step drive sequence.

Step	A	B	A/	B/	Hex Value
1	1	1	0	0	0x0C
2	0	1	1	0	0x06
3	0	0	1	1	0x03
4	1	0	0	1	0x09

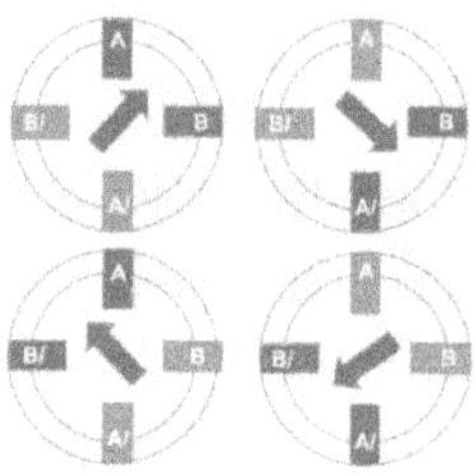

Stepper motor Connector:

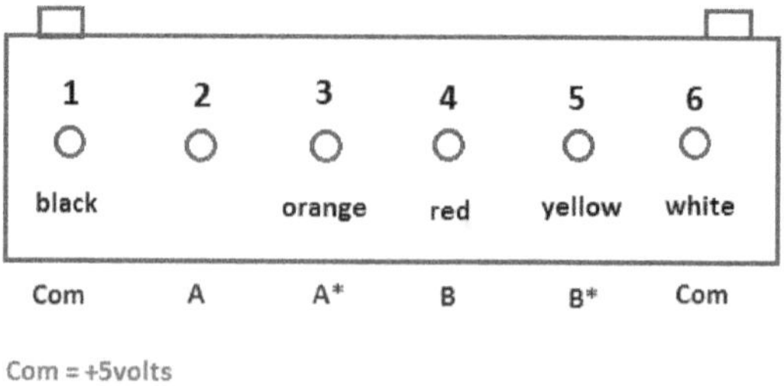

Algorithm:

1. Define the PIC18 configuration bits using the pragma directive, include xc.h, and set the crystal frequency for _XTAL_FREQ to utilize the built-in delay function.
2. Configure PORTD for the stepper motor interface and set it as an output port.
3. Declare and initialize the step sequences for both clockwise and counterclockwise rotation.
4. Use FOR loops to send 200 steps to the stepper motor driver for a 360-degree clockwise rotation.
5. Wait for 2 seconds.
6. Use FOR loops to send 200 steps to the stepper motor driver for a 360-degree counterclockwise rotation.
7. Wait for 2 seconds.
8. Halt the program execution.

Circuit Diagram:

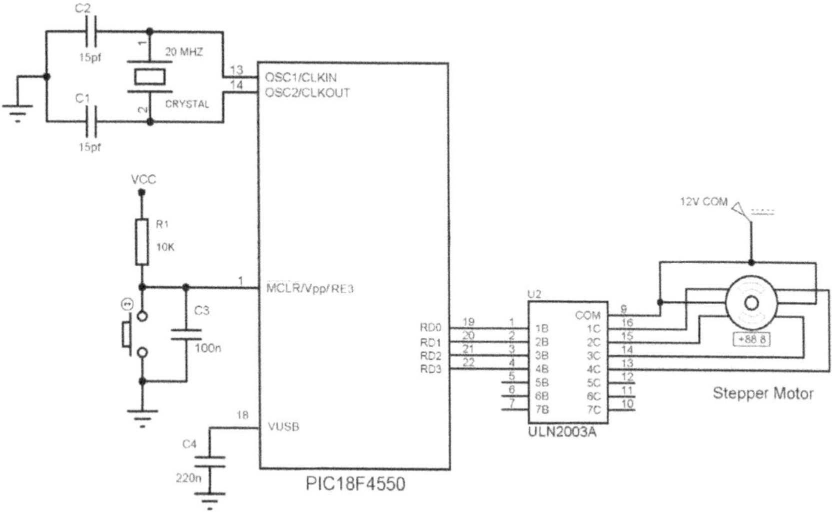

Program:

```
#pragma config PLLDIV = 5, CPUDIV = OSC1_PLL2, USBDIV = 2, FOSC = HS, FCMEN = 
OFF, IESO = OFF
#pragma config PWRT = OFF, BOR = OFF, BORV = 3, VREGEN = OFF, WDT = OFF,
```

```
WDTPS = 32768
#pragma config CCP2MX = ON, PBADEN = OFF, LPT1OSC = OFF, MCLRE = ON
#pragma config STVREN = ON, LVP = OFF, ICPRT = OFF, XINST = OFF
#pragma config CP0 = OFF, CP1 = OFF, CP2 = OFF, CP3 = OFF, CPB = OFF, CPD = OFF
#pragma config WRT0 = OFF, WRT1 = OFF, WRT2 = OFF, WRT3 = OFF, WRTC = OFF,
WRTB = OFF, WRTD = OFF
#pragma config EBTR0 = OFF, EBTR1 = OFF, EBTR2 = OFF, EBTR3 = OFF, EBTRB = OFF

#include <xc.h>
#define _XTAL_FREQ 20000000
#define step PORTD


void main()     {                  // Main Function
unsigned int i,j;
unsigned char cw[]={0x0C,0x06,0x03,0x09};
unsigned char ccw[]={0x09,0x03,0x06,0x0C};
TRISD = 0x00;

// for 360 clk-wise rotation, 360/1.8 = 200 steps to the stepper motor
for (i=0; i<50; i++)               // Loop count 50 x inner loop count 4
{
        for(j=0; j<4; j++)         // 4 step sequence
        {
        step = cw[j];              // Move each step to the stepper motor
        __delay_ms(15);            // 15 ms delay between steps
        }
}
__delay_ms (2000);                 // Hold rotation for 2 sec

// for 360 Anti-clk-wise rotation, 360/1.8 = 200 steps to the stepper motor
for (i=0; i<50; i++)               // Loop count 50 x inner loop count 4
{
        for(j=0; j<4; j++)         // 4 step sequence
        {
        step = ccw[j];             // Move each step to the stepper motor
```

```
        __delay_ms(15);          // 15 ms delay between steps
        }
}
__delay_ms (2000);               // Hold rotation for 2 sec
while(1);
}
```

Conclusion:

The embedded system for controlling the stepper motor's rotation by 360 degrees clockwise and 360 degrees counterclockwise, using a PIC18F4550 Microcontroller and an embedded C program, has been successfully demonstrated.

36. INTERFACING PROXIMITY SENSOR USING INTERRUPT

Aim:

Develop an embedded system with a proximity sensor to showcase the external hardware interrupt functionality of the PIC18F4550 Microcontroller using an embedded C program.

Hardware Requirements:

- PIC18F4550 Microcontroller, 20 MHz Crystal (1), 15 pF Disc Capacitors (2), 220 nF Disc Capacitor (1), 100 nF Disc Capacitor (1), Resistor 10K (1), and Push Button (1)
- Proximity Sensor, NPN Transistor BC547 (1), Relay 5V (1), IN4007 Diode (1), LED (1), Resistor 100, Resistor 1 K

Software Used:

- IDE: MPLAB X IDE v5.45
- Compiler: XC8 - v2.31

Theory:

An interrupt is an event that prompts the CPU to pause its normal program execution and execute a specific routine related to the event.

An interrupt can be

- Hardware Interrupt
    - External Interrupt: External circuitry asserts an interrupt signal
    - Internal Interrupt: On-chip peripherals generating an interrupt signal
- Software Interrupt
    - Raised by user program during overflow, divided-by-zero and underflow.

Maskable Interrupt

Interrupts provide the capability to selectively enable or disable them. A hardware interrupt can be ignored by setting a bit in an interrupt mask register (IMR). When an interrupt is disabled (by setting the bit), the CPU will ignore it, and this interrupt is referred to as a pending interrupt..

Non-Maskable Interrupt (NMI)

A hardware interrupt that can not be ignored. It has highest priority task.

Interrupt Priority

The priority of interrupts determines their order of servicing. If two interrupts occur simultaneously, the one with the higher priority is handled first.

Interrupt Service

The CPU provides service to an interrupt by executing a program called an interrupt service routine (ISR). After providing service to an interrupt, the CPU must resume normal program execution.

The interrupt service cycle typically includes the following steps:

- Interrupt Occurrence: An interrupt signal is generated by an external or internal source.
- Interrupt Detection: The CPU detects the interrupt and temporarily halts the current program execution.

- Context Saving: The CPU saves the state of the current program (e.g., registers, program counter) to ensure that it can resume from the same point after handling the interrupt.
- Interrupt Vectoring: The CPU identifies the appropriate ISR based on the interrupt vector and priority.
- ISR Execution: The CPU executes the ISR to address the interrupt, performing the necessary tasks or handling the event.
- Context Restoration: After the ISR execution, the CPU restores the saved state of the interrupted program.
- Resume Normal Execution: The CPU resumes normal program execution from where it was interrupted.

PIC18 Interrupts

The PIC18 MCU features the following interrupt sources:

- Four edge-triggered INT pin interrupts: These are triggered by changes on the external interrupt pins (INT0 through INT3).
- Port B pins change interrupts: These interrupts occur when there is a change in any of the upper four Port B pins.
- On-chip peripheral function interrupts: These interrupts are generated by various internal peripherals and functions of the microcontroller.

PIC18 Interrupt Priority

Interrupts in the PIC18 MCU are categorized into two groups:

- High-Priority Interrupts: The interrupt vector address for high-priority interrupts is 0x000008.
- Low-Priority Interrupts: The interrupt vector address for low-priority interrupts is 0x000018.

When an interrupt occurs, the CPU checks the priority level and uses the appropriate vector address to service the interrupt based on its priority.

PIC18 Interrupt sources

The PIC18 MCU supports a variety of interrupt sources, including:

- Reset Interrupts:
    - Reset

    - Brown-Out Reset
    - Watch-Dog Reset
    - Power-On Reset
- External Interrupts:
    - External Interrupt 0 (INT0)
    - External Interrupt 1 (INT1)
    - External Interrupt 2 (INT2)
- Timer Interrupts:
    - Timer 0 Interrupt
    - Timer 1 Interrupt
    - Timer 2 Interrupt
    - Timer 3 Interrupt
- Port Change Interrupts:
    - RB Port Change Enable Interrupt
- EUSART Interrupts:
    - EUSART Receive Interrupt
    - EUSART Transmit Interrupt
- ADC Interrupt:
    - ADC Interrupt
- Analog Comparator Interrupt:
    - Analog Comparator Interrupt
- Other Peripherals:
    - Streaming Parallel Port Read/Write Interrupt
    - Master Synchronous Serial Port Interrupt
    - CCP1 Interrupt (Capture, Compare, PWM)
    - Oscillator Fail Interrupt
    - USB Interrupt
    - Data EEPROM/Flash Write Operation Interrupt
    - Bus Collision Interrupt
    - High/Low-Voltage Detect Interrupt
    - CCP2 Interrupt

PIC18 Interrupt Related Registers

Each interrupt source in the PIC18 MCU is controlled by three bits:

- Flag Bit: Indicates whether an interrupt event has occurred. This bit is set by the hardware when an interrupt event happens and must be cleared by the software in the interrupt service routine.
- Enable Bit: Controls whether the interrupt source is enabled or disabled. Setting this bit enables the interrupt source, while clearing it disables the interrupt.
- Priority Bit: Determines the priority level of the interrupt. This bit selects whether the interrupt is high-priority or low-priority, allowing the CPU to handle higher-priority interrupts before lower-priority ones.

PIC18 has 13 registers to control interrupt operations,

- RCON
- INTCON
- INTCON2
- INTCON3
- PIR1, PIR2, and PIR3
- PIE1, PIE2, and PIE3
- IPR1, IPR2, and IPR3

PIC18 Interrupt Operation

PIC18 MCU can enable or disable the priority scheme.

- IPEN bit of the RCON register

If the interrupt priority scheme is disabled (when IPEN is cleared), the PIC18 MCU operates in a mode compatible with the PIC16 MCU. In this mode:

- All peripheral interrupts are managed using a three-level enabling scheme.
- All interrupt sources share a common interrupt vector located at address 0x08.

If the priority scheme is enabled (when IPEN is set), the PIC18 MCU divides interrupts into high-priority and low-priority groups:

- High-priority interrupts are managed with a two-level enabling mechanism.
- To enable high-priority interrupts, both the GIE bit in the

INTCON register and the specific interrupt bit must be set.

High-priority interrupts include:

- External interrupts from the INT pin (INT0 - INT3)
- Timer 0 overflow interrupt
- PORTB input pin changes (upper four pins)

In the PIC18 MCU, low-priority interrupts are managed using a three-level enabling scheme:

- Global Interrupt Enable (GIE) Bit: Must be set to allow any interrupts to be processed. This bit is located in the INTCON register.
- Peripheral Interrupt Enable (PEIE) Bit: Must be set to enable peripheral interrupts. This bit is also found in the INTCON register.
- Interrupt Enable Bit for Specific Source: The individual interrupt source must be enabled by setting its specific enable bit. For instance, the ADC interrupt is controlled by the ADIE bit located in the PIE1 register.

Example for enabling the ADC interrupt:

- Set the GIE bit (INTCON<7>) to enable global interrupts.
- Set the PEIE bit (INTCON<6>) to enable peripheral interrupts.
- Set the ADIE bit (PIE1<6>) to enable the ADC interrupt.

INT Pin interrupts

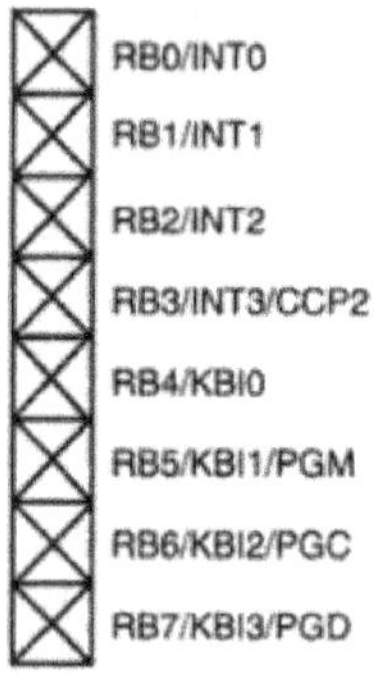

- All INT pin interrupts (INT0-INT3) are edge triggered.
- The edge-select bits are contained in the INTCON2 register.
- When an edge-select bit is set to logic '1' the corresponding INT pin interrupt is requested on the rising edge.
- Otherwise, the INT pin interrupt is requested on the falling edge.
- The lower four port B pins (RB3-RB0) are the external interrupt pins, INT3 to INT0.

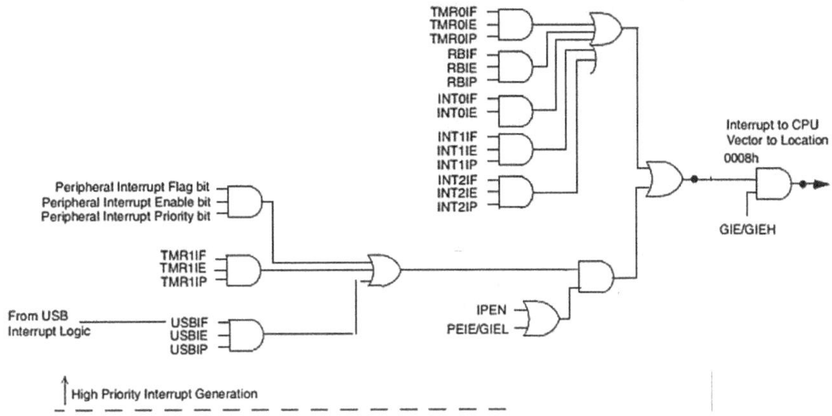

Algorithm:

Main Program: (Flashing an LED)

1. Define the PIC18 configuration bits using the pragma directive, include xc.h, and set the crystal frequency for _XTAL_FREQ to use the built-in delay function.
2. Configure PORTB0 as an input port for the interrupt pin.
3. Set PORTD0 and PORTC0 as output ports and initialize them to low.
4. Configure interrupt settings:
   - Enable global interrupts by setting the GIE bit in the INTCON register.
   - Enable the interrupt priority scheme by setting the IPEN bit in the RCON register.
   - Enable External Interrupt 0 (INT0) by setting the INT0IE bit in the INTCON register.
   - Configure the interrupt to trigger on the falling edge by clearing the INTEDG0 bit in the INTCON2 register.
   - Clear the INT0IF bit in the INTCON register.
5. Turn off RC0 (LED).
6. Wait for 100 ms.
7. Turn on RC0 (LED).
8. Wait for 100 ms.
9. Repeat steps 5 through 8.

ISR:

1. If the INT0F flag is set, proceed with the following steps; otherwise, skip them.
2. Toggle the state of PORTD0 (Relay).
3. Clear the INT0F flag.
4. Return to the main function.

Program:

```
#pragma config PLLDIV = 5, CPUDIV = OSC1_PLL2, USBDIV = 2, FOSC = HS, FCMEN =
OFF, IESO = OFF
#pragma config PWRT = OFF, BOR = OFF, BORV = 3, VREGEN = OFF, WDT = OFF,
WDTPS = 32768
#pragma config CCP2MX = ON, PBADEN = OFF, LPT1OSC = OFF, MCLRE = ON
#pragma config STVREN = ON, LVP = OFF, ICPRT = OFF, XINST = OFF
#pragma config CP0 = OFF, CP1 = OFF, CP2 = OFF, CP3 = OFF, CPB = OFF, CPD = OFF
#pragma config WRT0 = OFF, WRT1 = OFF, WRT2 = OFF, WRT3 = OFF, WRTC = OFF,
WRTB = OFF, WRTD = OFF
#pragma config EBTR0 = OFF, EBTR1 = OFF, EBTR2 = OFF, EBTR3 = OFF, EBTRB = OFF

#include <xc.h>
#define _XTAL_FREQ 20000000

void __interrupt() Relay(void)
{
  if (INT0F == 1){
  LATD0 = ~LATD0;
  INT0F = 0;                    // Clear the interrupt 0 flag
  }
}

void main()
{
INTCONbits.GIE = 1;             // Enable the Global Interrupt
RCONbits.IPEN = 1;              // Interrupt priority scheme enable
INTCONbits.INT0IE = 1;          // Enable INT0
INTCON2bits.INTEDG0 = 0;        // Set Falling Edge Trigger for INT0
```

```
INTCONbits.INT0F = 0;        // Clear the interrupt 0 flag
TRISB0=1;                    // RB0/INT0 as input
TRISD0=0;                    // Configure RD0 as output port
TRISC0=0;                    // Configure RC0 as output port
LATD0=0;                     // Clear RD0
while(1)
  {
  LATC0=0;                   // Reset RC0
  __delay_ms(100);           // Delay for 100 msec
  LATC0=1;                   // Set RC0
  __delay_ms(100);           // Delay for 100 msec
  }
}
```

Circuit Diagram:

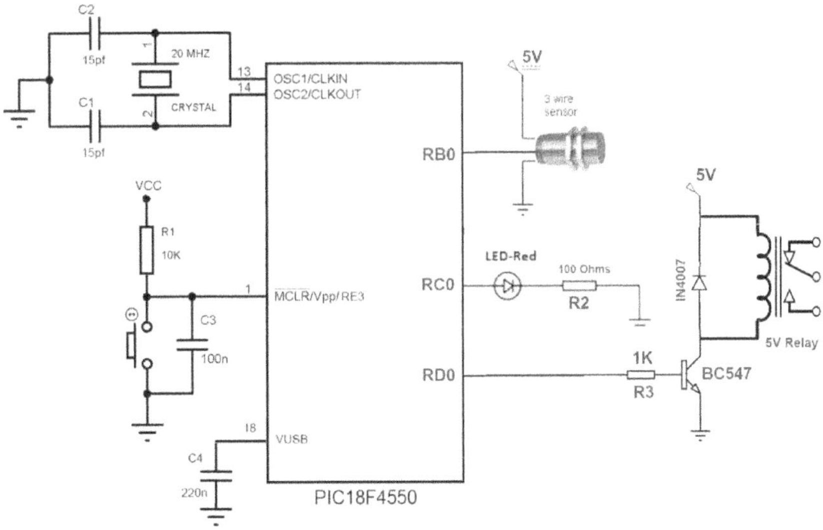

Conclusion:

An embedded system with a proximity sensor has been developed, demonstrating the external hardware interrupt functionality of the PIC18F4550 Microcontroller using an embedded C program.

37. FLASHING LED USING ON-CHIP TIMER

Aim:

Develop an embedded system to flash an LED using the on-chip timer of the PIC18F4550 Microcontroller and an embedded C program. Verify its functionality.

Hardware Requirements:

- PIC18F4550 Microcontroller, 20 MHz Crystal (1), 15 pF Disc Capacitors (2), 220 nF Disc Capacitor (1), 100 nF Disc Capacitor (1), Resistor 10K (1), and Push Button (1)
- LED (1) and Resistor 220 (1)

Software Used:

- IDE: MPLAB X IDE v5.45
- Compiler: XC8 - v2.31

Theory:

A PIC18 microcontroller may feature four or five timers: Timer0, Timer1, Timer2, Timer3, and Timer4. Note that Timer4 is specific to the PIC18F8xxx family.

Timer Types:

- Timer0, Timer1, and Timer3 are 16-bit timers.
- Timer2 and Timer4 are 8-bit timers.

Timer Operation:

- When a 16-bit timer (Timer0, Timer1, Timer3) rolls over from 0xFFFF to 0x0000, or an 8-bit timer (Timer2, Timer4) rolls over from 0xFF to 0x00, the timer flag/interrupt is set.

Clock Sources:

- Timers generally use an internal clock source.
- Counters can use an external clock source.
- Specifically, Timer2 and Timer4 use only the internal clock source, while Timer0, Timer1, and Timer3 can use either internal or external clock sources.

Timer0:

The Timer0 module incorporates the following features:

- Software selectable operation as a timer or counter in both 8-bit or 16-bit modes
- Software programmable prescaler
- Selectable clock source (internal or external)
- Edge select for external clock
- Interrupt on overflow
- T0CON register controls all aspects of the module's operation, including the prescale selection.

T0CON Register

R/W-1	R/W-1	R/W-1	R/W-1	R/W-1	R/W-1	R/W-1	R/W-1
TMR0ON	T08BIT	T0CS	T0SE	PSA	T0PS2	T0PS1	T0PS0
bit 7							bit 0

bit 7 **TMR0ON:** Timer0 On/Off Control bit
1 = Enables Timer0
0 = Stops Timer0

bit 6 **T08BIT**: Timer0 8-Bit/16-Bit Control bit
1 = Timer0 is configured as an 8-bit timer/counter
0 = Timer0 is configured as a 16-bit timer/counter

bit 5 **T0CS**: Timer0 Clock Source Select bit
1 = Transition on T0CKI pin
0 = Internal instruction cycle clock (CLKO)

bit 4 **T0SE**: Timer0 Source Edge Select bit
1 = Increment on high-to-low transition on T0CKI pin
0 = Increment on low-to-high transition on T0CKI pin

bit 3 **PSA**: Timer0 Prescaler Assignment bit
1 = Timer0 prescaler is NOT assigned. Timer0 clock input bypasses prescaler.
0 = Timer0 prescaler is assigned. Timer0 clock input comes from prescaler output.

bit 2-0 **T0PS2:T0PS0**: Timer0 Prescaler Select bits
111 = 1:256 Prescale value
110 = 1:128 Prescale value
101 = 1:64 Prescale value
100 = 1:32 Prescale value
011 = 1:16 Prescale value
010 = 1:8 Prescale value
001 = 1:4 Prescale value
000 = 1:2 Prescale value

Timer0 Configuration:

Timer0 can operate in either 8-bit or 16-bit mode, or as a counter.

- Mode Selection: This is controlled by the T0CS bit in the T0CON register (T0CON<5>):
  - '0': Configures Timer0 as a timer.
  - '1': Configures Timer0 as a counter.

- Timer Mode: In Timer mode, the TMR0 register increments with each clock cycle, based on the prescaler value.
- Counter Mode: In Counter mode, Timer0 increments on each rising or falling edge of the RA4/T0CKI pin:
    - o The Timer0 Source Edge Select bit (T0SE, T0CON<4>) determines the edge:
      Clearing T0SE selects the rising edge.
      Setting T0SE selects the falling edge.
- To divide the clock signal by a prescaler before it is applied to the Timer0 clock input.

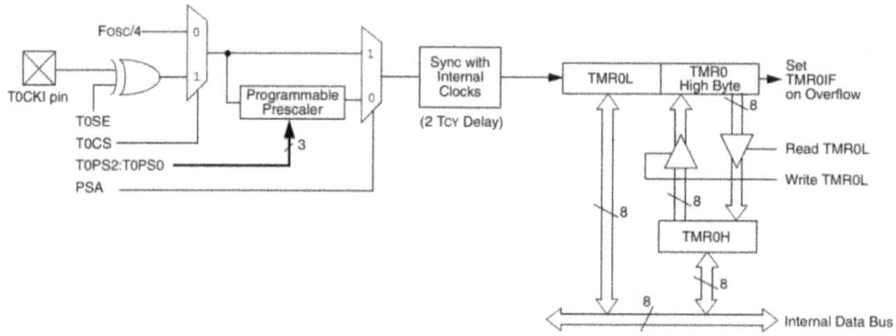

TIMER0 Block Diagram (16-Bit Mode)

- T0SE (T0CON<4>): The Source Edge Select bit. When set to 1, Timer0 increments on a high-to-low transition of the input signal.
- T0CS (T0CON<0>): Selects the clock source for Timer0:
    - o '0': Internal clock source (Timer mode).
    - o '1': External clock source (Counter mode).
- Prescaler Value: Set using the PSA bit and the T0PS2
- bits in the T0CON register (T0CON<3:0>).
- Instruction Cycle Overhead: Writing to the TMR0 register results in a loss of two instruction cycles.
- Interrupt Generation: A TMR0 interrupt occurs when the TMR0 register overflows from 0xFF to 0x00 in 8-bit mode or from 0xFFFF to 0x0000 in 16-bit mode. This overflow sets the TMR0IF flag bit. The interrupt can be disabled by clearing the TMR0IE bit (INTCON<5>).

- TMR0H: In 16-bit mode, TMR0H is a buffer holding the higher byte of Timer0. It is not directly readable or writable.

Write a delay subroutine for 10ms using Timer0.

Step-1: Find the value of timer register TMR0L for required time delay

- Fosc/4 = 20MHZ/4 = 5MHZ => Timer clock | | TCY = 1/5MHZ = 0.2 us.
- Timer increments every 0.2 us * prescaler = 0.2 us * 256 = 51.2 uS.
- For 10ms, the timer value would be 10mS/51.2 uS = 195.3 ~=195 counts.
- **8-bit mode: TMR0L = 256-195 = 61 or 0x3D**
- **16-bit mode: TMR0 = 65536-195 = 65341 or 0x FF3D**

Step-2: Timer0 interrupt configurations (INTCON Reg.)

- GIEH = 0; // Timer interrupt is disabled
- TMR0IE = 0;
- TMR0IF = 0; // Clear timer0 flag

Step-3: Timer0 configurations (T0CON Reg.)

- TMR0ON = 1; // ON the timer
- T08BIT = 1; // 1 for 8-bit mode and 0 for 16-bit mode
- T0CS = 0; // Use system clock to increment timer
- PSA = 0; // A prescaler is assigned for Timer0
  - T0PS2 = 1; // Use a 1:256 prescaler
  - T0PS1 = 1;
  - T0PS0 = 1;
- **T0CON = 0xC7**

Step-4: wait and clear timer flag

- while (!(TMR0IF)); // wait until timer flag is set
- TMR0IF=0; // Clear timer0 flag

// delay program for 10ms using TMR0 in 8-bit mode

```
Void T0_delay_10ms (void)
{
TMR0L = 61;                    // with 1:256 prescaler
INTCONbits.TMR0IF = 0;
```

```
T0CON = 0xC7;
while(!(INTCONbits.TMR0IF));
INTCONbits.TMR0IF=0;
return;
}
```

// delay program for 10ms using TMR0 in 16-bit mode

```
Void T0_delay_10ms (void)
{
TMR0 = 65341;                    // TMR0H = 0xFF; TMR0L = 0x3D;
INTCONbits.TMR0IF = 0;
T0CON = 0x87;
while(!(INTCONbits.TMR0IF));
INTCONbits.TMR0IF=0;
return;
}
```

Algorithm:

Main Program:

1. Define the PIC18 configuration bits using the pragma directive, include xc.h, and set the crystal frequency for _XTAL_FREQ to use the built-in delay function.
2. Configure PORTD0 as an output port.
3. Timer0 Settings:
   GIEH = 0; // Disable all interrupts
   TMR0IF = 0; // Clear the TMR0 flag bit
   T08BIT = 0; // Set to 16-bit timer mode
   T0CS = 0; // Select internal clock source (Timer mode)
   PSA = 0; // Enable prescaler assignment
   T0PS2 = 1; // Set prescaler to 1:256
   T0PS1 = 1;
   T0PS0 = 1;
4. Clear RD0.
5. Create a time delay of 200 ms using Timer0.

6. Set RD0.
7. Create another time delay of 200 ms using Timer0.
8. Repeat steps 4 through 7.

Subroutine: timer0_200ms:

1. Clear the Timer0 Interrupt Flag (TMR0IF = 0).
2. Load the TMR0 register with the value 61630 to achieve a 200 ms delay.
3. Enable Timer0.
4. Wait until the Timer0 Interrupt Flag is set.
5. Clear the Timer0 Interrupt Flag (TMR0IF = 0).
6. Disable Timer0.

Program:

```
#pragma config PLLDIV = 5, CPUDIV = OSC1_PLL2, USBDIV = 2, FOSC = HS, FCMEN = OFF, IESO = OFF
#pragma config PWRT = OFF, BOR = OFF, BORV = 3, VREGEN = OFF, WDT = OFF, WDTPS = 32768
#pragma config CCP2MX = ON, PBADEN = OFF, LPT1OSC = OFF, MCLRE = ON
#pragma config STVREN = ON, LVP = OFF, ICPRT = OFF, XINST = OFF
#pragma config CP0 = OFF, CP1 = OFF, CP2 = OFF, CP3 = OFF, CPB = OFF, CPD = OFF
#pragma config WRT0 = OFF, WRT1 = OFF, WRT2 = OFF, WRT3 = OFF, WRTC = OFF, WRTB = OFF, WRTD = OFF
#pragma config EBTR0 = OFF, EBTR1 = OFF, EBTR2 = OFF, EBTR3 = OFF, EBTRB = OFF

#include <xc.h>
#define _XTAL_FREQ 20000000

void timer0delay()                  // Subroutine
{
   TMR0IF = 0;                      // Clear TMR0 Interrupt flag
   TMR0 = 61630;                    // TMR0 value for 200 ms delay time
   TMR0ON = 1;                      // Turn-on timer 0
   while(TMR0IF == 0);              // Wait until TMR0IF is zero
   TMR0IF = 0;                      // Clear TMR0IF
   TMR0ON = 0;                      // Turn-off timer 0
}
```

```
void main() {
TRISD0=0;                  // PORTD0 is output port
GIEH = 0;                  // disable all interrupts
TMR0IF = 0;                // Clear TMR0 flag bit
T08BIT = 0;                // Setting 16-bit timer
T0CS = 0;                  // Select internal clock source (Timer mode)
PSA = 0;                   // Prescaler assignment ON
T0PS2 = 1;                 // 1:256 prescale
T0PS1 = 1;
T0PS0 = 1;
while(1)    {
  LATD0=0;                 // Reset RD0
  timer0delay();           // Delay for 200 msec
  LATD0=1;                 // Set RD0
  timer0delay();           // Delay for 200 msec
  }
}
```

Circuit Diagram:

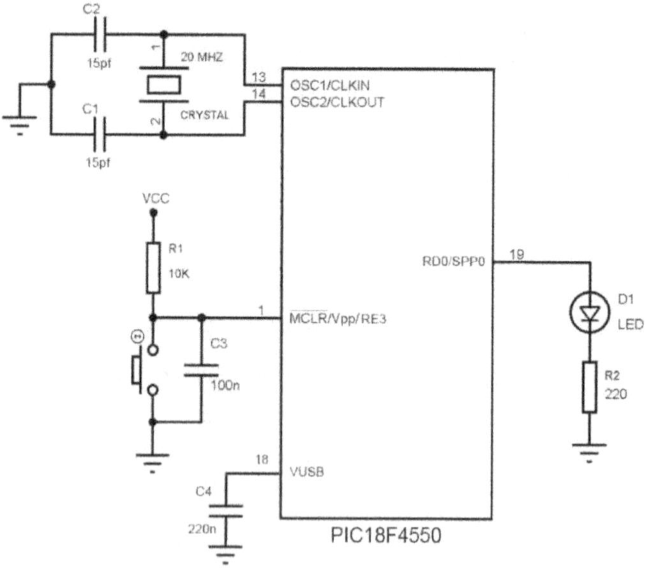

Conclusion:

The embedded system for flashing an LED using the on-chip timer of the PIC18F4550 Microcontroller, implemented with an Embedded C program, has been successfully demonstrated.

38. SPEED CONTROL OF DC MOTOR USING PWM

Aim:

Develop an embedded system to control the speed of a DC motor using the PWM functionality of the PIC18F4550 Microcontroller and an Embedded C program. Verify the system's performance.

Hardware Requirements:

- PIC18F4550 Microcontroller, 20 MHz Crystal (1), 15 pF Disc Capacitors (2), 220 nF Disc Capacitor (1), 100 nF Disc Capacitor (1), Resistor 10K (1), and Push Button (1)
- NPN Transistor TIP122 (1), DC Motor (1), IN4007 Diode (1), Resistor 1K, Resistor 2.2K, 100 nF Disc Capacitor, and Push Button (1)

Software Used:

- IDE: MPLAB X IDE v5.45
- Compiler: XC8 - v2.31

Theory:

CCP – PWM Module

The PWM (Pulse Width Modulation) signal can be generated in the PIC Microcontroller using the CCP (Compare Capture PWM) module. This module supports:

- Capture Operation: Captures the contents of a timer and stores it in a capture register.
- Compare Operation: Compares the value in a CCPR register with the value in Timer1 (or Timer3) on each clock cycle. When the values match, the associated pin can be set to high, low, or toggled.

- PWM Mode: In this mode, the CCP module generates a waveform with a specific frequency and duty cycle. This is achieved using Timer2 or Timer4 to control the timing of the PWM signal.

A PIC18 device may feature one, two, or even five capture/compare/PWM (CCP) modules. Each module includes the following components:

- 16-bit Capture Register
- 16-bit Compare Register
- PWM Master/Slave Duty Cycle Register

The operation of a CCP module is managed by:

- Control Register (CCPxCON): Configures the module's operation.
- Data Register (CCPRx): Comprises two 8-bit registers:
  - CCPRxL: Lower byte of the data register.
  - CCPRxH: Upper byte of the data register.

CCPxCON: CCPx Control Register

U-0	U-0	R/W-0	R/W-0	R/W-0	R/W-0	R/W-0	R/W-0
—(1)	—(1)	DCxB1	DCxB0	CCPxM3	CCPxM2	CCPxM1	CCPxM0
bit 7							bit 0

bit 7-6 **Unimplemented:** Read as '0'(1)

bit 5-4 **DCxB1:DCxB0**: PWM Duty Cycle Bit 1 and Bit 0 for CCPx Module

Capture mode:
Unused.

Compare mode:
Unused.

PWM mode:
These bits are the two LSbs (bit 1 and bit 0) of the 10-bit PWM duty cycle. The eight MSbs of the duty cycle are found in CCPR1L.

bit 3-0 **CCPxM3:CCPxM0**: CCPx Module Mode Select bits

0000 = Capture/Compare/PWM disabled (resets CCPx module)
0001 = Reserved
0010 = Compare mode: toggle output on match (CCPxIF bit is set)
0011 = Reserved
0100 = Capture mode: every falling edge
0101 = Capture mode: every rising edge
0110 = Capture mode: every 4th rising edge
0111 = Capture mode: every 16th rising edge
1000 = Compare mode: initialize CCPx pin low; on compare match, force CCPx pin high (CCPxIF bit is set)
1001 = Compare mode: initialize CCPx pin high; on compare match, force CCPx pin low (CCPxIF bit is set)
1010 = Compare mode: generate software interrupt on compare match (CCPxIF bit is set, CCPx pin reflects I/O state)
1011 = Compare mode: trigger special event, reset timer, start A/D conversion on CCP2 match (CCPxIF bit is set)
11xx = PWM mode

- CCP Modules use Timers 1, 2, 3, or 4, depending on the selected module.

- In Capture or Compare Mode, Timer 1 or Timer 3 is used.
- In PWM Mode, Timer 2 or Timer 4 is required.
- The assignment of a specific timer to a module is determined by bits 6 and 3 of the T3CON register.

T3CON: TIMER3 CONTROL REGISTER

R/W-0	R/W-0	R/W-0	R/W-0	R/W-0	R/W-0	R/W-0	R/W-0
RD16	T3CCP2	T3CKPS1	T3CKPS0	T3CCP1	$\overline{\text{T3SYNC}}$	TMR3CS	TMR3ON

bit 6, 3 **T3CCP2:T3CCP1:** Timer3 and Timer1 to CCPx Enable bits
1x = Timer3 is the capture/compare clock source for both CCP modules
01 = Timer3 is the capture/compare clock source for CCP2;
Timer1 is the capture/compare clock source for CCP1
00 = Timer1 is the capture/compare clock source for both CCP modules

In PWM mode, the CCPx pin can produce a PWM output with up to 10-bit resolution. For the CCP2 pin, which is multiplexed with a PORTB or PORTC data latch, the corresponding TRIS bit must be cleared to configure the CCP2 pin as an output.

- Changing the duty cycle is defined as PWM.
    - CCP pin is set as an output
    - Value for duty cycle to be loaded into CCP register
    - Value for period to be loaded in base timer register
    - Varying the duty cycle will generate PWM
- Duty cycle to be generated is a 10-bit value (resolution)
    - Upper 8-bits stored in CCPRxH register (from CCPRxL)
    - Lower 2-bits stored in bit 5 and bit 4 of CCPxCON register

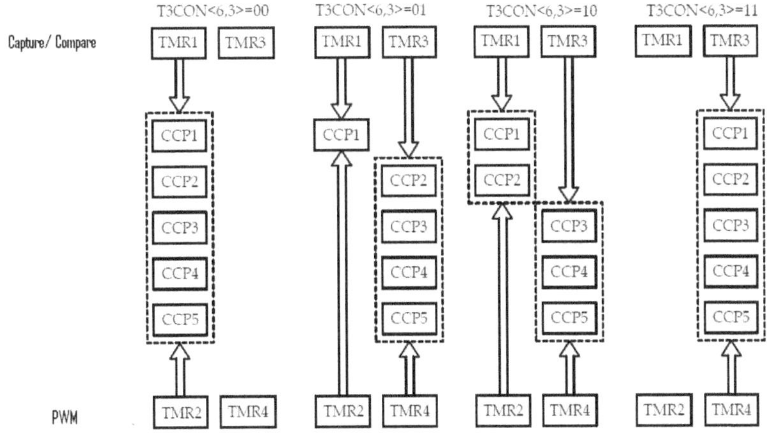

Base Timer for CCP Operations

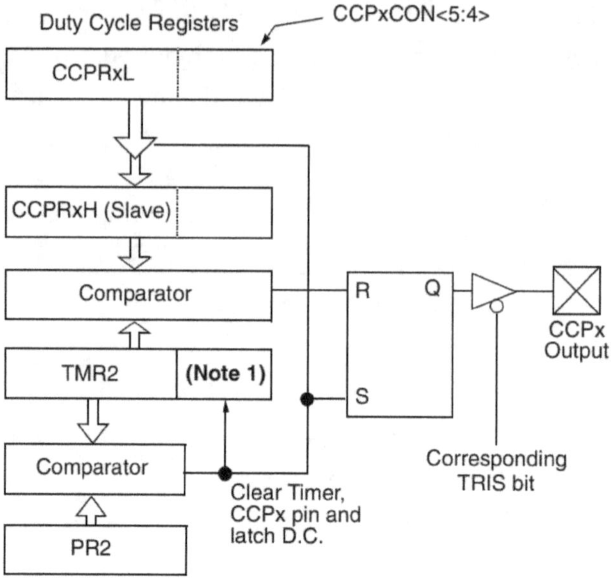

PWM Block Diagram

In PWM mode, the duty cycle value is compared with the TMRy register in every instruction cycle. When the values are equal, the CCPx pin is pulled low.

The TMRy register is compared with the PRy register in every crystal oscillator cycle. When these values are equal, the following events occur on the next increment cycle:

- The CCPx pin is pulled high.
- The TMRy register is cleared.
- The PWM duty cycle is latched from CCPRxL into CCPRxH.

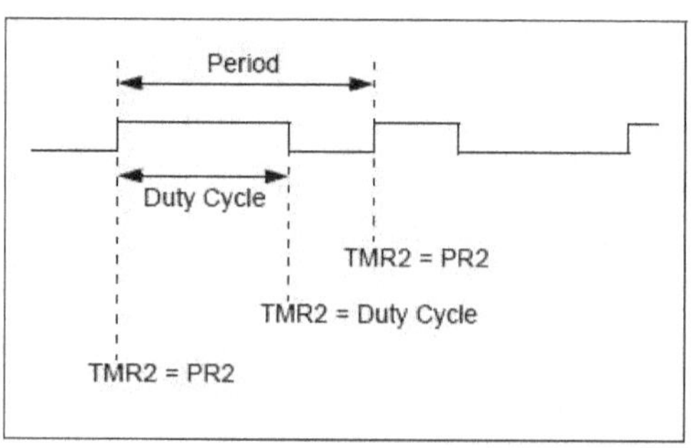

The PWM period can be calculated using the following formula:

PWM period = [(PRy) + 1] × 4 × TOSC × (TMRy prescale factor)

Time unit used in period calculation is instruction cycle.

The PWM duty cycle can be calculated using the following formula:

PWM duty cycle = (CCPRxL:CCPxCON<5:4>) × TOSC × (TMRy prescale factor)

Time unit used in duty cycle calculation is crystal oscillator cycle.

To configure the CCP module for PWM operation, follow these steps:

- Set the PWM Period:
  - Write to the PRy (where y = 2 or 4) register.
- Set the PWM Duty Cycle:
  - Write to the CCPRxL register.
  - Configure the CCPxCON<5:4> bits accordingly.
- Make the CCPx Pin an Output:
  - Ensure the CCPx pin is set as an output.
- Configure Timer Prescale and Enable:
  - Set the TMRy prescale value and enable TMRy by writing to the TMRyCON register.
- Configure the CCPx Module for PWM Operation:
  - Set up the CCPx module for PWM operation by configuring the appropriate registers.

If using Timer2 for PWM:

- Set Up PWM Period:
  - Write to the PR2 register.
- Set Up PWM Duty Cycle:
  - Write to the CCPR1L register.
  - Configure Bit5-Bit4 of the CCP1CON register.
- Configure the CCP Pin:
  - Set up pin RC2/CCP1 of PORTC as an output.
- Set Up Timer2:
  - Configure the TMR2 prescale value and set Timer2 in timer mode by writing to the T2CON register.

- Configure CCP1 for PWM:
  - Write to the CCP1CON register to enable PWM operation.

Algorithm:

Main Program:

1. Define the PIC18 configuration bits using the pragma directive, include xc.h, and set the crystal frequency for _XTAL_FREQ to utilize the built-in delay function.
2. Define a key at PORTB0 to control the PWM duty cycles.
3. Call the function pwm_config() to set up the PWM mode.
4. Set the duty cycle to 0% and wait for the key to be pressed and released.
5. Set the duty cycle to 20% and wait for the key to be pressed and released.
6. Set the duty cycle to 40% and wait for the key to be pressed and released.
7. Set the duty cycle to 60% and wait for the key to be pressed and released.
8. Set the duty cycle to 80% and wait for the key to be pressed and released.
9. Set the duty cycle to 100% and wait for the key to be pressed and released.
10. Repeat the steps from step 4.

Subroutine: pwm_config():

1. Configure the RC2/CCP1 pin as an output port.
2. Set up Timer 2 to serve as the base timer for CCP1, using a 1:16 prescaler.
3. Write to the PR2 register to define the PWM frequency at 2 kHz.
4. Set the Duty Cycle register (CCPR1L) to 0 for a 0% duty cycle.
5. Configure the CCP1 module for PWM output.

Program:

```
#pragma config PLLDIV = 5, CPUDIV = OSC1_PLL2, USBDIV = 2, FOSC = HS, FCMEN =
OFF, IESO = OFF
#pragma config PWRT = OFF, BOR = OFF, BORV = 3, VREGEN = OFF, WDT = OFF,
WDTPS = 32768
#pragma config CCP2MX = ON, PBADEN = OFF, LPT1OSC = OFF, MCLRE = ON
#pragma config STVREN = ON, LVP = OFF, ICPRT = OFF, XINST = OFF
#pragma config CP0 = OFF, CP1 = OFF, CP2 = OFF, CP3 = OFF, CPB = OFF, CPD = OFF
#pragma config WRT0 = OFF, WRT1 = OFF, WRT2 = OFF, WRT3 = OFF, WRTC = OFF,
WRTB = OFF, WRTD = OFF
#pragma config EBTR0 = OFF, EBTR1 = OFF, EBTR2 = OFF, EBTR3 = OFF, EBTRB = OFF

#include <xc.h>
#define _XTAL_FREQ 20000000
#define key PORTBbits.RB0

// subroutines
void pwm_config()
{
TRISC2 = 0;             // configure RC2 / CCP1 pin as output for PWM
T3CON = 0x80;           // use Timer2 as base timer for CCP1
PR2=155;                // period for 2KHz
//PR2=[(1/2KHZ)/(4*(1/20MHZ))*16]?1 =10000/64 - 1 = 156-1 =155
T2CON = 0x07;
CCPR1L = 0;             // 0% duty cycle
CCP1CON = 0x0C;         // Enable PWM mode
}

void delay_100ms (unsigned int x)
{
   int i;
   for (i=0; i<x; i++)
   {
      TMR0 = 63583;
      TMR0IF = 0;
      T0CON = 0x87;
```

```
        while(TMR0IF==0);
        TMR0IF=0;
    }
return;
}

void main (void)
{
pwm_config();
TRISB0=1;                   // Pushbutton Normally high
while(1)
{
CCPR1L = 0;                 //0% duty cycle
while(key==1);              // Wait until key press
delay_100ms (2);
while(key==0);

CCPR1L = 31;                //20% duty cycle = 155 x 0.2 = 31
while(key==1);              // Wait until key press
delay_100ms (2);
while(key==0);

CCPR1L = 62;                //40% duty cycle = 155 x 0.4 = 62
while(key==1);              // Wait until key press
delay_100ms (2);
while(key==0);

CCPR1L = 93;                //60% duty cycle = 155 x 0.6 = 93
while(key==1);              // Wait until key press
delay_100ms (2);
while(key==0);

CCPR1L = 124;               //80% duty cycle = 155 x 0.8 = 124
while(key==1);              // Wait until key press
```

```
delay_100ms (2);
while(key==0);

CCPR1L = 155;           //100% duty cycle = 155 x 1.0 = 155
while(key==1);          // Wait until key press
delay_100ms (2);
while(key==0);
}
}
```

Circuit Diagram:

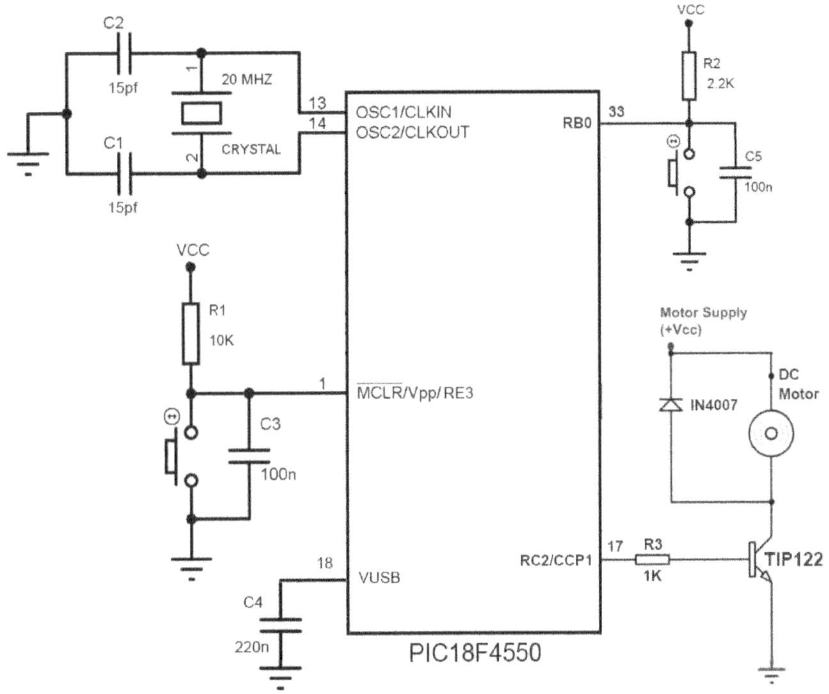

Conclusion:

The embedded system for controlling the speed of a DC motor using the PWM functionality of the PIC18F4550 Microcontroller and an Embedded C program has been successfully demonstrated.

39. SERVO MOTOR CONTROL USING PWM

Aim:

Develop an embedded system to control the angle of rotation of a servo motor using the PWM functionality of the PIC18F4550 Microcontroller and an Embedded C program. Verify the system's output to ensure proper operation.

Hardware Requirements:

- PIC18F4550 Microcontroller, 20 MHz Crystal (1), 15 pF Disc Capacitors (2), 220 nF Disc Capacitor (1), 100 nF Disc Capacitor (1), Resistor 10K (1), and Push Button (1)
- Servo motor

Software Used:

- IDE: MPLAB X IDE v5.45
- Compiler: XC8 - v2.31

Theory:

A servo motor is a sophisticated device that includes a DC motor, a reduction gearbox, a positional feedback device, and error correction circuits. It operates as an automatic closed-loop control system, where its position is continuously adjusted based on feedback. The system compares the actual output signal from the motor's shaft with the reference input signal. An error detection amplifier determines if the shaft is in the correct position. If there is a discrepancy, the controller adjusts the motor's speed—either accelerating or decelerating it—to correct the position. Typically, a servo motor can control angular motion between 0 and 180 degrees. Servo motors are commonly used in applications such as robotics, CNC machinery, and automated manufacturing.

Servo motor Control:

Servo motors are controlled using pulse width modulation (PWM). The control signal is an electrical pulse with a variable width sent through the control wire. The key characteristics of the PWM signal for servo motors are:

- Frequency: The signal should have a frequency of 50Hz, meaning a pulse is sent every 20ms.
- Pulse Width: The width of the pulse determines the angular position of the servo motor shaft.

Typically, a servo motor can rotate 90° in either direction, providing a total range of 180° movement. The length of the pulse (measured in milliseconds) adjusts the position of the servo within this range.
For example, a 1.5ms pulse will make the motor turn to the 90° position.

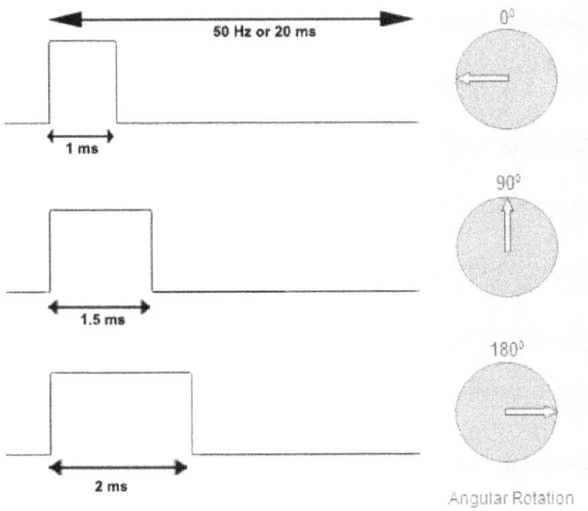

Servo motors have three wires: two for power (positive and ground) and one for the control signal. To control the servo motor, you need to program the MCU to send PWM signals to the control wire. The servo motor's internal circuitry reads the duty cycle of the PWM signal and adjusts the motor's shaft to the desired position.
For the SG90 servo motor, the duty cycle times corresponding to different angles of rotation are as follows:

- 0° Rotation: Approximately 0.8 ms pulse width (4% duty cycle)
- 90° Rotation: Approximately 1.4 ms pulse width (7% duty cycle)
- 180° Rotation: Approximately 2.2 ms pulse width (11% duty cycle)

CCP1 in Compare mode to generate PWM signal:

The lowest frequency achievable with Timer2 is 1220.7 Hz (calculated as 20000000 / (4 * 16 * 256)), which is insufficient for generating a 50 Hz PWM signal using CCP1. Instead, Timer1 can be utilized to produce a 50 Hz PWM signal in Compare mode with CCP1.

In CCP1's Compare mode, the 16-bit CCPRx register is compared with Timer1 (or Timer3). When the values match, one of the following actions occurs on the CCPx pin, and the CCPxIF interrupt flag bit is set:

- Driven High: The pin is set to a high state.
- Driven Low: The pin is set to a low state.
- Toggled: The pin switches state between high and low.
- Remain Unchanged: The pin retains its current state.

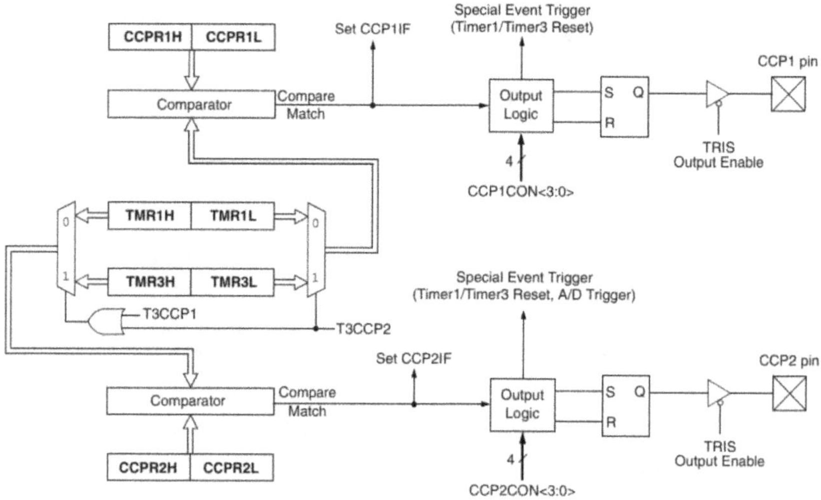

The required settings are

1. CCP1 (RC2): It should be an output port.
2. T1CON: Enable Timer 1 with 1:8 prescale (0xB1)

RD16	--	T1CKPS1	T1CKPS0	T1OSCEN	T1SYN	TMR1CS	TMR1ON
1	0	1	1	0	0	0	1

- TCY = 4/FOSC = 4/20MHz = 0.2 us.
- Timer increments every 0.2 us * prescaler = 0.2 us * 8 = 1.6 us.

- Number of ticks that corresponds to 20 ms PWM period = 20 ms/1.6 us = 12500

3. CCP1CON: Configure CCP1 in compare mode
   - 1000 = Compare mode, set output on match (CCP1IF bit is set)
   - 1001 = Compare mode, clear output on match (CCP1IF bit is set)
4. Load CCPR1 Register

   CCPR1 = Number of ticks for On-Time of 20ms pulse width
   - 0.8 ms (4% duty cycle) => CCPR1 = 500
   - 1.4 ms (7% duty cycle) => CCPR1 = 875
   - 2.2 ms (11% duty cycle) => CCPR1 = 1375
5. Wait for CCP1IF
6. Disable CCP1

Algorithm:

1. Define the PIC18 configuration bits using the pragma directive, include xc.h, and set the crystal frequency for _XTAL_FREQ to utilize the built-in delay function.
2. Initialize an array with DutyCycle values for 0.8 ms, 1.5 ms, and 2.2 ms, corresponding to 0°, 90°, and 180° angles of rotation, respectively.
3. Configure PORTC2 as the CCP1 pin and set it as an output port. Clear RC2.
4. Select Timer1 as the base timer (set T3CON to 0x00).
5. Enable Timer1 with a 1:8 prescaler and 16-bit mode (set T1CON to 0xB1).
6. Clear the Timer1 register.
7. Clear the CCP1 interrupt flag (CCP1IF).
8. Assign the DutyCycle value (from the array) to the CCP1 register.
9. Enable CCP1 in compare mode (clear RC2 on a match).
10. Wait for the CCP1IF flag to be set.
11. Clear the CCP1IF flag.
12. Set the CCP1 register to 12500 - DutyCycle value (from the array).
13. Enable CCP1 in compare mode (set RC2 on a match).
14. Wait for the CCP1IF flag to be set.

15. Clear the CCP1IF flag.
16. Disable CCP1.
17. Repeat steps 5 to 16 a total of 50 times, with a 2-second delay between each cycle.

Program:

```
#pragma config PLLDIV = 5, CPUDIV = OSC1_PLL2, USBDIV = 2, FOSC = HS, FCMEN =
OFF, IESO = OFF
#pragma config PWRT = OFF, BOR = OFF, BORV = 3, VREGEN = OFF, WDT = OFF,
WDTPS = 32768
#pragma config CCP2MX = ON, PBADEN = OFF, LPT1OSC = OFF, MCLRE = ON
#pragma config STVREN = ON, LVP = OFF, ICPRT = OFF, XINST = OFF
#pragma config CP0 = OFF, CP1 = OFF, CP2 = OFF, CP3 = OFF, CPB = OFF, CPD = OFF
#pragma config WRT0 = OFF, WRT1 = OFF, WRT2 = OFF, WRT3 = OFF, WRTC = OFF,
WRTB = OFF, WRTD = OFF
#pragma config EBTR0 = OFF, EBTR1 = OFF, EBTR2 = OFF, EBTR3 = OFF, EBTRB = OFF

#include <xc.h>
#define _XTAL_FREQ 20000000

void main (void)
{
unsigned int i, j;
// Initialize DutyCycle value for 0.8 ms, 1.4 ms and 2.2 ms
unsigned int DCycle[4]={500, 875, 1375, 875};
TRISCbits.TRISC2 = 0;            // Set RC2/CCP1 as output
LATCbits.LATC2 = 0;              // Clear LATC2
T3CON = 0x00;                    // Select Timer1 as base timer
while (1)
{
  for (i=0; i<4; i++){
  for (j=0; j<50; j++){          // Sending 50 pulses to the servo motor
  T1CON = 0xB1;                  // Enable timer1 use 1:8 prescaler and 16-bit mode
  TMR1 = 0;                      // Clear timer1 register
  PIR1bits.CCP1IF = 0;           // Clear CCP1 flag
  CCPR1 = DCycle[i];             // Assign DutyCycle value to CCPR1
```

```
      CCP1CON = 0x09;              // Compare mode, clear output on match
      while(PIR1bits.CCP1IF == 0); // Wait for CCP1 flag
      PIR1bits.CCP1IF = 0;         // Clear CCP1 flag
      CCPR1 = 12500 - DCycle[i];   // Assign TOFF value to CCPR1
      CCP1CON = 0x08;              // Compare mode, set output on match
      while(PIR1bits.CCP1IF == 0); // Wait for CCP1 flag
      PIR1bits.CCP1IF = 0;         // Clear CCP1 flag
      CCP1CON = 0x00;              // Disable CCP1 module
      }
   __delay_ms(2000);               // Wait for 2 sec
   }
  }
}
```

Circuit Diagram:

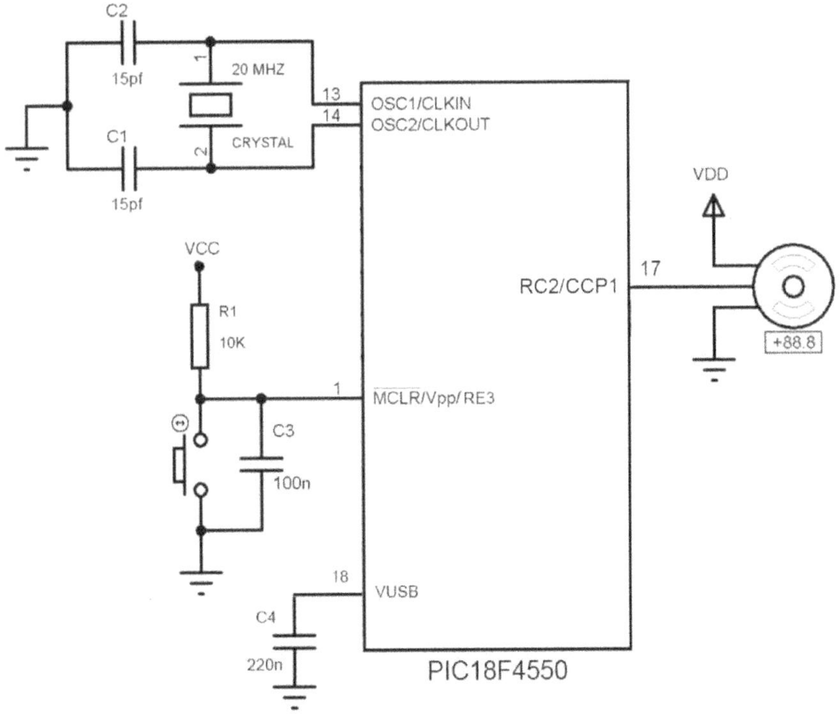

Conclusion:

The embedded system for controlling the angle of rotation of a servo motor using PWM mode on the PIC18F4550 Microcontroller, along with an Embedded C program, has been successfully demonstrated.

40. FREQUENCY MEASUREMENT

Aim:

Develop an embedded system for frequency measurement utilizing the capture mode of the PIC18F4550 Microcontroller and an Embedded C program. Verify the output using a function generator.

Hardware Requirements:

- PIC18F4550 Microcontroller, 20 MHz Crystal (1), 15 pF Disc Capacitors (2), 220 nF Disc Capacitor (1), 100 nF Disc Capacitor (1), Resistor 10K (1), and Push Button (1)
- 16x2 LCD and Function Generator

Software Used:

- IDE: MPLAB X IDE v5.45
- Compiler: XC8 - v2.31

Theory:

Capture Mode

In Capture Mode, the 16-bit CCPR1 register (comprising CCPR1H and CCPR1L) records the 16-bit value of the TMR1 register whenever an event occurs on the CCP1 pin (RC2). The types of events that can trigger the capture signal are:

- Every rising edge
- Every falling edge
- Every 4th rising edge
- Every 16th rising edge

Signal Event

The choice of which event will trigger the capture signal is made by the programmer. Timer 1 serves as the base timer for capture mode, and its register value (TMR1) increments with each event that occurs.

T1CKPS1:T1CKPS0: Timer1 Input Clock Prescaler Select bits

11 = 1:8 prescaler value

10 = 1:4 prescaler value

01 = 1:2 prescaler value

00 = 1:1 prescaler value

The CCP module should be configured to operate in capture mode with a selectable trigger event via the **CCP1CON** register.

CCP1M3: CCP1M0: CCP1 Mode Select bits

0100 = Capture mode is selected for every falling edge detected.

0101 = Capture mode is selected for every rising edge detected.

0110 = Capture mode is selected for every 4th rising edge detected.

0111 = Capture mode is selected for every 16th rising edge detected.

Configuring CCP1 Module for Capture Mode:

Configure the RC2/CCP1 Pin:

- Set the RC2/CCP1 pin as an input.

Set Timer1 Module:

- Configure Timer1 to operate in timer/counter mode.

Configure CCP1 Module:

- Set the CCP1 module to operate in Capture Mode by configuring the CCP1CON register.
- Choose the event that triggers the capture using the CCP1Mx bits.

Clear Flag Bits:

- Clear the CCP1 interrupt flag (CCP1IF) and the Timer1 interrupt flag (TMR1IF).

Initialize Registers:

- Clear the TMR1 register to start counting from 0.
- Clear the CCPR1 register (the capture count register) initially.

Turn On Timer1:

- Enable the Timer1 module to start counting.

Algorithm:

1. Define the PIC18 configuration bits using the pragma directive, include xc.h, and set the crystal frequency for _XTAL_FREQ to utilize the inbuilt delay functions.
2. Assign the RS and EN pins of the LCD to RD2 and RD3, respectively, and connect the data bus lines (D4-D7) of the LCD to RD4-RD7.
3. Include the lcd.h header file, which is the same one used in the LCD interface experiment.
4. Configure Timer1 with a tick time of 0.2 μs, suitable for a 20 MHz crystal oscillator with a 1:1 prescaler.
5. Declare local variables including start, stop, TimerCount, frequency, period, d1, d2, d3, d4, and d5.
6. Set the CCP1 pin as an input port and configure PORTD as an output port.
7. Initialize the 16x2 LCD for 4-bit mode to ensure proper operation.
8. Display "Signal Frequency" on the first line of the 16x2 LCD and "Hz" on the second line starting from address 0xCA.
9. Set Timer1 for 16-bit mode, choose the internal clock source for its operation, and set the prescaler to 1:1.
10. Clear the CCP1 interrupt flag and Timer1 interrupt flag.
11. Clear both the CCP1 register and the Timer1 register.
12. Configure the CCP1 module for capture mode, selecting capture on every rising edge of the event.
13. Enable Timer1 to start counting.
14. Wait until the CCP1 interrupt flag (CCP1IF) is set.
15. Clear the CCP1 interrupt flag (CCP1IF).
16. Move the TimerCount value from the first rising edge captured in the CCP1 register to the start variable.
17. Wait until the CCP1 interrupt flag (CCP1IF) is set again.
18. Clear the CCP1 interrupt flag (CCP1IF).
19. Move the TimerCount value from the second rising edge captured in the CCP1 register to the stop variable.
20. Disable both the CCP1 module and Timer1 module.
21. Calculate the frequency based on the time duration between the start

and stop variables.

22. Display the calculated frequency value on the second line of the LCD screen.
23. Repeat the steps from step 10 to continuously measure and display the frequency.

lcd.h() header file: (see the 16x2 LCD interface experiment)

Program:

```
#pragma config PLLDIV = 5, CPUDIV = OSC1_PLL2, USBDIV = 2, FOSC = HS, FCMEN =
OFF, IESO = OFF
#pragma config PWRT = OFF, BOR = OFF, BORV = 3, VREGEN = OFF, WDT = OFF,
WDTPS = 32768
#pragma config CCP2MX = ON, PBADEN = OFF, LPT1OSC = OFF, MCLRE = ON
#pragma config STVREN = ON, LVP = OFF, ICPRT = OFF, XINST = OFF
#pragma config CP0 = OFF, CP1 = OFF, CP2 = OFF, CP3 = OFF, CPB = OFF, CPD = OFF
#pragma config WRT0 = OFF, WRT1 = OFF, WRT2 = OFF, WRT3 = OFF, WRTC = OFF,
WRTB = OFF, WRTD = OFF
#pragma config EBTR0 = OFF, EBTR1 = OFF, EBTR2 = OFF, EBTR3 = OFF, EBTRB = OFF

#include <xc.h>
#define _XTAL_FREQ 20000000

#define tick 0.0000002              // timer1 clock time = 0.2us (for 20MHZ
with 1:1 prescaler)
#define RS       LATD2              // LATD2 is named as RS
#define EN       LATD3              // LATD3 is named as EN
#define D4       LATD4              // 4-bit mode (LATD4-D4, LATD5-D5
#define D5       LATD5              // LATD6-D6, LATD7-D7)
#define D6       LATD6
#define D7       LATD7
#include "lcd4bit_head.h"           // Include header file - lcd4bit_head.h

void main ()
{
unsigned long start, stop, TimerCount, frequency;
```

```
float period;
unsigned int d1, d2, d3, d4, d5;
TRISC = 0x0F;                    // LATC2/CCP1 is input pin
TRISD = 0x00;
lcd_init ();                     // LCD initialization
lcd_cmd (0x80);                  // Display the message on LCD screen
lcd_display ("Signal Frequency");
lcd_cmd (0xca);
lcd_data ('H');
lcd_data ('z');

T3CON=0x00;                      // Setting Timer1 as a base timer
// Setting Timer1
TMR1CS = 0;                      // Timer mode
T1CKPS0 = 0;                     // 1:1 prescale
T1CKPS1 = 0;
T1SYNC = 1;
while(1)
{
//clear flags
  CCP1IF = 0;
  TMR1IF = 0;
//clear registers
  TMR1 = 0;
  CCPR1 = 0;
//setting CCP1
  CCP1CON = 0x05;      // Capture mode: every rising edge
//Turn ON Timer1
  TMR1ON = 1;

  while (!(CCP1IF));   // Wait for first rising edge of a signal
  CCP1IF = 0;
  start = CCPR1;       // Copy TimerCount of 1st rising edge detected
```

```
    while (!(CCP1IF));      // Wait for second rising edge of a signal
    CCP1IF = 0;
    stop = CCPR1;           // Copy TimerCount of 2nd rising edge detected
    CCP1CON = 0x00;         // Turn-off CCP1 and Timer 1
    TMR1ON = 0;

//Calculation for Frequency Measurement
TimerCount = stop - start;
period = (float)(tick * TimerCount);
frequency = (float)(1/period);

// Display numbers on LCD display
d1= (frequency /10000) + 48;
d2= ((frequency /1000) % 10) + 48;
d3= ((frequency /100) % 10) + 48;
d4= ((frequency /10) % 10) + 48;
d5= (frequency % 10) + 48;
lcd_cmd (0xC4);
lcd_data (d1);
lcd_data (d2);
lcd_data (d3);
lcd_data (d4);
lcd_data (d5);
__delay_ms(500);
}
}
-----------------------------------------------------------------------------------------

// Header file: lcd4bit_head.h
void Lcd_WriteBit(unsigned char bt)      //write the nibble on 4-bit data bus of LCD
{
   if(bt & 1)
      D4 = 1;
   else
      D4 = 0;
```

```
    if(bt & 2)
        D5 = 1;
    else
        D5 = 0;
    if(bt & 4)
        D6 = 1;
    else
        D6 = 0;
    if(bt & 8)
        D7 = 1;
    else
        D7 = 0;
}

void lcd_cmd(unsigned char CMD)           // Definition of lcd_cmd() function
{
    RS = 0;                               // Make RS pin low to select CMD reg.
    Lcd_WriteBit((CMD >> 4) & 0x0FU);     // Send Higher Nibble of CMD
    EN = 1;                               // Give High to Low pulse to Enable (E)
    __delay_ms(2);
    EN = 0;
    __delay_ms(5);
    RS = 0;
    Lcd_WriteBit(CMD & 0x0FU);            // Send Lower Nibble of CMD
    EN = 1;                               // Give High to Low pulse to Enable (E)
    __delay_ms(2);
    EN = 0;
    __delay_ms(5);
}

void lcd_data(unsigned char DAT)          // Definition of lcd_data() function
{
    RS = 1;                               // Make RS pin high to select data reg.
    Lcd_WriteBit((DAT >> 4) & 0x0FU);     // Send Higher Nibble of data
```

```
    EN = 1;                              // Give High to Low pulse to Enable (E)
    __delay_ms(2);
    EN = 0;
    __delay_ms(5);
    RS = 1;
    Lcd_WriteBit(DAT & 0x0FU);           // Send Lower Nibble of data
    EN = 1;                              // Give High to Low pulse to Enable (E)
    __delay_ms(2);
    EN = 0;
    __delay_ms(5);
}

void lcd_display(char *x)                // Definition of lcd_display () function
{
    while(*x!=0x0) {                     // Condition is true until null character
    lcd_data(*x);                        // Send a character to LCD screen
    __delay_ms(10);                      // Make 10 ms delay
    x++;                                 // Increment pointer variable
    }
}

void lcd_init ()
{
    lcd_cmd(0x02); __delay_ms(12);       // 16X2 LCD in 4-bit mode
    lcd_cmd(0x28); __delay_ms(12);       // 2 lines, 5X7 dots in 4-bit mode
    lcd_cmd(0x0C); __delay_ms(12);       // Display ON Cursor OFF
    lcd_cmd(0x06); __delay_ms(12);       // Auto Increment cursor
    lcd_cmd(0x01); __delay_ms(12);       // Clear Display
}
```

Circuit Diagram:

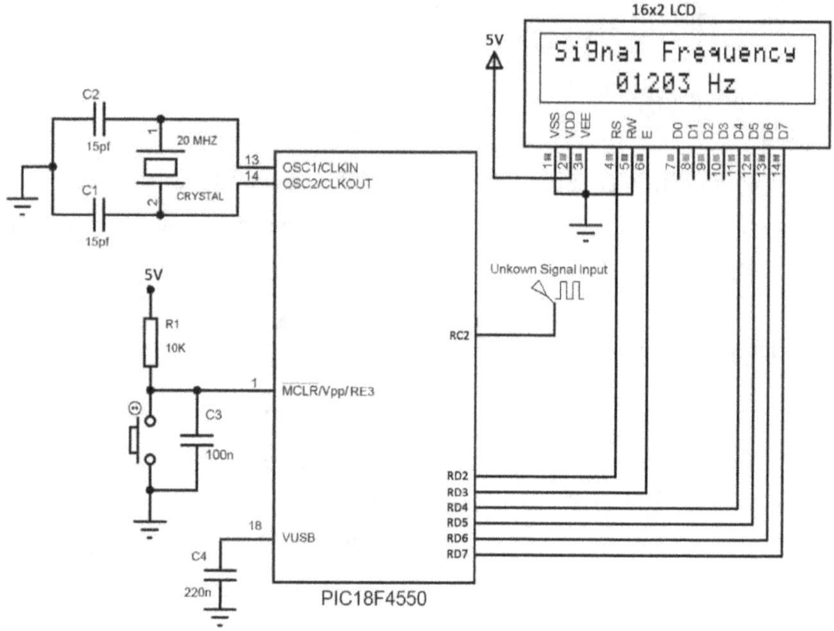

Conclusion:

The embedded system for frequency measurement using the PIC18F4550 Microcontroller and an Embedded C program has been successfully demonstrated.

41. ANALOG TO DIGITAL CONVERSION

Aim:

Write and execute an Embedded C program to verify the operation of the on-chip Analog-to-Digital Converter (ADC) of the PIC18F4550 Microcontroller.

Hardware Requirements:

- PIC18F4550 Microcontroller, 20 MHz Crystal (1), 15 pF Disc Capacitors (2), 220 nF Disc Capacitor (1), 100 nF Disc Capacitor (1),

Resistor 10K (1), and Push Button (1)
- POT 10K, Resistor 1K (1), LEDs (10), Resistor 120 (10)

Software Used:
- IDE: MPLAB X IDE v5.45
- Compiler: XC8 - v2.31

Theory:
- The number of analog inputs varies from device to device.
    - PIC18F4550: 13 channels (13 analog inputs)
    - PIC18F458: 8 channels (8 analog inputs)
- PIC18 has 10-bit A/D converter.
    - 10-bit resolution -> 10-bit digital output
    - Resolution = (Vref+ – Vref-)/(2^n – 1) = 5/1023 = 0.00488V
    - ADC resolution is 4.88mV, which is the minimum required voltage to change a bit.
- The analog input voltage of 3.65v will be represented by decimal number 748 or by binary number 1011101100.

$$\begin{Bmatrix} 5V & \rightarrow 1024 \\ 3.65V & \rightarrow X \end{Bmatrix} \rightarrow X = \frac{1024 * 3.65}{5} = 747.52 \approx 748$$

- External reference voltages: Vref+ and Vref- are applied through RA3 and RA2 respectively.
- 8 selectable clock options.
- ADC can be in auto-triggering mode for continuous A/D conversion.

PIC18F4550 ADC module has five 8-bit registers:

1. A/D Control Register 0 (ADCON0)
2. A/D Control Register 1 (ADCON1)
3. A/D Control Register 2 (ADCON2)
4. A/D Result High Register (ADRESH)
5. A/D Result Low Register (ADRESL)

ADCON0: A/D Control Register 0

—	—	CHS3	CHS2	CHS1	CHS0	GO/$\overline{DONE}$	ADON
bit 7							bit 0

bit 7-6 **Unimplemented:** Read as '0'

bit 5-2 **CHS3:CHS0:** Analog Channel Select bits

0000 = Channel 0 (AN0)
0001 = Channel 1 (AN1)
0010 = Channel 2 (AN2)
0011 = Channel 3 (AN3)
0100 = Channel 4 (AN4)
0101 = Channel 5 (AN5)(1,2)
0110 = Channel 6 (AN6)(1,2)
0111 = Channel 7 (AN7)(1,2)
1000 = Channel 8 (AN8)
1001 = Channel 9 (AN9)
1010 = Channel 10 (AN10)
1011 = Channel 11 (AN11)
1100 = Channel 12 (AN12)
1101 = Unimplemented(2)
1110 = Unimplemented(2)
1111 = Unimplemented(2)

bit 1 **GO/$\overline{DONE}$:** A/D Conversion Status bit

When ADON = 1:
1 = A/D conversion in progress
0 = A/D Idle

bit 0 **ADON:** A/D On bit

1 = A/D converter module is enabled
0 = A/D converter module is disabled

ADCON1: A/D Control Register 1

—	—	VCFG0	VCFG0	PCFG3	PCFG2	PCFG1	PCFG0
bit 7							bit 0

bit 7-6 **Unimplemented:** Read as '0'

bit 5 **VCFG0:** Voltage Reference Configuration bit (VREF- source)

1 = VREF- (AN2)
0 = VSS

bit 4 **VCFG0:** Voltage Reference Configuration bit (VREF+ source)

1 = VREF+ (AN3)
0 = VDD

bit 3-0 **PCFG3:PCFG0:** A/D Port Configuration Control bits:

PCFG3: PCFG0	AN12	AN11	AN10	AN9	AN8	AN7(2)	AN6(2)	AN5(2)	AN4	AN3	AN2	AN1	AN0
0000(1)	A	A	A	A	A	A	A	A	A	A	A	A	A
0001	A	A	A	A	A	A	A	A	A	A	A	A	A
0010	A	A	A	A	A	A	A	A	A	A	A	A	A
0011	D	A	A	A	A	A	A	A	A	A	A	A	A
0100	D	D	A	A	A	A	A	A	A	A	A	A	A
0101	D	D	D	A	A	A	A	A	A	A	A	A	A
0110	D	D	D	D	A	A	A	A	A	A	A	A	A
0111(1)	D	D	D	D	D	A	A	A	A	A	A	A	A
1000	D	D	D	D	D	D	A	A	A	A	A	A	A
1001	D	D	D	D	D	D	D	A	A	A	A	A	A
1010	D	D	D	D	D	D	D	D	A	A	A	A	A
1011	D	D	D	D	D	D	D	D	D	A	A	A	A
1100	D	D	D	D	D	D	D	D	D	D	A	A	A
1101	D	D	D	D	D	D	D	D	D	D	D	A	A
1110	D	D	D	D	D	D	D	D	D	D	D	D	A
1111	D	D	D	D	D	D	D	D	D	D	D	D	D

A = Analog input D = Digital I/O

ADCON2: A/D Control Register 2

ADFM	—	ACQT2	ACQT1	ACQT0	ADCS2	ADCS1	ADCS0
bit 7							bit 0

bit 7 **ADFM:** A/D Result Format Select bit
1 = Right justified
0 = Left justified

bit 6 **Unimplemented:** Read as '0'

bit 5-3 **ACQT2:ACQT0:** A/D Acquisition Time Select bits
111 = 20 TAD
110 = 16 TAD
101 = 12 TAD
100 = 8 TAD
011 = 6 TAD
010 = 4 TAD
001 = 2 TAD
000 = 0 TAD(1)

bit 2-0 **ADCS2:ADCS0:** A/D Conversion Clock Select bits
111 = FRC (clock derived from A/D RC oscillator)(1)
110 = FOSC/64
101 = FOSC/16
100 = FOSC/4
011 = FRC (clock derived from A/D RC oscillator)(1)
010 = FOSC/32
001 = FOSC/8
000 = FOSC/2

Selecting the A/D Conversion Clock

- A/D conversion clock time is defined as TAD.
- If Fosc=20 MHz,
  - 32 Tosc = 32 * (1/20MHz) = 1.6 us
- The length of TAD must be at least 1.6 us for 20 MHz
- Each 10-bit A/D conversion takes (0-20) TAD to complete
- TAD versus Crystal oscillator frequency

AD Clock Source (TAD)		Maximum Device Frequency	
Operation	**ADCS2:ADCS0**	**PIC18FXXXX**	**PIC18LFXXXX(4)**
2 TOSC	000	2.86 MHz	1.43 MHz
4 TOSC	100	5.71 MHz	2.86 MHz
8 TOSC	001	11.43 MHz	5.72 MHz
16 TOSC	101	22.86 MHz	11.43 MHz
32 TOSC	010	45.71 MHz	22.86 MHz
64 TOSC	110	48.0 MHz	45.71 MHz
RC(3)	x11	1.00 MHz(1)	1.00 MHz(2)

A/D Acquisition Requirements

The capacitor CHOLD holds the voltage to be converted.

The required minimum acquisition time TACQ is computed as follows:

- TACQ = Amplifier settling time (TAMP) + Holding capacitor charging time (TC) + Temperature coefficient (TCOFF) where,

$T_{AMP} = 2\ \mu s$

$T_{COFF} = (\text{temp} - 25°C) \times (0.05\ \mu s/°C)$, 0 for temp < 25°C.

$$T_C = 120\ pF \times (1\ K\Omega + R_{SS} + R_S) \log(2047)$$
$$= 120\ pF \times (1\ K\Omega + 7K\Omega + 2\ K\Omega) = 9.61\ \mu s$$

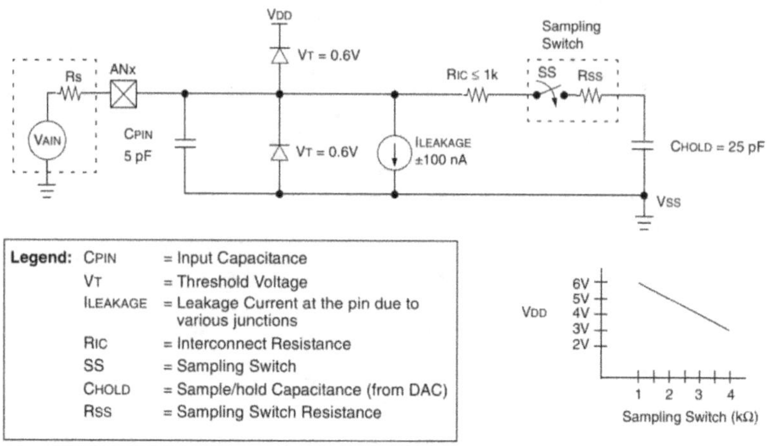

The acquisition time at 70°C = 2 us + 2.25 us + 9.61 us
= 13.86 us.

If the Acquisition time is 13.86 us (at 70°C), have to select 12 TAD using ACQT2:ACQT0 bits.

=> ~~8 TAD = 8 * 1.6 = 12.8 us~~

=> 12 TAD = 12 * 1.6 us = 19.2 us

The operation of A/D converter starts after the GO/DONE bit is set and have to wait for 12 TAD (101) to complete the conversion.

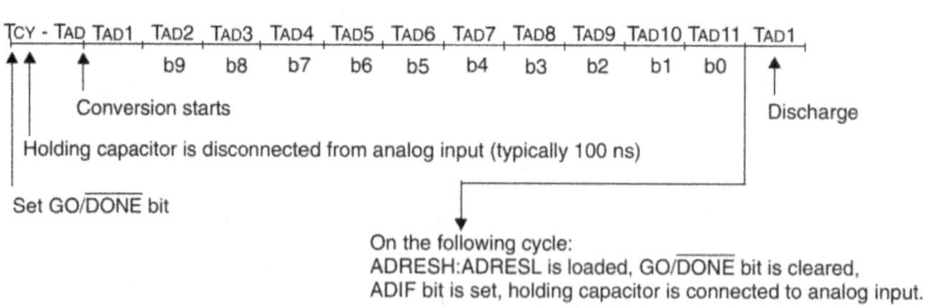

Automatic Acquisition Time

In newer devices, the acquisition time is automatically managed. If the ACQT2 bits (ADCON2<5:3>) are non-zero, the A/D module will continue sampling for the specified acquisition time after the GO/DONE bit is set and will then automatically begin the conversion. Once the conversion starts, the holding capacitor is disconnected from the analog input. It will be reconnected to the analog input at the end of the conversion. Therefore, there is no need to wait for an acquisition time between selecting a channel and setting the GO/DONE bit.

How to configure the ADC of PIC18F4550 to operate with the following parameters?

1. Fosc = 32 MHz, the highest ambient temperature may reach at 60°C, Use VDD and VSS as the high and low reference voltage, convert analog value from AN0, Conversion result right justified
2. TCOFF = (60-25) x 0.05 = 1.75 us
3. The required acquisition time = (9.61 + 2 + 1.75) us = 13.36 us
4. Fosc = 32MHz, the ADC clock source must be 64 Tosc (110) which makes TAD = 2 us (at least 1.6 us)
5. PIC18F supports automatic acquisition time, it must be set to at least 8 TAD (100) to make it greater than 13.36 us
   8 * TAD = 8 * 2 = 16 us

The following steps to be used for the A/D Conversion:

1. Configure the A/D module:
   - Select the A/D input channel (ADCON0)
   - Configure the analog pins and reference voltages (ADCON1)
   - Select the A/D acquisition time (ADCON2)
   - Select the AID conversion clock source (ADCON2)
   - Enable the A/D module (ADCON0)
2. Configure the A/D interrupt (if desired):
   - Set the GIE bit and PEIE bit (INTCON)
   - Clear the ADIF bit (PIR1)
   - Set the ADIE bit (PIE1)
3. Start the conversion by setting the GO/DONE bit.

4. Wait for the A/D conversion to complete by either waiting for the GO/DONE bit to be cleared or waiting for the A/D interrupt flag.
5. Read the A/D result registers; clear the ADIF flag

Algorithm:

1. Define the PIC18 configuration bits using the pragma directive, include xc.h, and define the crystal frequency for _XTAL_FREQ to use the built-in delay functions.
2. Configure PORTA as an input port, and PORTB and PORTD as output ports.
3. Clear PORTB and PORTD.
4. Configure the ADC using the ADCON0, ADCON1, and ADCON2 registers. Set the analog channel to AN0, use an ADC clock of FOSC/64, set the acquisition time to 8 TAD, right justify the result, and use VDD and VSS as reference inputs. Turn on the ADC.
5. Set the GO bit to start the conversion.
6. Wait for the DONE bit or ADIF to be set.
7. Clear the ADC interrupt flag by setting ADIF to 0.
8. Move the ADC result to LATB and LATD.
9. Wait for 100 ms.
10. Repeat the steps from step 4.

Program:

```
#pragma config PLLDIV = 5, CPUDIV = OSC1_PLL2, USBDIV = 2, FOSC = HS, FCMEN =
OFF, IESO = OFF
#pragma config PWRT = OFF, BOR = OFF, BORV = 3, VREGEN = OFF, WDT = OFF,
WDTPS = 32768
#pragma config CCP2MX = ON, PBADEN = OFF, LPT1OSC = OFF, MCLRE = ON
#pragma config STVREN = ON, LVP = OFF, ICPRT = OFF, XINST = OFF
#pragma config CP0 = OFF, CP1 = OFF, CP2 = OFF, CP3 = OFF, CPB = OFF, CPD = OFF
#pragma config WRT0 = OFF, WRT1 = OFF, WRT2 = OFF, WRT3 = OFF, WRTC = OFF,
WRTB = OFF, WRTD = OFF
#pragma config EBTR0 = OFF, EBTR1 = OFF, EBTR2 = OFF, EBTR3 = OFF, EBTRB = OFF

#include <xc.h>
#define _XTAL_FREQ 20000000
```

```
unsigned char ResH, ResL;

void adc_ch0 (void)
{
        // Select Channel 0 & ADC off
        ADCON0 = 0x01;
        // use VDD & VSS as reference voltages &
        // Make RA0/AN0 pin as analog pin  (other pins to be digital I/O)
        ADCON1 = 0x0E;
        // Right justified, 8TAD acquisition time,
        // Fosc/64 clock option
        ADIF=0;
        // Clear ADC flag
        ADCON2=0xA6;
        GO_nDONE = 1;           // Start the conversion
        while (ADIF==0);        // wait for ADIF=1 for end of conversion
        ADIF=0;
        ResL= ADRESL;           // Result of ADC to ResH & ResL
        ResH= ADRESH;
        ADON=0;                 // Turn-off ADC
}

void main(void)
{
TRISA=0xFF;             // Make PORTA as input port
TRISB=0x00;             // Make PORTB as output port
TRISD=0x00;             // Make PORTD as output port
LATB=0x00;              // Clear LATB and LATD
LATD=0x00;
while(1) {
adc_ch0();              // Call adc_ch0() function to configure the ADC
LATB = ResL;            // LSB of 10-bit Digital result
LATD = ResH;            // MSB of 10-bit Digital result
__delay_ms(100);        // Wait for 100ms
```

```
}
}
```

Circuit Diagram:

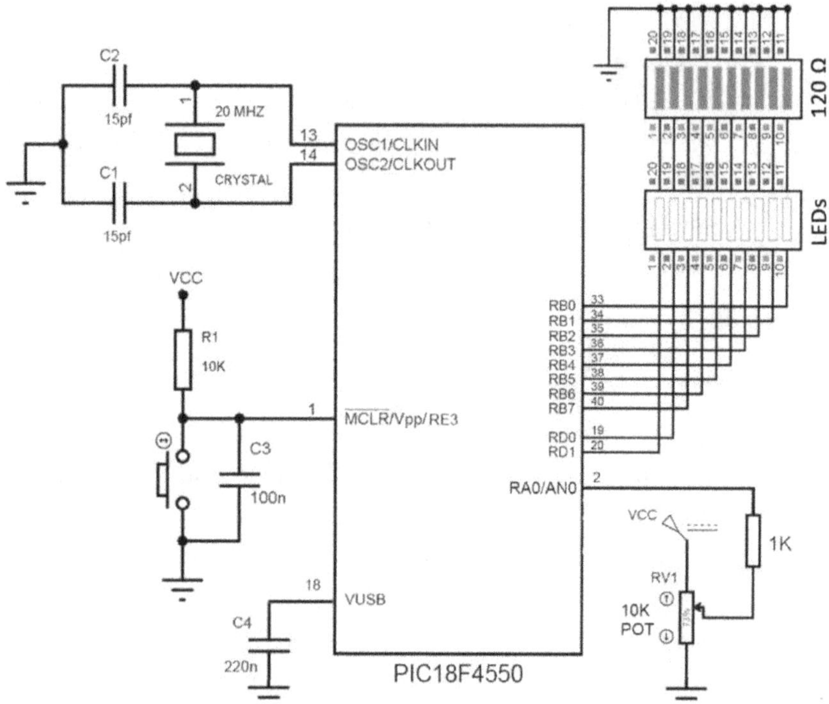

Conclusion:

The operation of the on-chip analog-to-digital converter in the PIC18F4550 Microcontroller has been successfully verified.

42. TEMPERATURE MONITOR USING ON-CHIP ADC

Aim:

Develop an embedded system to measure temperature using the on-chip ADC of the PIC18F4550 Microcontroller and an Embedded C program, and verify its accuracy.

Hardware Requirements:

- PIC18F4550 Microcontroller, 20 MHz Crystal (1), 15 pF Disc Capacitors (2), 220 nF Disc Capacitor (1), 100 nF Disc Capacitor (1), Resistor 10K (1), and Push Button (1)
- LM35 sensor and 16x2 LCD

Software Used:

- IDE: MPLAB X IDE v5.45
- Compiler: XC8 - v2.31

Theory:

The LM35 is an analog temperature sensor that outputs a voltage proportional to the temperature in degrees Celsius. With a sensitivity of 10 mV per degree Celsius, it provides a direct measurement of temperature without the need for additional calibration circuitry.

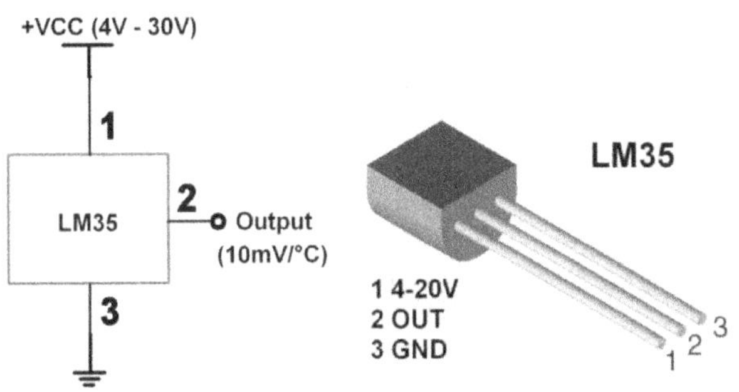

As the temperature rises, the output voltage of the LM35 increases proportionally. For instance, an output voltage of 275 mV corresponds to a temperature of 27.5°C. The LM35 is a 3-terminal sensor designed to measure ambient temperatures ranging from -55°C to 150°C.

Algorithm:

1. Define the PIC18 configuration bits using the pragma directive, include xc.h, and set the crystal frequency for _XTAL_FREQ to utilize the built-in delay function.
2. Assign the RS and EN pins of the LCD to LATD2 and LATD3, respectively. Assign the data bus pins (D4-D7) of the LCD to LATD4-

LATD7.

3. Include the lcd4bit_head.h header file, which is the same header file used in the LCD interface experiment.

main function:

4. Declare the local variable adc_res for storing ADC results.
5. Configure PORTD as an output port.
6. Initialize the 16x2 LCD in 4-bit mode.
7. Display "TEMPERATURE" on the first line of the LCD.
8. Read an analog value from AN0 and store it in the adc_res variable.
9. Convert the adc_res value to its corresponding temperature and display it on the second line of the LCD.
10. Wait for 1 second.
11. Repeat the steps from step 8.

float adc_ch0() function:

1. Configure the on-chip ADC module: select AN0, set ADC clock to FOSC/64, right-justify the result, set acquisition time to 19.72μs, use VDD and VSS as reference inputs, and enable the ADC. (ADCON0 = 0x01; ADCON1 = 0x0E; ADCON2 = 0xAA;)
2. Set the GO bit to start the conversion.
3. Wait for the DONE bit to indicate the conversion is complete.
4. Convert the 16-bit binary result into a decimal value.
5. Turn off the ADC.
6. Scale the decimal result to match a range of 0 to 100, considering the ADC input span, and return the result to the main function.

lcd_num(int) function:

1. Extract the digit in the 10's position from the given value, convert it to its ASCII representation, and then display it on the LCD screen.
2. Extract the digit in the 1's position from the given value, convert it to its ASCII representation, and then display it on the LCD screen.

Program:

Main Source File:

```
#pragma config PLLDIV = 5, CPUDIV = OSC1_PLL2, USBDIV = 2, FOSC = HS, FCMEN =
OFF, IESO = OFF
```

```
#pragma config PWRT = OFF, BOR = OFF, BORV = 3, VREGEN = OFF, WDT = OFF,
WDTPS = 32768
#pragma config CCP2MX = ON, PBADEN = OFF, LPT1OSC = OFF, MCLRE = ON
#pragma config STVREN = ON, LVP = OFF, ICPRT = OFF, XINST = OFF
#pragma config CP0 = OFF, CP1 = OFF, CP2 = OFF, CP3 = OFF, CPB = OFF, CPD = OFF
#pragma config WRT0 = OFF, WRT1 = OFF, WRT2 = OFF, WRT3 = OFF, WRTC = OFF,
WRTB = OFF, WRTD = OFF
#pragma config EBTR0 = OFF, EBTR1 = OFF, EBTR2 = OFF, EBTR3 = OFF, EBTRB = OFF

#include <xc.h>
#define _XTAL_FREQ 20000000
#define RS      LATD2         // LATD2 is named as RS
#define EN      LATD3         // LATD3 is named as EN
#define D4      LATD4         // 4-bit mode (LATD4-D4, LATD5-D5
#define D5      LATD5         // LATD6-D6, LATD7-D7)
#define D6      LATD6
#define D7      LATD7
#include "lcd4bit_head.h"     // Include header file - lcd4bit_head.h

float adc_ch0()
{
  unsigned int a;
        TRISA = 0x01;         // RA0 input port
        ADCON1 = 0x0E;        // Vref and channel selection
        ADCON2 = 0xAA;        // ADC clock and Acq time
        ADCON0 = 0x01;        //  Select Channel 0 & ADC ON
        ADCON0bits.GO_nDONE = 1;              // start ADC
        while (ADCON0bits.GO_nDONE == 1);     // wait for conversion
        a = ((ADRESH*256) + ADRESL);          // Move the result to 'a'
        ADCON0bits.ADON=0;                    // Turn-off the ADC
        return (a *(5.0/1023)*100);
}

void lcd_num(int n) {
  lcd_data((n/10)+48);        // n=12.45 --> n/10 = 1+48 (+48 for ASCII value in decimal)
  lcd_data((n%10)+48);        // n%10 --> 2 (modules) + 48
```

```
}

void main()                          // Main function
{
   float adc_res;                    // Variable declaration
   TRISD = 0x00;                     // set PORT D as output ports
   lcd_init ();                      // Call lcd_init() function
   lcd_cmd(0x80);                    // cursor position at 0th addr of line1
   lcd_display(" TEMPERATURE  ");    // Call lcd_display() function
   while (1)
   {
      adc_res = adc_ch0();           // Read the analog value from AN0
      lcd_cmd(0xc4);                 // LCD cursor at C4
      lcd_num( (int) adc_res);       // Write the 1st and 10th position digits
      lcd_cmd(0xC6);                 // Put decimal point at C6
      lcd_data('.');
      lcd_cmd(0xc7);                 // Write the 1/10th & 1/100th position digits
      lcd_num(( adc_res - (int) adc_res)*100);
      lcd_cmd(0xCA);                 // LCD cursor at CA
      lcd_data(0xdf);                // 0xdf for degree symbol
      lcd_data('C');                 // Write 'C' on LCD for Celsius
      __delay_ms(1000);              // Make 1 sec delay for next cycle
   }
}
```

```
// Header file: lcd4bit_head.h
void Lcd_WriteBit(unsigned char bt)      //write the nibble on 4-bit data bus of LCD
{
  if(bt & 1)
     D4 = 1;
  else
     D4 = 0;
  if(bt & 2)
     D5 = 1;
```

```
    else
        D5 = 0;
    if(bt & 4)
        D6 = 1;
    else
        D6 = 0;
    if(bt & 8)
        D7 = 1;
    else
        D7 = 0;
}

void lcd_cmd(unsigned char CMD)          // Definition of lcd_cmd() function
{
    RS = 0;                              // Make RS pin low to select CMD reg.
    Lcd_WriteBit((CMD >> 4) & 0x0FU);    // Send Higher Nibble of CMD
    EN = 1;                              // Give High to Low pulse to Enable (E)
    __delay_ms(2);
    EN = 0;
    __delay_ms(5);
    RS = 0;
    Lcd_WriteBit(CMD & 0x0FU);           // Send Lower Nibble of CMD
    EN = 1;                              // Give High to Low pulse to Enable (E)
    __delay_ms(2);
    EN = 0;
    __delay_ms(5);
}

void lcd_data(unsigned char DAT)         // Definition of lcd_data() function
{
    RS = 1;                              // Make RS pin high to select data reg.
    Lcd_WriteBit((DAT >> 4) & 0x0FU);    // Send Higher Nibble of data
    EN = 1;                              // Give High to Low pulse to Enable (E)
    __delay_ms(2);
```

```
    EN = 0;
    __delay_ms(5);
    RS = 1;
    Lcd_WriteBit(DAT & 0x0FU);              // Send Lower Nibble of data
    EN = 1;                                 // Give High to Low pulse to Enable (E)
    __delay_ms(2);
    EN = 0;
    __delay_ms(5);
}

void lcd_display(char *x){                  // Definition of lcd_display () function
    while(*x!=0x0) {                        // Condition is true until null character
    lcd_data(*x);                           // Send a character to LCD screen
    __delay_ms(10);                         // Make 10 ms delay
    x++;                                    // Increment pointer variable
    }
}
void lcd_init ()
{
    lcd_cmd(0x02); __delay_ms(12);          // 16X2 LCD in 4-bit mode
    lcd_cmd(0x28); __delay_ms(12);          // 2 lines, 5X7 dots in 4-bit mode
    lcd_cmd(0x0C); __delay_ms(12);          // Display ON Cursor OFF
    lcd_cmd(0x06); __delay_ms(12);          // Auto Increment cursor
    lcd_cmd(0x01); __delay_ms(12);          // Clear Display
}
```

Circuit Diagram:

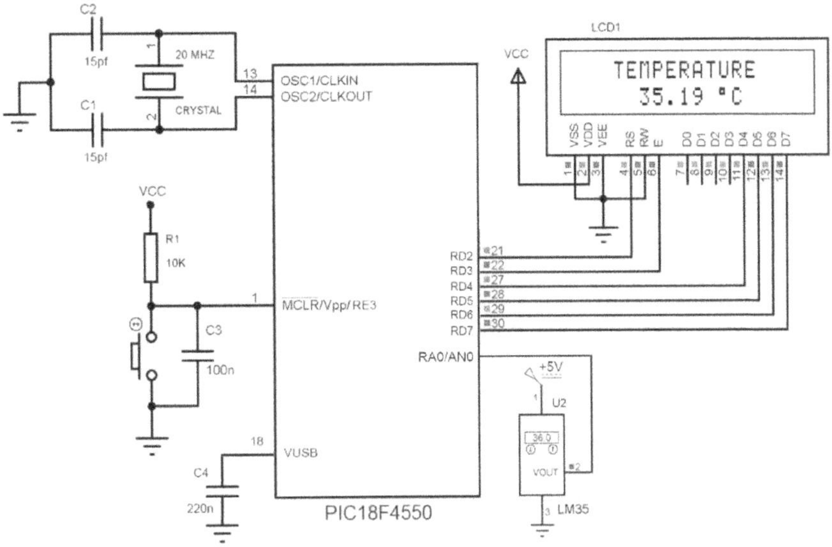

Conclusion:

The embedded system for temperature measurement using the PIC18F4550 Microcontroller and an Embedded C program has been successfully demonstrated.

43. SERIAL DATA TRANSFER USING UART

Aim:

Write and execute an Embedded C program to verify the operation of the asynchronous mode of the on-chip USART in the PIC18F4550 Microcontroller.

Hardware Requirements:

- PIC18F4550 Microcontroller, 20 MHz Crystal (1), 15 pF Disc Capacitors (2), 220 nF Disc Capacitor (1), 100 nF Disc Capacitor (1), Resistor 10K (1), and Push Button (1)
- IC MAX232 (1), Capacitor 1 uF (4), and DB9 Connector Female

Software Used:

- IDE: MPLAB X IDE v5.45
- Compiler: XC8 - v2.31
- Any serial window software

Theory:

USART stands for Universal Synchronous and Asynchronous Receiver/Transmitter. In asynchronous mode, it enables full duplex communication between two devices using separate data lines for transmitting (TX) and receiving (RX) data. It is essential that the ground of both devices is connected. One of the most common asynchronous communication protocols is the RS232 standard, which defines serial communication over a COM port.

- Standard for serial communication (COM port)
  1: -3V to -25V
  0: +3V to +25V

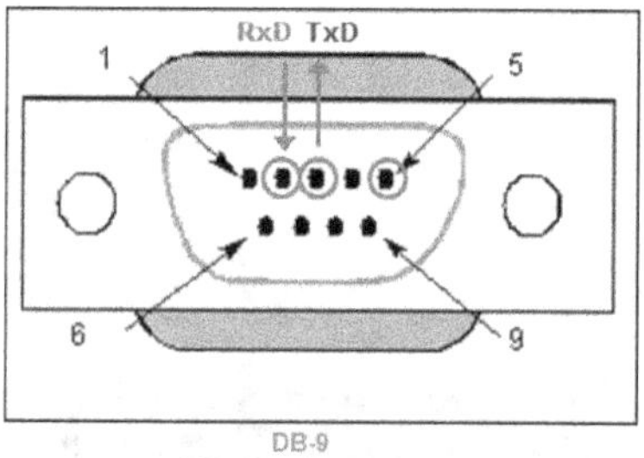

9-Pin Male Connector

- A null modem is a communication method used to connect two Data Terminal Equipment (DTE) devices, such as computers, terminals, or printers, directly using an RS-232 serial cable. In a null modem connection, the transmit and receive lines are cross-linked to allow for direct communication between the devices.
- The PIC18F4550 microcontroller supports one or two USART modules, each of which can be configured independently for asynchronous serial communication.
- For the PIC18F4550, the USART functionality is available on Pin 25 (RC6/Tx) for transmitting data and Pin 26 (RC7/Rx) for receiving data.

The USART module can be configured in three modes:

- Asynchronous (Full Duplex): This mode is used for full-duplex communication, allowing data to be transmitted and received simultaneously. It's commonly used to connect the PIC18F4550 to a PC serial port or other peripherals, facilitating communication one byte at a time.
- Synchronous – Master (Half Duplex): In this mode, data is transferred in half-duplex, meaning data can only flow in one direction at a time. The PIC18F4550 acts as the master, coordinating data transfer to external peripherals.
- Synchronous – Slave (Half Duplex): This mode is also half-duplex, but the PIC18F4550 operates as a slave device, receiving data from a master device. This setup is used for transferring blocks of data between the PIC and external peripherals like ADCs or EEPROMs.

In the asynchronous method, each character is placed between start and stop bits (framing)

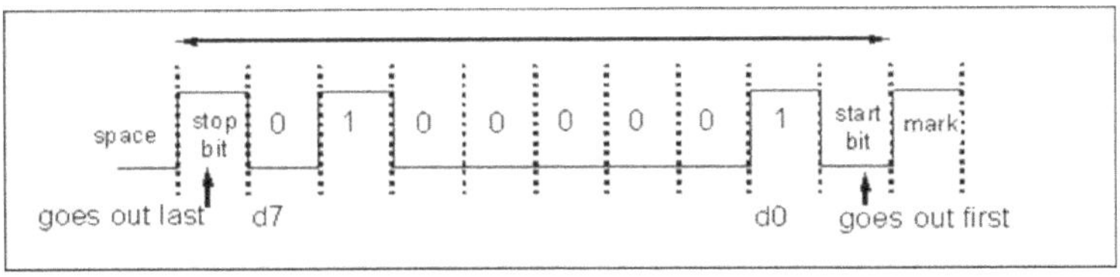

USART in PIC18F4550:

Each USART module having the following registers to control its operation:

- Transmit status register (TXSTA)
- Receive status register (RCSTA)
- Baud rate generate register(SPBRG)
- Transmit register(TXREG)
- Receive register(RCREG)

TXSTA – Transmit Status and Control Register:

R/W-0	R/W-0	R/W-0	R/W-0	U-0	R/W-0	R-1	R/W-0
CSRC	TX9	TXEN	SYNC	—	BRGH	TRMT	TX9D
bit 7							bit 0

- **TX9D**: This is the 9th bit of data in the 9-bit transmission mode which is commonly used as a Parity Bit.
- **TRMT**: This is the Transmit Shift Register (TSR) status bit. This can be used to check whether the data written to the transmit register is transmitted or not. When the TRS is empty this bit is set and when the TSR is full this bit will be 0.
- **BRGH**: This is the High Baud Rate Select bit for Asynchronous mode operation and is unused in Synchronous mode.
- **SYNC**: This is the USART Mode select bit. Setting this bit selects Synchronous mode while clearing this bit selects Asynchronous mode.
- **TXEN**: Setting this bit enables the transmission.
- **TX9**: Setting this bit enables the 9-bit transmission otherwise 8-bit transmission is used.
- **CSRC**: Clock Source Select Bit, this bit has no application in the Asynchronous mode. It is used to select master or slave mode in Synchronous mode operation.

RCSTA – Receive Status and Control Register:

R/W-0	R/W-0	R/W-0	R/W-0	R/W-0	R-0	R-0	R-x
SPEN	RX9	SREN	CREN	ADDEN	FERR	OERR	RX9D
bit 7							bit 0

- **RX9D**: This is the 9th bit of Received Data and is commonly used as Parity Bit.
- **OERR**: Overrun Error bit. 1 at this bit indicates that Overrun error has occurred.
- **FERR**: Framing Error bit. 1 at this bit stands for Framing Error has occurred.
- **ADDEN**: Address Detect Enable bit. This bit is applicable only in Asynchronous 9-bit mode. Setting this bit enables the Address Detect.
- **CREN**: Continuous Receive Enable bit. Setting this bit will enable Continuous Receive. In the Synchronous Mode, CREN overrides SREN.

- **SREN**: Setting this bit will enable Single Receive. This bit will be cleared after the reception is complete.
- **RX9**: Setting this bit enables 9-bit reception otherwise it will be in 8-bit reception mode.
- **SPEN**: Serial Port Enable bit. Setting this bit enables the serial port and configures RC7, RC6 as serial port pins.

USART Baud Rate Generator (BRG):

The Baud Rate Generator supplies the clock needed for data transmission and reception. The USART module features an 8-bit baud rate generator that supports both Synchronous and Asynchronous modes. In Asynchronous mode, the baud rate is influenced by the BRGH bit, which is the 2nd bit of the TXSTA register. However, in Synchronous mode, the BRGH bit has no effect. The baud rate can be calculated using the following equations, where $FOSC$ represents the microcontroller's clock frequency.

SYNC	BRGH = 0 (Low Speed)	BRGH = 1 (High Speed)
0	(Asynchronous) Baud Rate = FOSC/(64 (X + 1))	Baud Rate = FOSC/(16 (X + 1))
1	(Synchronous) Baud Rate = FOSC/(4 (X + 1))	N/A

Legend: X = value in SPBRG (0 to 255)

Once the TXREG register transfers its data to the TSR register (which happens in one instruction cycle, TCY), the TXREG register is considered empty, and the TXIF flag bit (PIR1<4>) is set. The TRMT bit (TXSTA<1>) indicates the status of the TSR register. This TRMT bit is set when the TSR register is empty, signaling that it is time to transfer new data from TXREG to TSR. Similarly, when data is received in the RSR register and transferred to the RCREG register (if it is not empty), the RCIF flag bit (PIR1<5>) is set to indicate that the data transfer is complete.

Programming the PIC18F to Transfer Data Serially:

1. Set the TXSTA register to 0x20, which configures the USART for asynchronous mode with an 8-bit data frame, low baud rate, and transmit enabled.
2. Load the SPBRG register to set the baud rate using the formula:

SPBRG = (((FOSC / 64) / baud_rate) - 1).

3. Configure the TX pin (RC6/TX) as an output.
4. Enable the serial port by setting SPEN to 1 in the RCSTA register.
5. Write the character byte to be transmitted into the TXREG register.
6. Monitor the TXIF bit to check if the transmission is complete.
7. To transmit the next character, return to step 5.

Programming the PIC18F to Receive Data Serially:

1. Set the RCSTA register to 0x90 to enable continuous receive mode and select the 8-bit data size option.
2. Configure the TXSTA register to 0x00 to choose the low baud rate option by setting BRGH to 0 and SYNC to 0.
3. Load the SPBRG register to set the baud rate using the formula: SPBRG = (((FOSC / 64) / baud_rate) - 1).
4. Configure the RX pin (RC7/RX) as an input.
5. Monitor the RCIF bit to check if the data is received.
6. Read the value from the RCREG register.
7. To receive the next character, return to step 5.

Algorithm:

1. Define the PIC18 configuration bits using the pragma directive, include xc.h, and define the crystal frequency with _XTAL_FREQ to use the built-in delay function.
2. Declare global variables.

main function:

3. Call the function to configure the USART with a baud rate of 9600.
4. Call the function to print a string on the serial port.
5. Check for an overrun error; if an error occurs, re-enable the CREN bit.
6. Repeat the steps from step 5.

USART_Init function (unsigned long):

1. Configure the RC7 (Rx) pin as an input port and the RC6 (Tx) pin as an output port.
2. Set the baud rate to 9600 using the SPBRG register.

3. Configure the USART for asynchronous mode by setting the TXSTA and RCSTA registers.
4. Enable global interrupts, peripheral interrupts, and serial receive interrupts.
5. Clear the serial port flags RCIF and TXIF.

USART_Tx_string function:

1. Move the character from the string argument to the TXREG register.
2. Wait for the TRMT flag to indicate that the character has been sent.
3. Clear the transmit flag.
4. Increment the address of the string argument.

__interrupt()ISR:

1. Read the received serial data from the RCREG register and clear the RCIF flag.
2. Place the received character in the TXREG register.
3. Wait for the TRMT flag to indicate that the character has been sent.
4. Clear the transmit flag.

Program:

```
#pragma config PLLDIV = 5, CPUDIV = OSC1_PLL2, USBDIV = 2, FOSC = HS, FCMEN = OFF, IESO = OFF
#pragma config PWRT = OFF, BOR = OFF, BORV = 3, VREGEN = OFF, WDT = OFF, WDTPS = 32768
#pragma config CCP2MX = ON, PBADEN = OFF, LPT1OSC = OFF, MCLRE = ON
#pragma config STVREN = ON, LVP = OFF, ICPRT = OFF, XINST = OFF
#pragma config CP0 = OFF, CP1 = OFF, CP2 = OFF, CP3 = OFF, CPB = OFF, CPD = OFF
#pragma config WRT0 = OFF, WRT1 = OFF, WRT2 = OFF, WRT3 = OFF, WRTC = OFF, WRTB = OFF, WRTD = OFF
#pragma config EBTR0 = OFF, EBTR1 = OFF, EBTR2 = OFF, EBTR3 = OFF, EBTRB = OFF

#include <xc.h>
#define _XTAL_FREQ 20000000
unsigned char c=0;

void USART_Init(unsigned long Baud_rate){
  TRISC6 = 0;                    // TX Pin set as output
```

```
    TRISC7 = 1;                     // RX Pin set as input
    SPBRG = (_XTAL_FREQ/(64UL * Baud_rate)) - 1;
    TXSTAbits.BRGH  = 0;            // for high baud_rate
    TXSTAbits.SYNC  = 0;            // Asynchronous
    TXSTAbits.TXEN  = 1;            // enable transmission
    TXSTAbits.TX9   = 0;            // 8-bit reception selected
    RCSTAbits.SPEN  = 1;            // Enable serial port pins
    RCSTAbits.CREN  = 1;            // enable reception
    RCSTAbits.RX9   = 0;            // 8-bit reception mode selected
    INTCONbits.GIE=1;               // Global interrupt enable
    INTCONbits.PEIE=1;              // Peripheral interrupt enable
    PIE1bits.RCIE=1;                // Receive interrupt enable
    PIR1bits.RCIF=0;                // Clear receive flag
    PIR1bits.TXIF=0;                // Clear transmit flag
}

void __interrupt() Rx_ISR(void)  {                 // ISR
if (PIR1bits.RCIF ==1)              // if RCIF is set
{
c = RCREG;                          // Read received data and move it to the variable c
PIR1bits.RCIF =0;                   // Clear receive flag
TXREG = c;                          // Transmit the recived character
while(TXSTAbits.TRMT ==0);
PIR1bits.TXIF=0;                    // Clear transmit flag
}
}

void USART_Tx_string(char *tx_str)  {              // Print a string on serial port
   unsigned char ch;
   while(*tx_str != 0x00)
   {
      ch = *tx_str;                 // Get the charcter from a string
      TXREG = ch;                   // Transmit to the serial port one by one
      while(!(TXSTAbits.TRMT));
```

```
        PIR1bits.TXIF=0;                // Clear TXIF
        tx_str++;                       // Increment pointer
    }
}

int main() {
    USART_Init(9600);                   //initialize the UART function
    USART_Tx_string ("Welcome to USART");       // Print a string on serial port
    while(1)  {
        if(RCSTAbits.OERR)   {          // Check overrun error
        RCSTAbits.CREN = 0;             // if error occurs, re-enable CREN
        RCSTAbits.CREN = 1;
        }
    __delay_ms(100);        // delay for 100 ms
    }
    return 0;
}
```

Circuit Diagram:

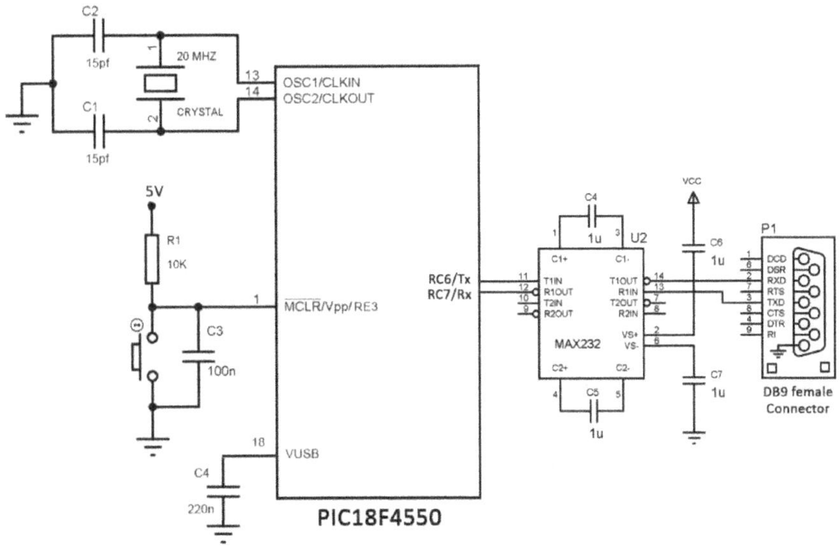

Conclusion:

The operation of the asynchronous mode of the on-chip USART in the PIC18F4550 Microcontroller has been successfully tested using an Embedded C program.

44. BLUETOOTH CONTROLLED SYSTEM

Aim:

Develop an embedded system to control an LED via a smartphone using the PIC18F4550 Microcontroller, a Bluetooth Module HC-05, and an Embedded C program. Verify the system's functionality.

Hardware Requirements:

- PIC18F4550 Microcontroller, 20 MHz Crystal (1), 15 pF Disc Capacitors (2), 220 nF Disc Capacitor (1), 100 nF Disc Capacitor (1), Resistor 10K (1), and Push Button (1)
- Bluetooth Module HC-05, Resistor 1K (1), and Resistor 2.2K (1)

Software Used:

- IDE: MPLAB X IDE v5.45
- Compiler: XC8 - v2.31

Theory:

The HC-05 is a Bluetooth module designed for wireless communication, operating via UART (Universal Asynchronous Receiver Transmitter) serial communication.

It can function in two modes: command mode and data mode. Command mode is used for configuring the Bluetooth module's settings using AT commands, while data mode facilitates data transfer between devices.

The module operates at either 5V or 3.3V and features six pins:

1. KEY : if set to HIGH, the module goes into command mode
2. Vcc : 5V supply
3. GND : Ground

4. TXD : TXD signal line
5. RXD : RXD signal line
6. State : Not connected

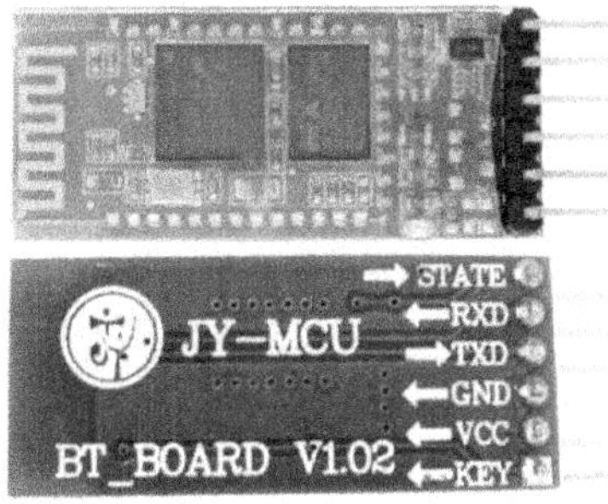

Step by step procedure:

- Install a Bluetooth application on your smartphone from the Play Store.
- Pair the HC-05 Bluetooth module with your smartphone. The default pairing code is 1234.
- Upload the following program to the PIC microcontroller.
- Use the Bluetooth app on your smartphone to control the LED connected to the MCU port. Send the character 'N' to turn the LED ON and the character 'F' to turn the LED OFF.

Algorithm:

1. Define the PIC18 configuration bits using the pragma directive, include xc.h, and define the crystal frequency for _XTAL_FREQ to utilize the inbuilt delay function.
2. Declare global variables.

main function:

3. Call the function to configure the USART with a baud rate of 9600.
4. Call the function to print a string to the serial port.
5. Check for overrun errors; if any occur, re-enable the CREN.
6. If the value in RCREG is 'n', turn ON the LED connected to RD0.
7. If the value in RCREG is 'f', turn OFF the LED connected to RD0.
8. Repeat the steps from step 6.

USART_Init function (unsigned long):

1. Configure the RC7 (Rx) pin as an input port and the RC6 (Tx) pin as an output port.
2. Set the baud rate to 9600 using the SPBRG register.
3. Configure the USART for asynchronous mode using the TXSTA and RCSTA registers.
4. Enable global interrupts, peripheral interrupts, and the serial receive interrupt.
5. Clear the serial port flags RCIF and TXIF.

USART_Tx_string function:

1. Move the character from the string argument to TXREG.
2. Wait for TRMT to indicate that the character has been sent.
3. Clear the transmit flag.
4. Increment the address of the string argument.

__interrupt()ISR:

1. Read the received serial data from RCREG.
2. Clear the RCIF flag.
3. Place the received character in TXREG.
4. Wait for TRMT to indicate that the character has been sent.
5. Clear the transmit flag.

Program:

```
#pragma config PLLDIV = 5, CPUDIV = OSC1_PLL2, USBDIV = 2, FOSC = HS, FCMEN =
OFF, IESO = OFF
#pragma config PWRT = OFF, BOR = OFF, BORV = 3, VREGEN = OFF, WDT = OFF,
WDTPS = 32768
#pragma config CCP2MX = ON, PBADEN = OFF, LPT1OSC = OFF, MCLRE = ON
#pragma config STVREN = ON, LVP = OFF, ICPRT = OFF, XINST = OFF
#pragma config CP0 = OFF, CP1 = OFF, CP2 = OFF, CP3 = OFF, CPB = OFF, CPD = OFF
#pragma config WRT0 = OFF, WRT1 = OFF, WRT2 = OFF, WRT3 = OFF, WRTC = OFF,
WRTB = OFF, WRTD = OFF
#pragma config EBTR0 = OFF, EBTR1 = OFF, EBTR2 = OFF, EBTR3 = OFF, EBTRB = OFF

#include <xc.h>
#define _XTAL_FREQ 20000000
unsigned char c=0;
```

```
void USART_Init(unsigned long Baud_rate){
   TRISC6 = 0;                    // TX Pin set as output
   TRISC7 = 1;                    // RX Pin set as input
   SPBRG = (_XTAL_FREQ/(64UL * Baud_rate)) - 1;
   TXSTAbits.BRGH  = 0;           // for high baud_rate
   TXSTAbits.SYNC  = 0;           // Asynchronous
   TXSTAbits.TXEN  = 1;           // enable transmission
   TXSTAbits.TX9   = 0;           // 8-bit reception selected
   RCSTAbits.SPEN  = 1;           // Enable serial port pins
   RCSTAbits.CREN  = 1;           // enable reception
   RCSTAbits.RX9   = 0;           // 8-bit reception mode selected
   INTCONbits.GIE=1;              // Global interrupt enable
   INTCONbits.PEIE=1;             // Peripheral interrupt enable
   PIE1bits.RCIE=1;               // Receive interrupt enable
   PIR1bits.RCIF=0;               // Clear receive flag
   PIR1bits.TXIF=0;               // Clear transmit flag
}

void __interrupt() Rx_ISR(void)  {                // ISR
if (PIR1bits.RCIF ==1)            // if RCIF is set
{
c = RCREG;                        // Read received data and move it to the variable c
PIR1bits.RCIF =0;                 // Clear receive flag
TXREG = c;                        // Transmit the recived character
while(TXSTAbits.TRMT ==0);
PIR1bits.TXIF=0;                  // Clear transmit flag
}
}

void USART_Tx_string(char *tx_str)  {             // Print a string on serial port
   unsigned char ch;
   while(*tx_str != 0x00)   {
      ch = *tx_str;               // Get the charcter from a string
```

```
        TXREG = ch;                  // Transmit to the serial port one by one
        while(!(TXSTAbits.TRMT));
        PIR1bits.TXIF=0;             // Clear TXIF
        tx_str++;                    // Increment pointer
    }
}

int main() {
    USART_Init(9600);                //initialize the UART function
    USART_Tx_string ("Welcome to USART");      // Print a string on serial port
    while(1)  {
      if(RCSTAbits.OERR)    {        // Check overrun error
      RCSTAbits.CREN = 0;            // if error occurs, re-enable CREN
      RCSTAbits.CREN = 1;
      }
      if (c=='n')                    // Check if received char is 'n'
      {
      LATDbits.LATD0=1;              // Make PORTD.0 as '1'
      }
      if (c=='f')                    // Check if received char is 'f'
      {
      LATDbits.LATD0=0;              // Make PORTD.0 as '0'
      }
      }
      return 0;
}
```

Circuit Diagram:

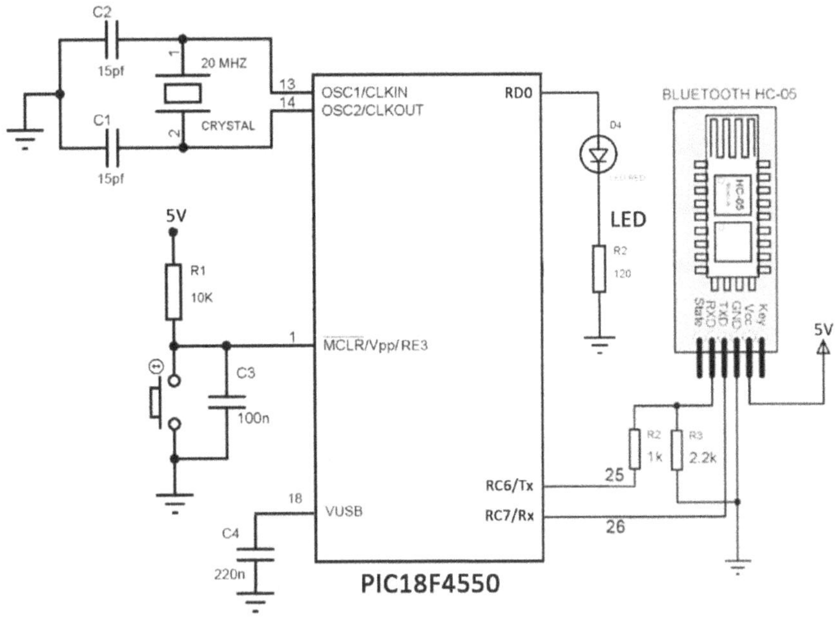

Conclusion:

The embedded system to control an LED through a smartphone using Bluetooth HC-05 and a PIC18F4550 microcontroller, along with an Embedded C program, has been successfully demonstrated.

45. OBSTACLE DETECTOR USING ULTRASONIC SENSOR

Aim:

Design and develop an embedded system using a PIC18F4550 microcontroller and an ultrasonic sensor to detect obstacles. Implement the system using Embedded C and verify its output.

Hardware Requirements:

- PIC18F4550 Microcontroller, 20 MHz Crystal (1), 15 pF Disc Capacitors (2), 220 nF Disc Capacitor (1), 100 nF Disc Capacitor (1), Resistor 10 K (1), and Push Button (1)
- Ultrasonic Sensor HC-SR04 (1), 16x2 LCD (1), NPN Transistor BC547 (1), Buzzer (1), and Resistor 1K (1)

Software Used:

- IDE: MPLAB X IDE v5.45
- Compiler: XC8 - v2.31

Theory:

The HC-SR04 is an ultrasonic range sensor module designed to measure distances between 2 cm and 500 cm. It works by sending an ultrasonic burst signal to an object and then picking up the echo. The time taken for the ultrasonic signal to travel to the target and back to the sensor is used to calculate the distance to the target. A microcontroller performs the necessary processing and displays the corresponding distance on an LCD. Obstacles can be detected within the specified distance range. The HC-SR04 has four pins: Vcc, Trigger, Echo, and GND.

1. Vcc: Connects to a 5V DC power supply.
2. Trigger: Requires a pulse with a 10μS ON time. Upon receiving a valid trigger signal, the module emits 8 pulses of 40 kHz ultrasonic sound from the transmitter.
3. Echo: This pin goes high when the module transmits the pulses and goes low when the receiver detects an echo signal from the target.
4. GND: Connects to ground.

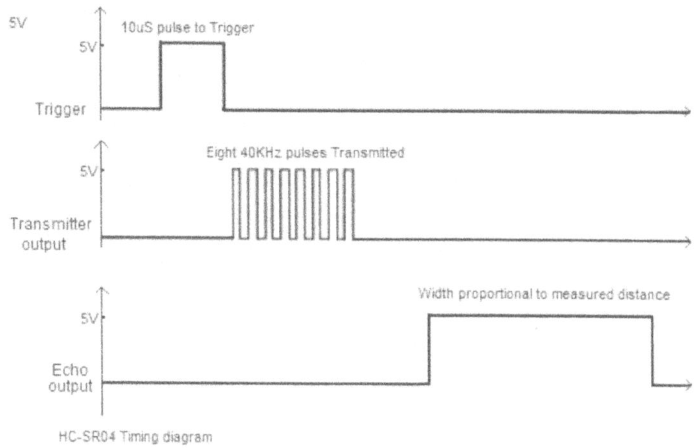

Working with the Ultrasonic sensor step by step:

1. Make the "Trig" pin of the sensor high for 10 µs.
2. The sensor will generate 8 pulses of 40 kHz ultrasonic signals, and the Echo pin will go high.
3. The 40 kHz sound wave will bounce off the target and return to the sensor.
4. When the sensor detects the reflected wave (Echo), the Echo pin will go low.
5. Calculate the distance between the target object and the sensor from the duration the Echo pin stays high.
6. If there is no object, the Echo pin will remain high for 38 ms before going low.

Algorithm:

1. Define the PIC18 configuration bits using the pragma directive, include xc.h, and define the crystal frequency for _XTAL_FREQ to use the inbuilt delay function.
2. Assign RS and EN of the LCD to RC6 and RC7, respectively. Assign the Data bus (D0-D7) of the LCD to PORTD.
3. Assign the Trig and Echo pins of the Ultrasonic sensor to RB0 and RB1, respectively.

4. Include the lcd4bit_head.h header file (the same header file used in the LCD interface experiment).

Main function:

5. Declare local variables: TimerCount and dist as unsigned long int variables, and d1, d2, d3 as char variables.
6. Configure PORTC and PORTD as output ports.
7. Configure RB0 as an output port and RB1 as an input port.
8. Initialize a 16x2 LCD in 4-bit mode.
9. Configure Timer 1 with an internal clock source and a 1:8 prescaler.
10. Clear TMR1.
11. Clear the TMR1IF flag.
12. Turn off the buzzer.
13. Clear the TimerCount and dist variables.
14. Display "Distance cm" on line 1 of the 16x2 LCD.
15. Clear the Trig pin.
16. Wait 10 ms for the ultrasonic sensor to stabilize.
17. Set the Trig pin.
18. Wait 10 μs to generate 8 cycles of 40 kHz ultrasonic waves.
19. Clear the Trig pin.
20. Enable Timer 1 and wait for the Echo pin to clear.
21. Disable Timer 1.
22. Calculate the time duration of the ultrasonic signal traveling between the sensor and the target object.
23. Display the distance in cm on the LCD.
24. If the target object's distance is less than or equal to 50 cm, display "Target Detected" on the LCD and turn on the buzzer for 1 second.
25. Repeat from step 10.

Program:

```
#pragma config PLLDIV = 5, CPUDIV = OSC1_PLL2, USBDIV = 2, FOSC = HS, FCMEN =
OFF, IESO = OFF
#pragma config PWRT = OFF, BOR = OFF, BORV = 3, VREGEN = OFF, WDT = OFF,
WDTPS = 32768
#pragma config CCP2MX = ON, PBADEN = OFF, LPT1OSC = OFF, MCLRE = ON
#pragma config STVREN = ON, LVP = OFF, ICPRT = OFF, XINST = OFF
```

```
#pragma config CP0 = OFF, CP1 = OFF, CP2 = OFF, CP3 = OFF, CPB = OFF, CPD = OFF
#pragma config WRT0 = OFF, WRT1 = OFF, WRT2 = OFF, WRT3 = OFF, WRTC = OFF,
WRTB = OFF, WRTD = OFF
#pragma config EBTR0 = OFF, EBTR1 = OFF, EBTR2 = OFF, EBTR3 = OFF, EBTRB = OFF

#include <xc.h>
#define _XTAL_FREQ 20000000
#define Trig LATB0                // Trigger pin is connected with RB0
#define Echo PORTBbits.RB1        // Echo pin is connected with RB1
#define Buzzer LATC0              // Buzzer circuit is connected with RC0
#define RS      LATD2             // RD2 is named as RS
#define EN      LATD3             // RD3 is named as EN
#define D4      LATD4             // 4-bit mode (RD4-D4, RD5-D5
#define D5      LATD5             // RD6-D6, RD7-D7)
#define D6      LATD6
#define D7      LATD7
#include "lcd4bit_head.h"         // Include header file - lcd4bit_head.h

void main() {                     // Main function
  unsigned long int TimerCount, dist;   // local variables declarations
  unsigned char d1, d2, d3;
  TRISB = 0x02;                   // Trig pin is output and Echo pin is input
  TRISC = 0x00;                   // set PORT C as output port
  TRISD = 0x00;                   // set PORT D as output port
  lcd_init ();                    // Call lcd_init() function to initialize 16x2 LCD
  TMR1CS = 0;                     // Set internal clock source for Timer 1
  T1CKPS0 = 1;                    // Prescaler is 1:8
  T1CKPS1 = 1;
   while (1) {                    // Forever loop
     TMR1 = 0;                    // Clear TMR1 Register value
     TMR1IF = 0;                  // Clear TIMER1 flag
     Buzzer = 0;                  // Turn-off buzzer
     TimerCount =dist=0;          // clear variables
     lcd_cmd(0x80);               // cursor position at 0th addr of line1
     lcd_display("Distance:   cm ");     // Call lcd_display() function
```

```
        Trig=0;                         // Clear Trig pin
        __delay_ms (10);                // Wait for 10 ms
        Trig=1;                         // Make Trig pin '1' to send ultrasonic pulses for 10us
        __delay_us (10);
        Trig=0;                         // Clear Trig pin
        while(Echo==0);                 // wait for sending 8 cycles of 40khz burst
        TMR1ON = 1;                     // Enable Timer1
        while(Echo==1);                 // wait for echo signal ( if target present)
        TMR1ON = 0;                     // Disable Timer1
        TimerCount = (TMR1H*256) + TMR1L; // Get decimal value of 16-bit binary
        // Ultrasonic Sound Velocity = 34029 (in cm per second)
        // Timer gets incremented for every 1.085 us
        // Distance in cm
        dist = TimerCount * 0.01846;            // distance in cm
        d1 = (dist/100) + 48;                   // Calculate ASCII value for each digit
        d2 = ((dist%100)/10) + 48;
        d3 = (dist%10) + 48;
        lcd_cmd(0x89);                          // Sending distance value to LCD
        lcd_data(d1);
        lcd_data(d2);
        lcd_data(d3);
        if (dist <= 50)                         // if obstacle with 50 cm
        {
          lcd_cmd(0xC0);                        // cursor position at 0th addr of line2
          lcd_display("Target Detected ");      // Display 'Target detected' in line 2
          Buzzer = 1;                           // Turn-on Buzzer
          __delay_ms(1000);                     // Make delay for 1000 ms
        }
        lcd_cmd(0x01);                          // clear the screen
    }
}
------------------------------------------------------------------------------------------
// Header file: lcd4bit_head.h
void Lcd_WriteBit(unsigned char bt) {   //write the nibble on 4-bit data bus of LCD
```

```
  if(bt & 1)
    D4 = 1;
  else
    D4 = 0;
  if(bt & 2)
    D5 = 1;
  else
    D5 = 0;
  if(bt & 4)
    D6 = 1;
  else
    D6 = 0;
  if(bt & 8)
    D7 = 1;
  else
    D7 = 0;
}

void lcd_cmd(unsigned char CMD) {        // Definition of lcd_cmd() function
  RS = 0;                                // Make RS pin low to select CMD reg.
  Lcd_WriteBit((CMD >> 4) & 0x0FU);      // Send Higher Nibble of CMD
  EN = 1;                                // Give High to Low pulse to Enable (E)
  __delay_ms(2);
  EN = 0;
  __delay_ms(5);
  RS = 0;
  Lcd_WriteBit(CMD & 0x0FU);             // Send Lower Nibble of CMD
  EN = 1;                                // Give High to Low pulse to Enable (E)
  __delay_ms(2);
  EN = 0;
  __delay_ms(5);
}

void lcd_data(unsigned char DAT) {       // Definition of lcd_data() function
```

```
    RS = 1;                              // Make RS pin high to select data reg.
    Lcd_WriteBit((DAT >> 4) & 0x0FU);    // Send Higher Nibble of data
    EN = 1;                              // Give High to Low pulse to Enable (E)
    __delay_ms(2);
    EN = 0;
    __delay_ms(5);
    RS = 1;
    Lcd_WriteBit(DAT & 0x0FU);           // Send Lower Nibble of data
    EN = 1;                              // Give High to Low pulse to Enable (E)
    __delay_ms(2);
    EN = 0;
    __delay_ms(5);
}

void lcd_display(char *x){               // Definition of lcd_display () function
    while(*x!=0x0) {                     // Condition is true until null character
    lcd_data(*x);                        // Send a character to LCD screen
    __delay_ms(10);                      // Make 10 ms delay
    x++;                                 // Increment pointer variable
    }
}
void lcd_init ()
{
    lcd_cmd(0x02); __delay_ms(12);       // 16X2 LCD in 4-bit mode
    lcd_cmd(0x28); __delay_ms(12);       // 2 lines, 5X7 dots in 4-bit mode
    lcd_cmd(0x0C); __delay_ms(12);       // Display ON Cursor OFF
    lcd_cmd(0x06); __delay_ms(12);       // Auto Increment cursor
    lcd_cmd(0x01); __delay_ms(12);       // Clear Display
}
```

Circuit Diagram:

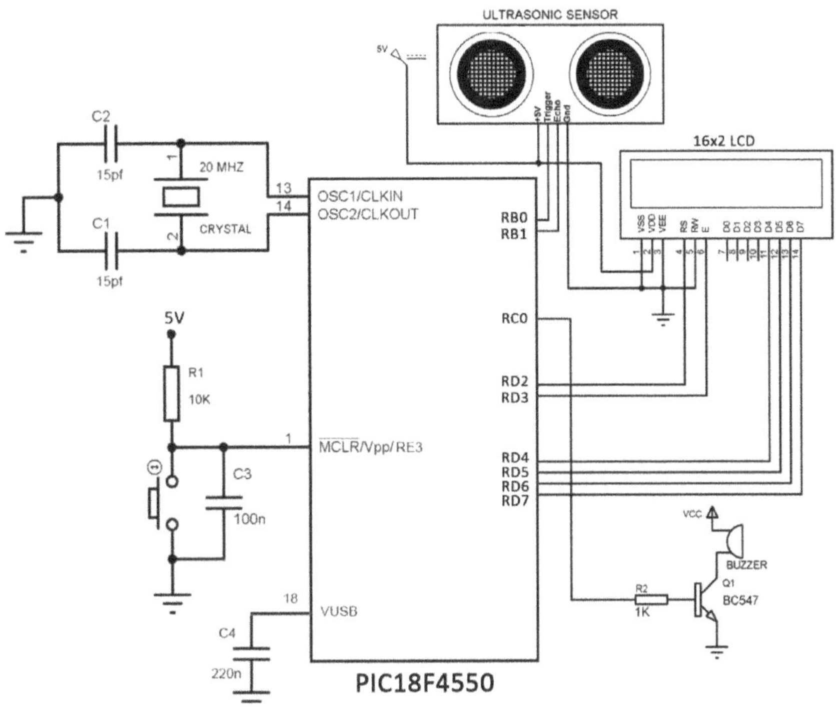

Conclusion:

The embedded system for obstacle detection using an Ultrasonic Sensor, a PIC18F4550 Microcontroller, and an Embedded C program has been successfully demonstrated.

46. SENDING SMS USING GSM MODULE

Aim:

Design and develop an embedded system for sending SMS using the SIM900 GSM module and a PIC18F4550 microcontroller. Implement the system using Embedded C and verify its output.

Hardware Requirements:

- PIC18F4550 Microcontroller, 20 MHz Crystal (1), 15 pF Disc Capacitors (2), 220 nF Disc Capacitor (1), 100 nF Disc Capacitor (1), Resistor 10 K (1), and Push Button (1)
- GSM SIM900 module, IC MAX232 (1), Capacitor 1 uF (4), and DB9 Connector Female

Software Used:

- IDE: MPLAB X IDE v5.45
- Compiler: XC8 - v2.31

Theory:

A GSM (Global System for Mobile Communications) module is used to interact with the GSM network using a computer or MCU. The GSM module only understands AT commands. Some of these commands are:

- AT+CSMS – Select message service.
- AT+CMGF – Message format.
- AT+CMGL – List messages.
- AT+CMGR – Read the message.
- AT+CMGS – Send the message.
- AT+CMGD – Delete the message.
- ATA – Answer a call.
- ATD – Dial a number.
- ATDL – Dial the last outgoing number.
- ATH – Hang up the call.

The GSM SIM900 module operates in the 900 MHz band, which includes both the primary GSM band (GSM-P) and the extended GSM band (E-GSM) as defined by the ETSI standard. Communication with the SIM900 module is achieved through the microcontroller's serial port using RxD (receive) and TxD (transmit) lines. The default baud rate for the GSM SIM900 is 9600 bps.

Algorithm:

1. Define the PIC18 configuration bits using the pragma directive, include xc.h, and define the crystal frequency for _XTAL_FREQ to use the built-in delay function.
2. Initialize the on-chip USART for asynchronous mode with a 9600 baud rate using the USART_Init function.
3. Wait for a few seconds.
4. Send the AT command AT+CMGF=1 to set SMS text mode using the USART_Tx_string function.
5. Wait for a few seconds.
6. Send the AT command AT+CMGS to specify the recipient's mobile number and send the SMS message in text mode.
7. Wait for a few seconds.
8. Send the CTRL+Z character to indicate the end of the SMS message.
9. Wait for a few seconds.
10. Send the AT command.
11. Halt the system.

USART_Init function (unsigned long):

1. Configure the RC7 (Rx) pin as an input port and the RC6 (Tx) pin as an output port.
2. Set the baud rate to 9600 using the SPBRG register.
3. Configure USART for asynchronous mode by setting the TXSTA and RCSTA registers.
4. Enable global interrupts, peripheral interrupts, and serial receive interrupts.
5. Clear the serial port flags RCIF and TXIF.

USART_Tx_string function:

1. Move the character from the string argument to TXREG.
2. Wait for TRMT to ensure the character has been sent and clear the

transmit flag.

3. Increment the address of the string argument.

USART_Tx_char(char):

1. Send the character data to TXREG.
2. Wait for TRMT to ensure the character has been sent and clear the TXIF flag.

Program:

```
#pragma config PLLDIV = 5, CPUDIV = OSC1_PLL2, USBDIV = 2, FOSC = HS, FCMEN =
OFF, IESO = OFF
#pragma config PWRT = OFF, BOR = OFF, BORV = 3, VREGEN = OFF, WDT = OFF,
WDTPS = 32768
#pragma config CCP2MX = ON, PBADEN = OFF, LPT1OSC = OFF, MCLRE = ON
#pragma config STVREN = ON, LVP = OFF, ICPRT = OFF, XINST = OFF
#pragma config CP0 = OFF, CP1 = OFF, CP2 = OFF, CP3 = OFF, CPB = OFF, CPD = OFF
#pragma config WRT0 = OFF, WRT1 = OFF, WRT2 = OFF, WRT3 = OFF, WRTC = OFF,
WRTB = OFF, WRTD = OFF
#pragma config EBTR0 = OFF, EBTR1 = OFF, EBTR2 = OFF, EBTR3 = OFF, EBTRB = OFF
#include <xc.h>
#define _XTAL_FREQ 20000000
unsigned char c=0;

void USART_Init(unsigned long Baud_rate){
  TRISC6 = 0;                    // TX Pin set as output
  TRISC7 = 1;                    // RX Pin set as input
  SPBRG = (_XTAL_FREQ/(64UL * Baud_rate)) - 1;
  TXSTAbits.BRGH  = 0;           // for high baud_rate
  TXSTAbits.SYNC  = 0;           // Asynchronous
  TXSTAbits.TXEN  = 1;           // enable transmission
  TXSTAbits.TX9   = 0;           // 8-bit reception selected
  RCSTAbits.SPEN  = 1;           // Enable serial port pins
  RCSTAbits.CREN  = 1;           // enable reception
  RCSTAbits.RX9   = 0;           // 8-bit reception mode selected
  INTCONbits.GIE=1;              // Global interrupt enable
  INTCONbits.PEIE=1;             // Peripheral interrupt enable
  PIE1bits.RCIE=1;               // Receive interrupt enable
```

```
  PIR1bits.RCIF=0;              // Clear receive flag
  PIR1bits.TXIF=0;              // Clear transmit flag
}

void USART_Tx_char(char c) {            // ISR
TXREG = c;                      // Transmit the recived character
while(TXSTAbits.TRMT ==0);
PIR1bits.TXIF=0;                // Clear transmit flag
}

void USART_Tx_string(char *tx_str) {    // Print a string on serial port
  unsigned char ch;
  while(*tx_str != 0x00)  {
    ch = *tx_str;               // Get the charcter from a string
    TXREG = ch;                 // Transmit to the serial port one by one
    while(!(TXSTAbits.TRMT));
    PIR1bits.TXIF=0;            // Clear TXIF
    tx_str++;                   // Increment pointer
  }
}

void main(void)  {                      // Main function
USART_Init(9600);                       // Initialize the USART
__delay_ms(2000);                       // Wait to get ready SIM900
USART_Tx_string ("AT\r\n");             // Send AT
__delay_ms(1000);                       // wait for 1 sec
// Send AT+CMGF=1
USART_Tx_string ("AT+CMGF=1\r\n");
__delay_ms(1000);                       // wait for 1 sec
// Send AT+CMGS =\"mobile number of receiver\"
USART_Tx_string ("AT+CMGS=\"0xxxxxxxxxx\";\r\n");
__delay_ms(2000);                       // wait for 2 sec
// Send "message block'
USART_Tx_string ("This is a test MESSAGE \r\n");
__delay_ms(1000); __delay_ms(1000);     // wait for 2 sec
```

```
USART_Tx_char (0x1A);              // Send return character
__delay_ms(2000);                  // wait for 2 sec
USART_Tx_string ("AT\r\n");        // Send AT
__delay_ms(1000);                  // wait for 1 sec
while(1);                          // Halt
}
```

Circuit Diagram:

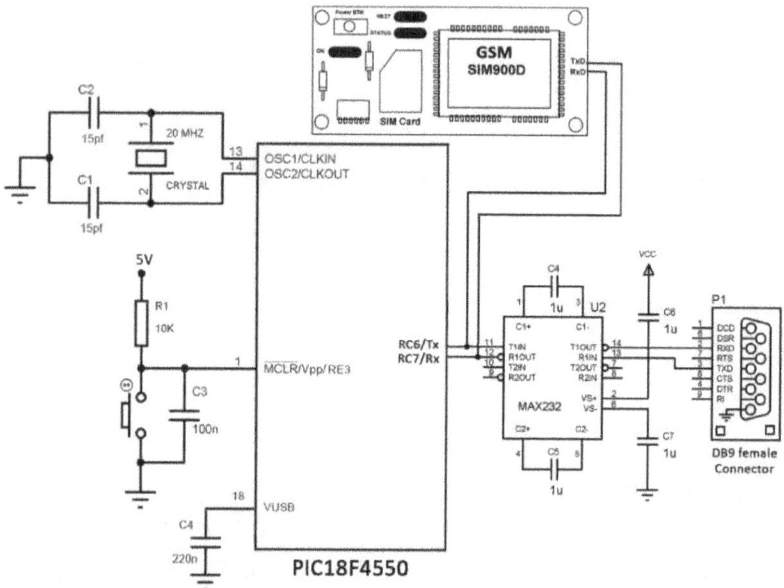

Conclusion:

The embedded system for controlling an LED via SMS using the SIM900 GSM module and the PIC18F4550 microcontroller has been successfully demonstrated.

47. LED ON/OFF CONTROL USING GSM MODULE

Aim:

Design and develop an embedded system to control an LED via SMS using a SIM900 GSM module and a PIC18F4550 microcontroller. Implement the system using Embedded C and verify its functionality.

Hardware Requirements:

- PIC18F4550 Microcontroller, 20 MHz Crystal (1), 15 pF Disc Capacitors (2), 220 nF Disc Capacitor (1), 100 nF Disc Capacitor (1), Resistor 10 K (1), and Push Button (1)
- GSM SIM900 module, IC MAX232 (1), Capacitor 1 uF (4), and DB9 Connector Female (1), LED (1) and Resistor 220 (1)

Software Used:

- IDE: MPLAB X IDE v5.45
- Compiler: XC8 - v2.31

Algorithm:

1. Define the PIC18 configuration bits using the pragma directive, include xc.h, and set the crystal frequency for _XTAL_FREQ to use the built-in delay function.
2. Define the LED port (LATD0) and global variables.
3. Initialize the on-chip USART for asynchronous mode with a 9600 baud rate.
4. Set PORTD as an output port.
5. Wait for a few seconds.
6. Send the AT command to disable echo.
7. Wait for a few seconds.
8. Send the AT command to store the current configuration.
9. Wait for a few seconds.
10. Send the AT command to select SMS text mode.
11. Wait for a few seconds.
12. Send the AT command to enable notifications for new SMS.
13. Wait for a few seconds.
14. Send the AT command to read SMS messages.
15. Wait for a few seconds.
16. Send the AT command to save the settings.
17. Wait for a few seconds.
18. Check the message body; it should start with '#' and end with '@'.
19. If the received message string is "ON," turn on the LED.

20. If the received message string is "OFF," turn off the LED.

USART_Init function (unsigned long):

1. Configure the RC7 (Rx) pin as an input port and the RC6 (Tx) pin as an output port.
2. Set the baud rate to 9600 using the SPBRG register.
3. Configure USART for asynchronous mode using the TXSTA and RCSTA registers.
4. Enable global interrupts, peripheral interrupts, and serial receive interrupts.
5. Clear the serial port flags RCIF and TXIF.

USART_Tx_string function:

1. Move the character from the string argument to TXREG.
2. Wait for TRMT to ensure the character is sent.
3. Clear the transmit flag.
4. Increment the address of the string argument.

__interrupt()ISR:

1. Read the received serial data from RCREG.
2. Clear the RCIF flag.
3. Place the received character in TXREG.
4. Wait for TRMT to ensure the character is sent.
5. Clear the transmit flag.

Program:

```
#pragma config PLLDIV = 5, CPUDIV = OSC1_PLL2, USBDIV = 2, FOSC = HS, FCMEN =
OFF, IESO = OFF
#pragma config PWRT = OFF, BOR = OFF, BORV = 3, VREGEN = OFF, WDT = OFF,
WDTPS = 32768
#pragma config CCP2MX = ON, PBADEN = OFF, LPT1OSC = OFF, MCLRE = ON
#pragma config STVREN = ON, LVP = OFF, ICPRT = OFF, XINST = OFF
#pragma config CP0 = OFF, CP1 = OFF, CP2 = OFF, CP3 = OFF, CPB = OFF, CPD = OFF
#pragma config WRT0 = OFF, WRT1 = OFF, WRT2 = OFF, WRT3 = OFF, WRTC = OFF,
WRTB = OFF, WRTD = OFF
#pragma config EBTR0 = OFF, EBTR1 = OFF, EBTR2 = OFF, EBTR3 = OFF, EBTRB = OFF

#include <xc.h>
#define _XTAL_FREQ 20000000
```

```
#define LED LATD0
unsigned char msg[25]={0x0}, RDS = '\0', t = '\0';
unsigned int c;

void USART_Init(unsigned long Baud_rate)
{
   TRISC6 = 0;                           // TX Pin set as output
   TRISC7 = 1;                           // RX Pin set as input
   SPBRG = (_XTAL_FREQ/(64UL * Baud_rate)) - 1;
   TXSTAbits.BRGH  = 0;                  // for high baud_rate
   TXSTAbits.SYNC  = 0;                  // Asynchronous
   TXSTAbits.TXEN  = 1;                  // enable transmission
   TXSTAbits.TX9   = 0;                  // 8-bit reception selected
   RCSTAbits.SPEN  = 1;                  // Enable serial port pins
   RCSTAbits.CREN  = 1;                  // enable reception
   RCSTAbits.RX9   = 0;                  // 8-bit reception mode selected
   __delay_ms(100);                      // Wait for serial port stable
   PIR1bits.RCIF=0;                      // Clear receive flag
   PIR1bits.TXIF=0;                      // Clear transmit flag
}

void USART_Tx_string(char *tx_str) {    // Print a string on serial port
   unsigned char ch;
   while(*tx_str != 0x00)
   {
      ch = *tx_str;                      // Get the charcter from a string
      TXREG = ch;                        // Transmit to the serial port one by one
      while(!(TXSTAbits.TRMT));
      PIR1bits.TXIF=0;                   // Clear TXIF
      tx_str++;                          // Increment pointer
   }
}

void __interrupt() Rx_ISR(void)          // ISR
```

```
{
if (PIR1bits.RCIF ==1)                     // if RCIF is set
{
if(RCSTAbits.OERR)   {                     // Check overrun error
RCSTAbits.CREN = 0;                        // if error occurs, re-enable CREN
RCSTAbits.CREN = 1;
}
RDS = RCREG;          // Read the received character from RCREG
if (t=='s'){          // if t='s', store the received character in msg[] array
msg[c]=RDS;
c++;                                       // Increment array index
}}
RCIF=0;                                    // Clear RCIF
}

void main (void)                           // Main function
{
USART_Init (9600);             // Initialize the USART for asynchronous mode
TRISD = 0x00;                              // Configure PORTD as output port
LED = 0;                                   // Clear LED
__delay_ms(1000);                          // Wait 2 sec to stabilize SIM900
__delay_ms(1000);
USART_Tx_string ("AT\r\n");                // Send AT
__delay_ms(1000);
USART_Tx_string ( "ATE1\r");               // Turn off echo
__delay_ms(1000);
USART_Tx_string ( "AT&W\r");               // Stores Current Configuration
__delay_ms(1000);
USART_Tx_string ( "AT+CMGF=1\r");  // Select text mode for sms
__delay_ms(1000);
USART_Tx_string ( "AT+CNMI= 1,2,0,0,0\r");     // notification of new sms
__delay_ms(1000);
__delay_ms(1000);
USART_Tx_string ( "AT+CMGR=1\r");              // AT command to read sms
```

```
__delay_ms(1000);
USART_Tx_string ("AT+CSAS\r");                  // Save settings
__delay_ms(1000); __delay_ms(1000);
__delay_ms(1000); __delay_ms(1000);
__delay_ms(1000); __delay_ms(1000);
USART_Tx_string ("AT\r\n");
INTCONbits.GIE=1;                     // Global interrupt enable
INTCONbits.PEIE=1;                    // Peripheral interrupt enable
PIE1bits.RCIE=1;                      // Receive interrupt enable
PIR1bits.RCIF=0;                      // Clear receive flag
PIR1bits.TXIF=0;                      // Clear transmit flag
while(1)
{
  while(RDS != '*');          // Check message body (message start from '*'
  t='s';                              // Move character 's' to variable t
  while(RDS != '@');                  // Check message end character '@'
  __delay_ms(1000);                   // Wait for 1 sec
  USART_Tx_string (msg);              // Send received char to serial port
  if (msg[0]=='O' && msg[1]=='N' )    // If msg is 'ON'
  {
  LED =1;                             // Turn-on LED
  }
  if (msg[0]=='O' && msg[1]=='F' && msg[2]=='F' )        // If msg is 'OFF'
  {
  LED =0;                             // Turn-off LED
  }
  c=0; RDS = '\0'; t='\0';            // Clear c, RDS and t
}
}
```

Circuit Diagram:

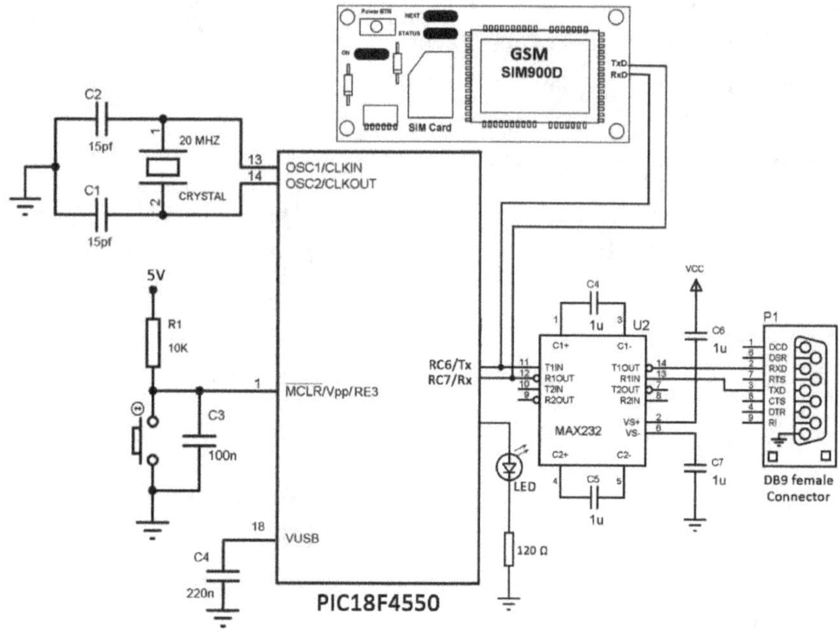

Conclusion:

The embedded system for controlling an LED via SMS, utilizing the SIM900 GSM module and the PIC18F4550 microcontroller, has been successfully demonstrated using an Embedded C program.

48. GPS MODULE INTERFACE

Aim:

Design and develop an embedded system to receive latitude and longitude values from a GPS module and display them on an LCD screen using a PIC18F4550 microcontroller. Implement the system using Embedded C and verify its output.

Hardware Requirements:

- PIC18F4550 Microcontroller, 20 MHz Crystal (1), 15 pF Disc

Capacitors (2), 220 nF Disc Capacitor (1), 100 nF Disc Capacitor (1), Resistor 10 K (1), and Push Button (1)

- GPS module and 16x2 LCD

Software Used:

- IDE: MPLAB X IDE v5.45
- Compiler: XC8 - v2.31

Theory:

The Global Positioning System (GPS) utilizes satellite navigation technology to provide location data. A GPS receiver delivers the location of an object in terms of latitude and longitude. In addition to location, GPS provides time in GMT and various other geographical details, such as the number of satellites in view, altitude, and direction of travel. This information is formatted in a specific string known as the NMEA format, which needs to be decoded by GPS modems.

An example of an NMEA format string is: $GPGGA,100908.00,2604.7041778,N,07047.8466270,E,4,08,1.00,495.144,M,29.310,M,0.10,0000*40

1. $: The string always starts with a dollar sign.
1. GPGGA: Indicates Global Positioning System Fix Data.
2. ,: Commas separate different values in the string.
3. 100908.00: GMT time formatted as 10 hours, 01 minute, 08 seconds, and 00 milliseconds.
4. 2604.7041778,N: Latitude 26 degrees, 04.7041778 minutes North.
5. 07047.8466270,E: Longitude 070 degrees, 47.8466270 minutes East.
6. 4: Fix quality indicator (0 = invalid, 1 = valid, 2 = DGPS fix, 4 = RTK Fix).
7. 08: Number of satellites currently in view.
8. 1.00: Horizontal Dilution of Precision (HDOP).
9. 495.144,M: Altitude above sea level in meters.
10. 29.310,M: Geoid height in meters.
11. 0.10: Age of the correction (if any).
12. 0000: Correction station ID (if any).

13. *40: Checksum for error checking.

The NEO-6M GPS module from u-blox, which tracks up to 22 satellites across 50 channels, provides data in RS232 logic level format. This data is converted to TTL using a MAX232 line converter for compatibility with the PIC18F4550 microcontroller. The latitude and longitude information from the GPS module will be displayed on a 16x2 LCD.

To verify the GPS module's functionality:

1. Download and install the u-center software on your Windows PC.
2. Connect the RS232 port of the GPS module to the RS232 port of the PC.
3. Run the u-center software to display GPS data and confirm that the NEO-6M GPS module is working correctly.
4. Check the baud rate of the GPS module using the u-center software and adjust your program accordingly if the baud rate is different from 9600 bps.

Algorithm:

1. Define the PIC18 configuration bits using the pragma directive, include xc.h, and set the crystal frequency for _XTAL_FREQ to utilize the built-in delay functions.
2. Include the header file for the LCD in 4-bit mode.
3. Declare PORTD to interface with the 16x2 LCD and initialize the LCD in 4-bit mode.
4. Initialize USART in asynchronous mode and set the baud rate to 9600 bps.
5. Receive serial data from the GPS module and compare it with the string '$GPGGA,' byte by byte.
6. Wait for the comma (,) as the string matches.

7. Store the data that appears after the comma and before the next 'N' into an array variable to hold the latitude.
8. After the subsequent comma (,), store the data into another array variable to hold the longitude.
9. Display both the latitude and longitude values on the LCD.
10. Repeat the process from step 5 to continuously update the latitude and longitude of the GPS receiver.

Program:

```
#pragma config PLLDIV = 5, CPUDIV = OSC1_PLL2, USBDIV = 2, FOSC = HS, FCMEN =
OFF, IESO = OFF
#pragma config PWRT = OFF, BOR = OFF, BORV = 3, VREGEN = OFF, WDT = OFF,
WDTPS = 32768
#pragma config CCP2MX = ON, PBADEN = OFF, LPT1OSC = OFF, MCLRE = ON
#pragma config STVREN = ON, LVP = OFF, ICPRT = OFF, XINST = OFF
#pragma config CP0 = OFF, CP1 = OFF, CP2 = OFF, CP3 = OFF, CPB = OFF, CPD = OFF
#pragma config WRT0 = OFF, WRT1 = OFF, WRT2 = OFF, WRT3 = OFF, WRTC = OFF,
WRTB = OFF, WRTD = OFF
#pragma config EBTR0 = OFF, EBTR1 = OFF, EBTR2 = OFF, EBTR3 = OFF, EBTRB = OFF

#include <xc.h>
#define _XTAL_FREQ 20000000
#define RS      LATD2          // RD2 is named as RS
#define EN      LATD3          // RD3 is named as EN
#define D4      LATD4          // 4-bit mode (RD4-D4, RD5-D5
#define D5      LATD5          // RD6-D6, RD7-D7)
#define D6      LATD6
#define D7      LATD7
#include "lcd4bit_head.h"      // Include header file - lcd4bit_head.h

unsigned char rx_data()
{
if(RCSTAbits.OERR)   {         // Check overrun error
RCSTAbits.CREN = 0;            // if error occurs, re-enable CREN
RCSTAbits.CREN = 1;
}
```

```
while(PIR1bits.RCIF==0);            // Wait until RCIF gets low
return RCREG;                       // Return RCREG value
}
void InitUSART(const long int baudrate)
{
SPBRG = (_XTAL_FREQ/(long)(64UL * baudrate)) - 1;
TRISC6 = 0;                         // Tx pin (output)
TRISC7 = 1;                         // Rx pin (input)
TXSTA = 0b00100000;                 // Setting UART for transmission
RCSTA = 0b10010000;                 // Setting UART for reception
__delay_ms(100);                    // Wait for serial port stable
PIR1bits.TXIF=0;                    // Clear transmit flag
PIR1bits.RCIF=0;                    // Clear receive flag
}
void main(void)
{
unsigned char i, gps=0, lati_data[11], long_data[12];
TRISD = 0x00;                       // set PORT D as output port
InitUSART(9600);                    // Initialize USART in asynchronous mode
lcd_init ();                        // Call lcd_init() function to initialize 16x2 LCD

while(1){
gps=rx_data();                      // Check the string '$GPGGA,'
if(gps=='$')
{
gps=rx_data();
if(gps=='G')
{
gps=rx_data();
if(gps=='P')
{
gps=rx_data();
if(gps=='G')
{
```

```
gps=rx_data();
if(gps=='G')
{
gps=rx_data();
if(gps=='A')
{
gps=rx_data();                    // Check first comma
if(gps==',')
{
gps=rx_data();
while(gps != ','){                // Check second comma
gps=rx_data();
}
for(i=0; gps != 'N'; i++){
gps=rx_data();
lati_data[i]=gps;                 // Store the Latitude data
}
gps=rx_data();                    // skip comma
for(i=0; gps != 'E'; i++){
gps=rx_data();
long_data[i]=gps;                 // Store the Longitude data
}                                 // End if cases
}}}}}}}
lcd_cmd(0x80);                    // cursor position at 0th addr of line1
lcd_display("Lt ");               // Display 'Lt' for Latitude
for (i=0; i<11; i++) {
  lcd_data(lati_data[i]);         // Display the Latitude data on LCD
}
lcd_cmd(0xC0);                    // Cursor position at 0th addr of line2
lcd_display("Lg ");               // Display 'Lg' for Longitude
for (i=0; i<12; i++) {
  lcd_data(long_data[i]);         // Display the Longitude data on LCD
}
__delay_ms(3000);                 // Wait for 3 sec
```

```
lcd_cmd(0x01);                    // Clear screen
}
}
```

Circuit Diagram:

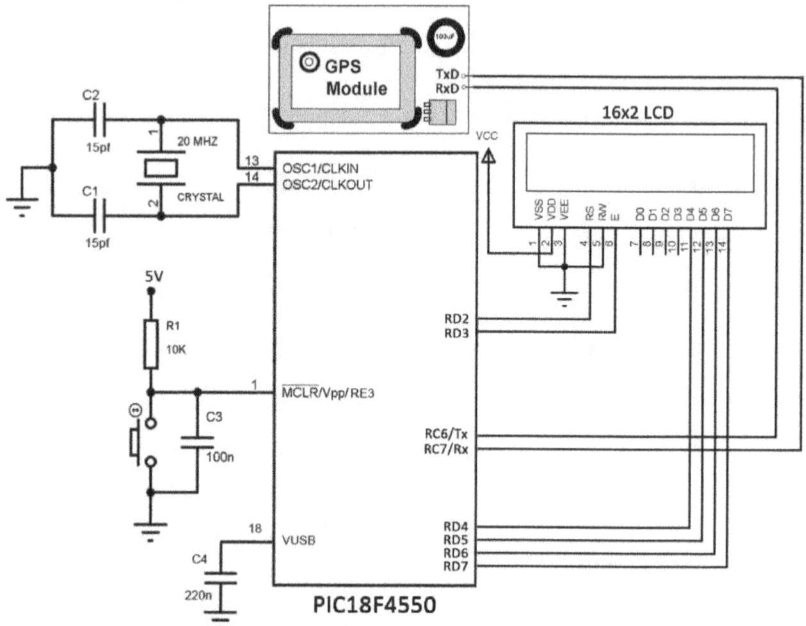

Conclusion:

The embedded system for displaying latitude and longitude values on a 16x2 LCD, utilizing a GPS module and a PIC18F4550 microcontroller, has been successfully demonstrated using an Embedded C program.

49. MOTION DETECTION ALARM USING PIR SENSOR

Aim:

Design and develop an embedded system to detect motion using a PIC18F4550 microcontroller and a Passive Infra-Red (PIR) sensor. Implement the system using Embedded C and verify its functionality.

Hardware Requirements:

- PIC18F4550 Microcontroller, 20 MHz Crystal (1), 15 pF Disc Capacitors (2), 220 nF Disc Capacitor (1), 100 nF Disc Capacitor (1), Resistor 10 K (1), and Push Button (1)
- PIR sensor, NPN transistor BC547 (1), Resistor 1K (1) and Buzzer (1)

Software Used:

- IDE: MPLAB X IDE v5.45
- Compiler: XC8 - v2.31

Theory:

The PIR sensor detects infrared (IR) radiation, which is emitted by living bodies above absolute zero. It responds to IR radiation at a wavelength of 10μm. The sensor has two slots connected to a differential amplifier. When a stationary object is present, both slots receive the same amount of radiation, resulting in a zero output. However, when an object moves, one slot receives more radiation than the other, causing the output to swing high or low, indicating motion.

The sensor is often enhanced with Fresnel lenses to extend its sensing range to about 10 meters and narrow its field of view to less than 180 degrees.

The PIR sensor has three pins:

1. VDD: +3.3-5V power supply.
2. Output: Digital output pin.
3. GND: Ground.

In the presence of human IR energy, the PIR sensor converts the detected IR energy into electrical pulses, which activate the sensor output. PIR sensors are widely used in thermal sensing applications such as security alarms, motion detection alarms, and automatic lighting systems.

Algorithm:

1. Define the PIC18 configuration bits using the pragma directive, include xc.h, and set the crystal frequency for _XTAL_FREQ to utilize the built-in delay function.
2. Configure RB0 as an input port for the external interrupt. Define PORTB2 for the buzzer.
3. Set the buzzer port (PORTB2) as an output port. Enable global interrupts and enable the INT0 interrupt.
4. Configure the interrupt to trigger on the rising edge.
5. Halt the main function to allow the interrupt service routine (ISR) to handle events.

ISR:

1. Clear the interrupt flag (INTF).
2. Turn on the buzzer.
3. Call the delay function for 500 ms to keep the buzzer on for a short period.
4. Turn off the buzzer.
5. Return from the ISR to resume normal operation.

Program:

```
#pragma config PLLDIV = 5, CPUDIV = OSC1_PLL2, USBDIV = 2, FOSC = HS, FCMEN =
OFF, IESO = OFF
#pragma config PWRT = OFF, BOR = OFF, BORV = 3, VREGEN = OFF, WDT = OFF,
WDTPS = 32768
#pragma config CCP2MX = ON, PBADEN = OFF, LPT1OSC = OFF, MCLRE = ON
#pragma config STVREN = ON, LVP = OFF, ICPRT = OFF, XINST = OFF
#pragma config CP0 = OFF, CP1 = OFF, CP2 = OFF, CP3 = OFF, CPB = OFF, CPD = OFF
#pragma config WRT0 = OFF, WRT1 = OFF, WRT2 = OFF, WRT3 = OFF, WRTC = OFF,
WRTB = OFF, WRTD = OFF
#pragma config EBTR0 = OFF, EBTR1 = OFF, EBTR2 = OFF, EBTR3 = OFF, EBTRB = OFF

#include <xc.h>
#define _XTAL_FREQ 20000000
#define buzzer PORTBbits.RB2

// RB0 (INT0) is connected with the output of PIR sensor
```

```
void __interrupt() isr (void)       // Interrupt Service Routine
{

// Check the occurrence of Ext. Hardware interrupt
if (INTCONbits.INT0IE && INTCONbits.INT0IF)
{
INTCONbits.INT0IF = 0;              // Clear external interrupt flag
buzzer = 1;                         // Turn-on the buzzer
__delay_ms(500);                    // Make 100 ms delay
buzzer = 0;                         // Turn-off the buzzer
}
}

void main(void) {
TRISB = 0x01;
buzzer = 0;                         // Clear RB2
INTCONbits.GIE = 1;                 // Enable Global Interrupt
// Enable RB0/INT external hardware Interrupt
INTCONbits.INT0IE = 1;
INTCONbits.PEIE = 0;                // Disable peripheral interrupt
INTCON2bits.INTEDG0 = 1;            // Interrupt on raising edge
while(1);                           // wait for forever
}
```

Circuit Diagram:

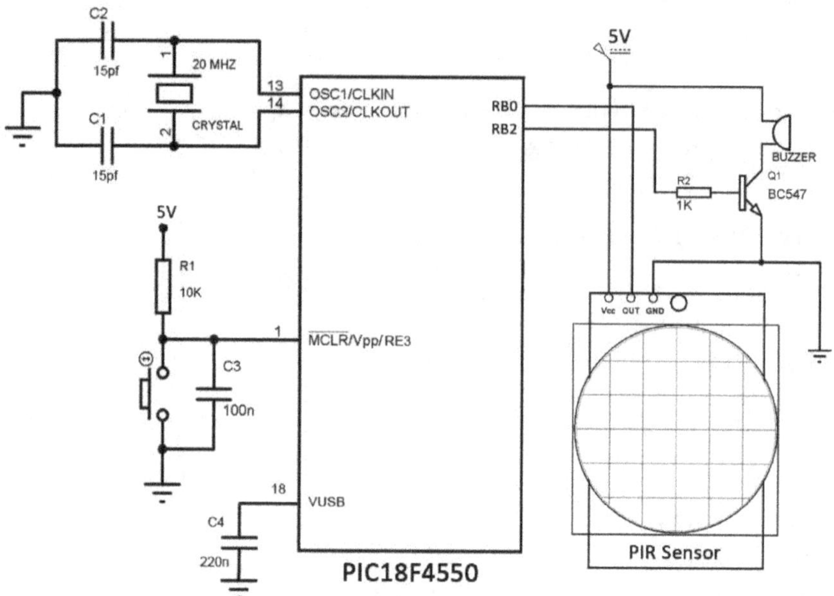

Conclusion:

The embedded system for motion detection, utilizing a PIR sensor, a PIC18F4550 microcontroller, and an Embedded C program, has been successfully demonstrated.

50. ACCELEROMETER SENSOR INTERFACE

Aim:

Develop an embedded system to read and print the X, Y, and Z axis values from an accelerometer sensor via a serial port using a PIC18F4550 microcontroller and an Embedded C program. Verify the accuracy and functionality of the output.

Hardware Requirements:

- PIC18F4550 Microcontroller, 20 MHz Crystal (1), 15 pF Disc Capacitors (2), 220 nF Disc Capacitor (1), 100 nF Disc Capacitor (1),

Resistor 10 K (1), and Push Button (1)

- ADXL 335 accelerometer, Line Driver IC MAX232 (1), Capacitor 1 uF (4), and DB9 Connector Female (1)

Software Used:

- IDE: MPLAB X IDE v5.45
- Compiler: XC8 - v2.31

Theory:

The ADXL335 is a three-axis analog accelerometer that measures acceleration forces along the X, Y, and Z axes. It outputs an analog voltage that is proportional to the acceleration in each axis. These analog voltages can be converted into digital values using the on-chip ADC of a microcontroller for various applications. The ADXL335 is commonly used in tilt sensing for applications such as automobiles, robots, drones, and gaming devices. It has a full sensing range of ±3g for all three axes.

The ADXL335 accelerometer has five pins:

1. VCC: 5V DC regulated power supply
2. Ground: Ground connection
3. X-axis Analog Output: Voltage corresponding to acceleration along the X-axis
4. Y-axis Analog Output: Voltage corresponding to acceleration along the Y-axis
5. Z-axis Analog Output: Voltage corresponding to acceleration along the Z-axis

To calculate angles of inclination and rotation using the ADXL335:

1. Convert the 10-bit ADC values into acceleration values in g units.
2. According to the ADXL335 datasheet, the sensor's output voltage at 0g is 1.65V with a sensitivity scale factor of 330mV/g.

The formula for acceleration value in g unit

$$A_{out} = \frac{ADCvalue * V_{ref} - VoltageLevel@0g}{SensitivityFactor}$$

Axout = (((X axis ADC value * Vref) / 1024) – 1.65) / 0.330

Ayout = (((Y axis ADC value * Vref) / 1024) – 1.65) / 0.330

Azout = (((Z axis ADC value * Vref) / 1024) – 1.65) / 0.330

Angle of Inclination:

The angle of inclination means by how much angle the device is tilted from its plane of the surface. It can be calculated as,

$$\theta(theta) = a\tan\left(\frac{A_{xout}}{\sqrt{A_{yout}^{2} + A_{zout}^{2}}}\right)$$

$$\psi(psi) = a\tan\left(\frac{A_{yout}}{\sqrt{A_{xout}^{2} + A_{zout}^{2}}}\right)$$

$$\phi(\text{phi}) = a\tan\left(\frac{\sqrt{A_{xout}^{2} + A_{yout}^{2}}}{A_{zout}}\right)$$

The above equations give angles in radians. To get angles in degrees, multiply these values by ($180/\pi \approx 57.29577951$) within range of -90° to +90° each axis.

Angle of Rotation:

A complete angle of rotation from 0° to 360° around X, Y, Z axes are called,

Roll - Angle of rotation about the X-axis

Pitch - Angle of rotation about the Y-axis

Yaw - Angle of rotation about the Z-axis

It can be calculated as,

Roll = (atan2(Ayout, Azout)) *57.29577951+180

Pitch = (atan2(Azout, Axout)) *57.29577951+180

Yaw = (atan2(Axout, Ayout)) *57.29577951+180

Algorithm:

1. Define the PIC18 configuration bits using the pragma directive, include xc.h, and define the crystal frequency for _XTAL_FREQ to use the inbuilt delay function.

2. Declare ADC_X, ADC_Y, and ADC_Z as integers and Axout, Ayout, and Azout as doubles.
3. Configure AN0, AN1, and AN2 as analog ports.
4. Initialize the on-chip USART for asynchronous mode with a 9600 baud rate.
5. Configure ADCON0 for Channel AN0, set ADC Clock to FOSC/64, and turn on the ADC.
6. Read the analog value for AN0 and store it in ADC_X.
7. Configure ADCON0 for Channel AN1, set ADC Clock to FOSC/64, and turn on the ADC.
8. Read the analog value for AN1 and store it in ADC_Y.
9. Configure ADCON0 for Channel AN2, set ADC Clock to FOSC/64, and turn on the ADC.
10. Read the analog value for AN2 and store it in ADC_Z.
11. Convert ADC_X, ADC_Y, and ADC_Z values to g units.
12. Print the X, Y, and Z axis values to the serial port.
13. Wait for 1 second.
14. Repeat the steps from step 5.

USART_Tx_string(char) function:

1. Send the string data to TXREG using the pointer variable.
2. Wait until TXIF is set.
3. Clear the TXIF flag.
4. Increment the pointer variable.

USART_Tx_char(char) function:

1. Send the character data to TXREG.
2. Wait until TXIF is set.
3. Clear the TXIF flag.

USART_Init(unsigned long) function:

1. Load the SPBRG register to set the baud rate to 9600.
2. Configure the TxD and RxD ports as output and input for serial communication, respectively.

3. Load the TXSTA and RCSTA registers to configure serial transmission and reception.
4. Clear the TXIF and RCIF flags.

SerialPrint() function:

1. Declare the array variable buf[].
2. Convert the double value into a char and store it in buf[].
3. Print the string.
4. Print the contents of buf[].
5. Wait for 10 ms.

adc_read() function:

1. Configure ADC Clock, set right-justified result, configure AN0-AN4 as analog ports, use VDD and VSS as references, and turn on the ADC.
2. Wait for the acquisition time (1 ms).
3. Set the GO bit to start the conversion.
4. Wait for the DONE bit.
5. Move the result of the ADC to adc_res.
6. Clear the ADIF flag.
7. Return the adc_res value.

Program:

```
#pragma config PLLDIV = 5, CPUDIV = OSC1_PLL2, USBDIV = 2, FOSC = HS, FCMEN =
OFF, IESO = OFF
#pragma config PWRT = OFF, BOR = OFF, BORV = 3, VREGEN = OFF, WDT = OFF,
WDTPS = 32768
#pragma config CCP2MX = ON, PBADEN = OFF, LPT1OSC = OFF, MCLRE = ON
#pragma config STVREN = ON, LVP = OFF, ICPRT = OFF, XINST = OFF
#pragma config CP0 = OFF, CP1 = OFF, CP2 = OFF, CP3 = OFF, CPB = OFF, CPD = OFF
#pragma config WRT0 = OFF, WRT1 = OFF, WRT2 = OFF, WRT3 = OFF, WRTC = OFF,
WRTB = OFF, WRTD = OFF
#pragma config EBTR0 = OFF, EBTR1 = OFF, EBTR2 = OFF, EBTR3 = OFF, EBTRB = OFF

#include <stdio.h>
#include <stdlib.h>
#include <math.h>
```

```
#include <xc.h>
#define _XTAL_FREQ 20000000

void USART_Tx_string(char *tx_str) {     // Print a string on serial port
unsigned char ch;
while(*tx_str != 0x00) {
ch = *tx_str;                    // Get the charcter from a string
TXREG = ch;                      // Transmit to the serial port one by one
while(!(TXSTAbits.TRMT));
PIR1bits.TXIF=0;                 // Clear TXIF
tx_str++;                        // Increment pointer
}
}

void USART_Tx_char(char c) {     // ISR
TXREG = c;                       // Transmit the recived character
while(TXSTAbits.TRMT ==0);
PIR1bits.TXIF=0;                 // Clear transmit flag
}

void USART_Init(unsigned long Baud_rate) {
TRISC6 = 0;                      // TX Pin set as output
TRISC7 = 1;                      // RX Pin set as input
SPBRG = (_XTAL_FREQ/(64UL * Baud_rate)) - 1;
TXSTAbits.BRGH = 0;              // for high baud_rate
TXSTAbits.SYNC = 0;              // Asynchronous
TXSTAbits.TXEN = 1;              // enable transmission
TXSTAbits.TX9 = 0;               // 8-bit reception selected
RCSTAbits.SPEN = 1;              // Enable serial port pins
RCSTAbits.CREN = 1;              // enable reception
RCSTAbits.RX9 = 0;               // 8-bit reception mode selected
__delay_ms(100);                 // Wait for serial port stable
PIR1bits.RCIF=0;                 // Clear receive flag
PIR1bits.TXIF=0;                 // Clear transmit flag
```

```
}

void SerialPrint(const char* str, double val, char unit) {
char buf[10];
sprintf(buf,"%.2f", val);              // Convert double into string
USART_Tx_string (str);                 // Send string
USART_Tx_string (buf);                 // Send value
USART_Tx_char (unit);                  // Send unit char
USART_Tx_char ('\t');                  // Send tab char
__delay_ms(10);
}

int adc_read() {
int adc_res;
// (1) ADC Clock, (1) Right justified, AN0-4 Analog ports & VDD and VSS references
ADCON1 = 0xC2;
__delay_ms(1);                         // Wait for acquisition time
ADCON0bits.GO_nDONE = 1;               // Start A/D conversion
while(ADCON0bits.GO_nDONE);            // Waiting for conversion to complete
adc_res = (ADRESH*256)+ ADRESL;        // ADC result in decimal
PIR1bits.ADIF = 0;                     // Clear ADC interrupt flag
ADCON0bits.ADON=0;                     // Turn-off ADC
return adc_res;                        // Return ADC result to main function
}

void main()
{
int ADC_X, ADC_Y, ADC_Z;
double Axout, Ayout, Azout;
TRISA = 0x07;                          // Analog pin AN0-2 as Input port
USART_Init (9600);
while(1) {
   ADCON0 = 0x81;      // Channel AN0, (10)ADC Clock FOSC/64 & Turn ON ADC
   ADC_X = adc_read();
   ADCON0 = 0x89;      // Channel AN1, (10)ADC Clock FOSC/64 & Turn ON ADC
```

```
  ADC_Y = adc_read();
  ADCON0 = 0x91;        // Channel AN2, (10)ADC Clock FOSC/64 & Turn ON ADC
  ADC_Z = adc_read();

  //Convert X, Y and Z values in g unit
   Axout = (((double)(ADC_X*5)/1.024)-1650.0)/330.0;
   Ayout = (((double)(ADC_Y*5)/1.024)-1650.0)/330.0;
   Azout = (((double)(ADC_Z*5)/1.024)-1650.0)/330.0;

  SerialPrint("Axout = ", Axout, 'g');      // Print X, Y, Z values in g unit
  SerialPrint("Ayout = ", Ayout, 'g');
  SerialPrint("Azout = ", Azout, 'g');
  USART_Tx_string ("\r\n");                 // Carriage Return & Move cursor to the new line
  __delay_ms(1000);                         // wait 1 sec for next cycle
  }
}
```

Circuit Diagram:

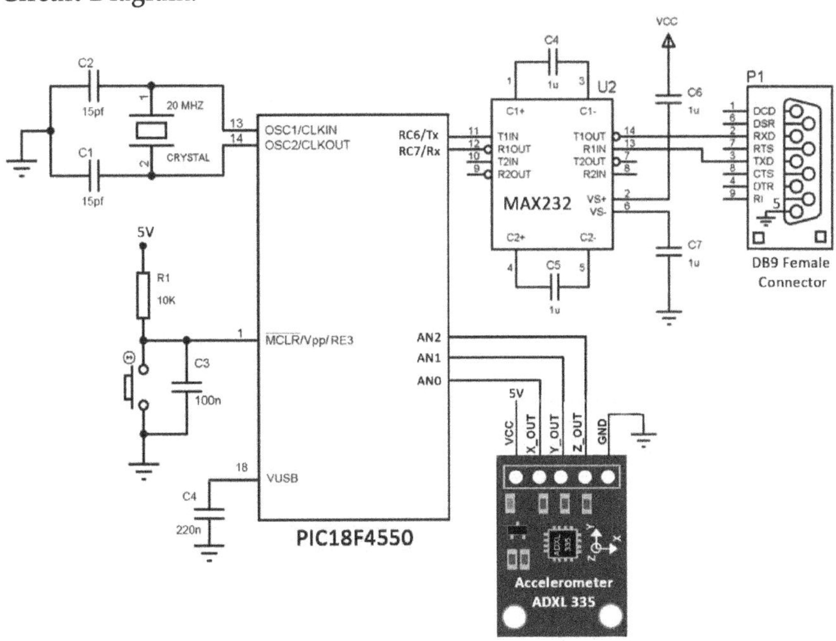

Conclusion:

The accelerometer sensor was successfully interfaced with the PIC18F4550 Microcontroller, and the acceleration values for the X, Y, and Z axes were accurately displayed in g units on the serial monitor.

51. GRAPHICAL LCD INTERFACE

Aim:

Develop an embedded system to display a message on a graphical LCD using a PIC18F4550 Microcontroller and an Embedded C program. Verify the system's output.

Hardware Requirements:

- PIC18F4550 Microcontroller, 20 MHz Crystal (1), 15 pF Disc Capacitors (2), 220 nF Disc Capacitor (1), 100 nF Disc Capacitor (1), Resistor 10 K (1), and Push Button (1)
- Graphical LCD and POT 1K (1)

Software Used:

- IDE: MPLAB X IDE v5.45
- Compiler: XC8 - v2.31

Theory:

A graphical LCD is an electronic display unit capable of showing not only alphanumeric characters but also images, fonts, and other graphical elements. With a resolution of 128×64, it has 128 columns and 64 rows, totaling 8192 pixels. The LCD screen is divided into two halves. The first half, from columns 1 to 64, is controlled by the first controller, which manages 4096 dots. The second half, from columns 65 to 128, is managed by the second controller. Each half is further divided into 8 pages, each with 8 rows and 64 columns, totaling 512 dots per page. Each pixel is made up of 8 vertical dots.

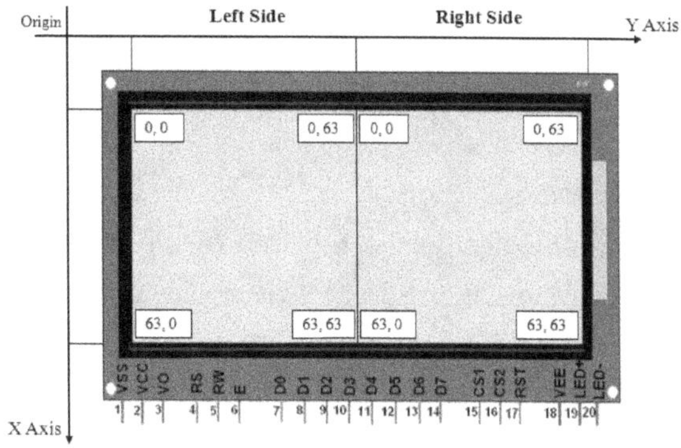

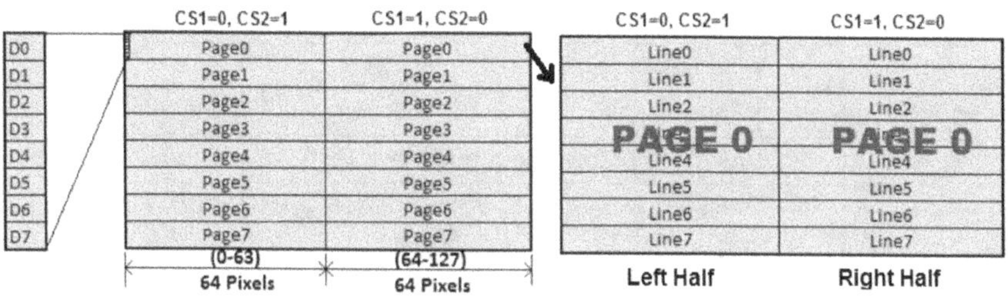

Page Selection (X address):

Page0 Address = 0xB8 (Separate X counter for both left and right half of the screen)

Page1 Address = 0xB9

Page2 Address = 0xBA

Page3 Address = 0xBB

Page4 Address = 0xBC

Page5 Address = 0xBD

Page6 Address = 0xBE

Page7 Address = 0xBF

Cursor/Char Position (Y address):

To set the cursor position (0-63), send the following address to GLCD. It is incremented by 1 automatically to read or write operations of display data.

Cursor Position 0 (Address = 0x40) (Left most pixel)

Cursor Position 1 (Address = 0x41)

.

.

Cursor Position 63 (Address = 0x7F)

Start Line (Z address):

The Z address will decide the top line of the liquid crystal display screen. It starts from 0xC0 (0th line) to 0xFF (63rd line). It is used for scrolling (y-axis) of the liquid crystal display screen.

KS0108/JHD12864E is a 20-pin GLCD module. It has 6 control & 8 data pins, and 6 power pins.

Pin No	*Name*	*Function*
1	VCC	Supply voltage (5V)
2	VSS	Ground
3	V0	Contrast adjustment (V0)
18	VEE	Negative voltage used along with VCC for brightness control
19	A	Backlight (+)
20	K	Backlight (-)
12	CS1	Chip select 1(enables left half)
13	CS2	Chip select 2 (enables right half)
14	RST	Reset
15	R/W	Read / Write (1/0)
16	D/I	Data/Instruction (1/0)
17	E	Enable

There are 4 modes of operation

D/I	*R/W*	*Mode*
0	0	Instruction write
0	1	Read the GLCD status
1	0	Data write to the RAM
1	1	Data read

Example: To display the character 'P' on the first line of the graphical LCD, we will use a 5x7 pixel font. This font leaves the first two columns, the 8th column, and the last row of the page as spacing.

To display 'P', you need to transfer the following bytes to the first page of the display by selecting the left controller (CS1) and setting the Y address from 0 to 7:

0x00, 0x00, 0x7F, 0x09, 0x09, 0x09, 0x06, 0x00

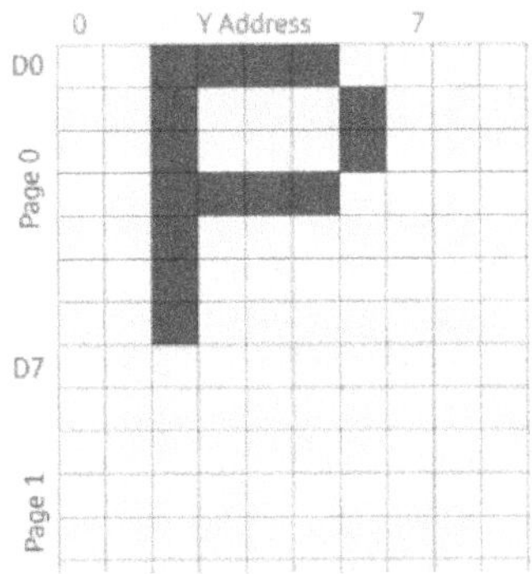

Initialize the display:

- Send 0x3E - Display OFF command.
- Send 0x40 - Y address (Start address).
- Send 0xB8 - X address (Page 0).
- Send 0xC0 - Z address (Start line).
- Send 0x3F - Display ON command.

Command Write:

- Send the command on the data pins.
- Set RS = 0 (Select Command Register) and RW = 0 (Write Operation).
- Make a High to Low transition on the Enable pin (greater than 1 µs).

Data Write:

- Send data on the data pins.
- Set RS = 1 (Select Data Register) and RW = 0 (Write Operation).
- Make a High to Low transition on the Enable pin (greater than 1 µs).

Algorithm:

1. Define the PIC18 configuration bits using pragma directive, include xc.h, and define the crystal frequency for _XTAL_FREQ to use the

inbuilt delay function.

2. Initialize the GLCD – Use PORTB and PORTD as output ports, configure both the left and right halves of the display, and set the X, Y, and Z addresses.
3. Clear the display.
4. Select the left half and set the addresses.
5. Display "ECS" on page 0.
6. Select the right half and set the addresses.
7. Display "DEPT" on page 0.
8. Halt.

Program:

```
#pragma config PLLDIV = 5, CPUDIV = OSC1_PLL2, USBDIV = 2, FOSC = HS, FCMEN =
OFF, IESO = OFF
#pragma config PWRT = OFF, BOR = OFF, BORV = 3, VREGEN = OFF, WDT = OFF,
WDTPS = 32768
#pragma config CCP2MX = ON, PBADEN = OFF, LPT1OSC = OFF, MCLRE = ON
#pragma config STVREN = ON, LVP = OFF, ICPRT = OFF, XINST = OFF
#pragma config CP0 = OFF, CP1 = OFF, CP2 = OFF, CP3 = OFF, CPB = OFF, CPD = OFF
#pragma config WRT0 = OFF, WRT1 = OFF, WRT2 = OFF, WRT3 = OFF, WRTC = OFF,
WRTB = OFF, WRTD = OFF
#pragma config EBTR0 = OFF, EBTR1 = OFF, EBTR2 = OFF, EBTR3 = OFF, EBTRB = OFF

#include <xc.h>
#define _XTAL_FREQ 20000000
#define GLCD_DataBus    LATD
#define EN      LATB0
#define RW      LATB1
#define RS      LATB2
#define CS2     LATB3
#define CS1     LATB4
char A[]={0x7e, 0x11, 0x11, 0x11, 0x7e, 0x00}; // 41 A
char B[]={0x7f, 0x49, 0x49, 0x49, 0x36, 0x00}; // 42 B
char C[]={0x3e, 0x41, 0x41, 0x41, 0x22, 0x00}; // 43 C
char D[]={0x7f, 0x41, 0x41, 0x22, 0x1c, 0x00}; // 44 D
char E[]={0x7f, 0x49, 0x49, 0x49, 0x41, 0x00}; // 45 E
```

```
char F[]={0x7f, 0x09, 0x09, 0x09, 0x01, 0x00}; // 46 F
char G[]={0x3e, 0x41, 0x49, 0x49, 0x7a, 0x00}; // 47 G
char H[]={0x7f, 0x08, 0x08, 0x08, 0x7f, 0x00}; // 48 H
char I[]={0x00, 0x41, 0x7f, 0x41, 0x00, 0x00}; // 49 I
char J[]={0x20, 0x40, 0x41, 0x3f, 0x01, 0x00}; // 4a J
char K[]={0x7f, 0x08, 0x14, 0x22, 0x41, 0x00}; // 4b K
char L[]={0x7f, 0x40, 0x40, 0x40, 0x40, 0x00}; // 4c L
char M[]={0x7f, 0x02, 0x0c, 0x02, 0x7f, 0x00}; // 4d M
char N[]={0x7f, 0x04, 0x08, 0x10, 0x7f, 0x00}; // 4e N
char O[]={0x3e, 0x41, 0x41, 0x41, 0x3e, 0x00}; // 4f O
char P[]={0x7f, 0x09, 0x09, 0x09, 0x06, 0x00}; // 50 P
char Q[]={0x3e, 0x41, 0x51, 0x21, 0x5e, 0x00}; // 51 Q
char R[]={0x7f, 0x09, 0x19, 0x29, 0x46, 0x00}; // 52 R
char S[]={0x46, 0x49, 0x49, 0x49, 0x31, 0x00}; // 53 S
char T[]={0x01, 0x01, 0x7f, 0x01, 0x01, 0x00}; // 54 T
char U[]={0x3f, 0x40, 0x40, 0x40, 0x3f, 0x00}; // 55 U
char V[]={0x1f, 0x20, 0x40, 0x20, 0x1f, 0x00}; // 56 V
char W[]={0x3f, 0x40, 0x38, 0x40, 0x3f, 0x00}; // 57 W
char X[]={0x63, 0x14, 0x08, 0x14, 0x63, 0x00}; // 58 X
char Y[]={0x07, 0x08, 0x70, 0x08, 0x07, 0x00}; // 59 Y
char Z[]={0x61, 0x51, 0x49, 0x45, 0x43, 0x00}; // 5a Z

void GLCD_LeftHalf()            // Select left half of GLCD screen
{
  CS1=0;
  CS2=1;
}
void GLCD_RightHalf()           // Select right half of GLCD screen
{
  CS1=1;
  CS2=0;
}
void GLCD_Cmd(char cmd)
{
```

```
    GLCD_DataBus = cmd;          //Send the Command to LCD
    RS = 0;                      // Make LOW RS pin for selecting Command register
    RW = 0;                      // Make LOW RW pin for Write operation
    EN = 1;                      // Generate a High-to-low pulse on EN pin
    __delay_us(10);
    EN = 0;
    __delay_us(10);
}
void GLCD_Data(char dat)
{
    GLCD_DataBus = dat;          //Send the Data to LCD
    RS = 1;                      // Make HIGH RS pin for selecting Command register
    RW = 0;                      // Make LOW RW pin for Write operation
    EN = 1;                      // Generate a High-to-low pulse on EN pin
    __delay_us(10);
    EN = 0;
    __delay_us(10);
}
void LCD_Char(char *pa)          // Sending Char to the LCD
{
    int i,s;
    for(i=0;i<6;i++) {           // 5x7 font, 1 char + 1 blank space
        GLCD_Data(pa[i]);
        __delay_us(5);
    }}
void GLCD_Init()                 // GLCD initialization function
{
    TRISB = 0x00;                // Make PORTC and PORTD as output ports
    TRISD = 0x00;
    CS1=0;                       // Select both left & right half of display
    CS2=0;
    __delay_ms(5);
    GLCD_Cmd(0x3E);              // Display OFF
    GLCD_Cmd(0x40);              // Set Y address (column=0)
```

```
  GLCD_Cmd(0xB8);               // Set x address (page=0)
  GLCD_Cmd(0xC0);               // Set z address (start line=0)
  GLCD_Cmd(0x3F);               // Display ON
}
void GLCD_ClearAll()            // GLCD all display clear function
{
  int i,j;
  CS1=0;                        // Select both left & right half of display
  CS2=0;
  for(i = 0; i <8; i++)         // Total pages are 8
  {
  GLCD_Cmd((0xB8) + i);         // Increment page
  for(j = 0; j < 64; j++)       // Total columns are 64
  {
  GLCD_Data(0x00);              // Write zeros to all 64 columns
  }
  }
  GLCD_Cmd(0x40);               // Set Y address (column=0)
  GLCD_Cmd(0xB8);               // Set X address (page=0)
}

void main()
{
GLCD_Init();                    // Initialize GLCD
GLCD_ClearAll();                // Clear all pixels in GLCD
GLCD_LeftHalf();                // Select Left Half
GLCD_Cmd(0x3F);                 // Display on
GLCD_Cmd(0x40);                 // Setting Y-address, Column 0
GLCD_Cmd(0xB8);                 // Setting X-address, Page 0
GLCD_Cmd(0xC0);                 // Setting Z-address, start line
__delay_ms(1);                  // Wait for 1 ms
LCD_Char(E);                    // Display " ECS " on left half in page 0
LCD_Char(C);
LCD_Char(S);
```

```
GLCD_RightHalf();
GLCD_Cmd(0x3F);          // Display on
GLCD_Cmd(0x40);          // Setting Y-address, Column 0
GLCD_Cmd(0xB8);          // Setting X-address, Page 0
GLCD_Cmd(0xC0);          // Setting Z-address, start line
__delay_ms(1);           // Wait for 1 ms
LCD_Char(D);             // Display " DEPT" on right half in page 0
LCD_Char(E);
LCD_Char(P);
LCD_Char(T);
while(1);                // Remain forever here
}
```

Circuit Diagram:

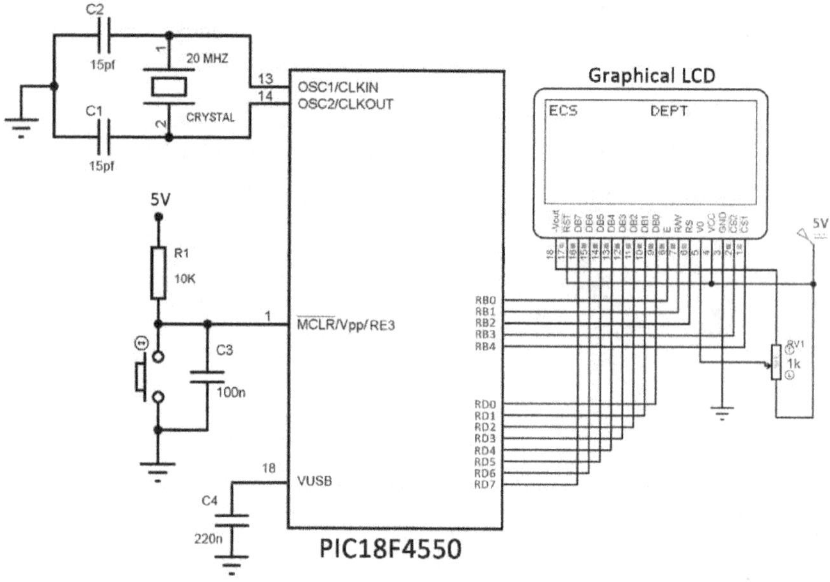

Conclusion:

The embedded system for displaying messages on a graphical LCD using the PIC18F4550 Microcontroller and an Embedded C program has been successfully demonstrated.

52. I2C COMMUNICATION

Aim:

Develop an embedded system to transfer data between two PIC18F4550 Microcontrollers using the I2C serial bus and an Embedded C program. Verify the data transfer functionality.

Hardware Requirements:

- PIC18F4550 Microcontroller (2), 20 MHz Crystal (2), 15 pF Disc Capacitors (4), 220 nF Disc Capacitor (2), 100 nF Disc Capacitor (2), Resistor 10 K (2), and Push Button (2)
- LED (1), Resistor 120 (1), LED Array 8-bit (1)

Software Used:

- IDE: MPLAB X IDE v5.45
- Compiler: XC8 - v2.31

Theory:

I2C (Inter Integrated Circuit):

The I2C (Inter-Integrated Circuit) bus is a bi-directional, two-wire serial bus that provides a communication link between integrated circuits (ICs). Developed by Philips Semiconductors in 1982, I2C is a synchronous protocol enabling communication between a master device and one or more slave devices. It operates in half-duplex mode, meaning data transfer can occur in both directions but not simultaneously.

The I2C bus supports various data transfer speeds:

- Standard Mode: Up to 100 kbit/s
- Fast Mode: Up to 400 kbit/s
- Fast Mode Plus: Up to 1 Mbit/s
- High-Speed Mode: Up to 3.4 Mbit/s
- Ultra-Fast Mode: Unidirectional data transfers up to 5 Mbit/s

I2C supports both 7-bit and 10-bit addressing. The bus consists of two signal lines:

- SCL (Serial Clock Line): Controlled by the master device, it synchronizes data transfer.

- SDA (Serial Data Line): Used for data transfer between devices.

The I2C bus lines are open-drain, meaning they are connected to VCC through pull-up resistors. Communication on the I2C bus is controlled by the master device, which initiates data transfers, while slave devices respond to the master's commands. Although multiple masters can be present on the bus, only one master is active at any given time. Applications of I2C include reading sensor values, interfacing with real-time clocks (RTCs), and accessing external EEPROM memory.

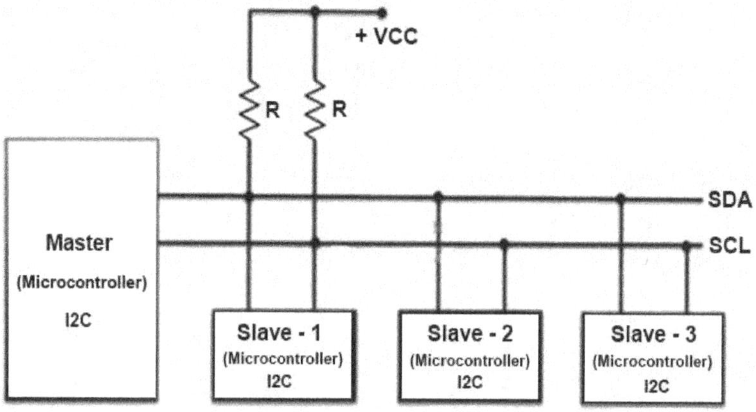

An I2C data transfer involves several fundamental signal components:

- Start (S): Indicates that a device intends to initiate communication on the I2C bus. It is signaled by the SDA line going low while the SCL line remains high.
- Stop (P): Indicates that a device wants to release control of the I2C bus, allowing other master devices to use it. This is signaled by the SDA line going high while the SCL line remains high.
- Repeated Start (R): Similar to the Start condition, this indicates that a device wants to continue data transfer without relinquishing control of the bus.
- Data: Represents the transfer of eight bits of information. The data is transmitted on the SDA line, with the clock pulses provided by the SCL line.
- Acknowledge (A): A positive acknowledgment of data transfer is

signaled by pulling the SDA line low during the 9th clock pulse of SCL.

- No Acknowledge (NACK): Indicates that the device does not acknowledge the data transfer by allowing the SDA line to float high during the 9th clock pulse. It is the opposite of an ACK.

In I2C communication, a master device can either read from or write to a slave device. This is indicated by a single bit transmitted following the address bits: a 1 signifies a read operation, while a 0 signifies a write operation.

The data transfer formats for 7-bit addressing:

Master Transmitter to Slave Receiver

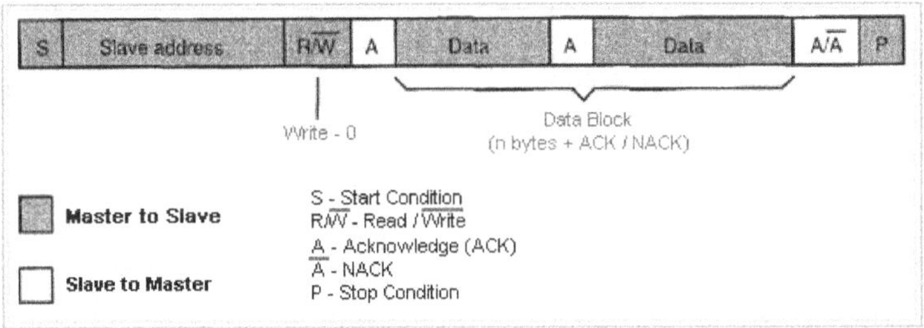

Master Receiver from Slave Transmitter

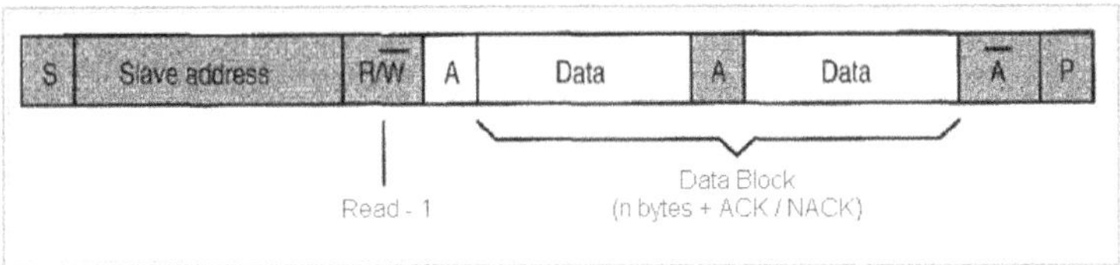

PIC18F4550 I2C Pins

The I2C communication is handled using the following pins:

PORTB.0: Used as the Serial Data Line (SDA).

PORTB.1: Used as the Serial Clock Line (SCL).

Since the I2C bus operates in an open-drain configuration, pull-up resistors must be connected to both the SCL and SDA pins to ensure proper operation.

PIC18F4550 I2C Registers

PIC18F4550 has different registers to establish the I2C communication.

SSPBUF: Serial Transmit/Receive Buffer

SSPBUF is a data register which is used for transmission and reception of data.

SSPSR: MSSP Shift Register

It is a shift register is used to shift data in and out on the SDA line. It is not directly accessible.

SSPADD Register: MSSP Address Register

In Master mode: SSPADD register is used to generate a baud/bit rate.

SSPADD = ((_XTAL_FREQ/4)/I2C_BaudRate) - 1;

In Slave mode: SSPADD register holds the address of the slave device.

SSPCON1: MSSP Control 1 Register

7	6	5	4	3	2	1	0
WCOL	SSPOV	SSPEN	CKP	SSPM3	SSPM2	SSPM1	SSPM0

Bit 7 – WCOL: Write Collision Detect bit

1 = SSPBUF Register is written while it is still transmitting the previous word.

0 = No collision.

Bit 6 – SSPOV: Receive overflow indicator flag

1 = A byte is received while SSPBUF Register is still holding the previous word.

0 = No overflow.

Bit 5 – SSPEN: Synchronous Serial Port Enable bit

1 = Enables the Serial Port and configures SDA and SCL pin as a serial port pin.

0 = Disable Serial Port and configure these pins as GPIO.

Bit 4 – CKP: SCK Release control bit

In slave mode:

1 = Release clock

0 = Holds clock low

Not used in master mode

Bit 3:0 – SSPM3:SSPM0:

0110 = I2C Slave mode, 7-bit address

0111 = I2C Slave mode, 10-bit address

1000 = I2C Master mode, Clock=FOSC / (4*(SSPADD+1))

1011 = I2C Firmware Controlled Master mode

1110 = I2C Slave mode, 7-bit address with Start and Stop interrupt enabled

1111 = I2C Slave mode, 10-bit address with Start and Stop interrupt enabled

SSPCON2: MSSP Control 2 Register

7	6	5	4	3	2	1	0
GCEN	ACKSTAT	ACKDT	ACKEN	RCEN	PEN	RSEN	SEN

Bit 6 – ACKSTAT: Acknowledgement Status bit
1 = acknowledgment signal was not received from the slave
0 = acknowledgment signal was received from the slave

Bit 5 – ACKDT: Acknowledge Data bit
This bit is used when the master requests to slave devices for reading/receiving of data.
1 = Not acknowledge which tells other devices stop sending data.
0 = Acknowledge which tells the device to send another data.

Bit 4 – ACKEN: Acknowledge Sequence Enable bit
1 = Initiate acknowledge sequence on SDA and SCL pins and transmit ACKDT data bit which is automatically cleared by hardware.
0 = Acknowledge sequence is disabled or not in use.

Bit 3 – RCEN: Receive Enable bit
1 = Enable receive mode for I2C.
0 = Disable receive mode.

Bit 2 – PEN: Stop Condition Enable bit
1 = Enable stop condition and cleared automatically by hardware.
0 = Stop condition is Idle.

Bit 1 – RSEN: Restart Condition Enable bit
1 = Enable repeated start condition and cleared automatically by hardware.
0 = Repeated start condition is Idle.

Bit 0 – SEN: Start Condition Enable bit
1 = Enable start condition and cleared automatically by hardware.
0 = Start condition is Idle.

SSPSTAT: MSSP Status Register

7	6	5	4	3	2	1	0
SMP	CKE	$D/\overline{A}$	P	S	$R/\overline{W}$	UA	BF

Bit 7 – SMP: Slew Rate Control bit
In Master or Slave mode:
1 = Slew rate control disabled for standard speed mode (100 kHz and 1MHz).
0 = Slew rate control enabled for high speed mode (400 kHz).

Bit 6 – CKE: SMBus Select bit
1 = Enable SMBus specific input.
0 = Disable SMBus specific input.

Bit 5 – D/A: Data/Address bit
In Slave mode:
1 = indicates that the last byte received or transmitted was data
0 = indicates that the last byte received or transmitted was address

Bit 4 – P: Stop bit
1 = indicates that the stop bit has been detected last
0 = stop bit was not detected last

Bit 3 – S: Start bit
1 = indicates that the start bit has been detected last
0 = start bit was not detected last

Bit 2 – R/W: Read/Write Information bit
In Slave mode:
1 = Read
0 = Write

In Master mode:
1 = Transmit is in progress
0 = Transmit is not in progress

Bit 1 – UA: Update Address bit.
It is used for 10-bit slave mode only.
1 = Indicates that the user needs to update the address in the SSPADD register.
0 = Address does not need to be updated

Bit 0 – BF: Buffer Full Status bit
In Transmit mode:
1 = SSPBUF is full.
0 = SSPBUF is empty.

In Receive mode:
1 = SSPBUF is full (does not include ACK and stop bit.)
0 = SSPBUF is empty.

<u>I2C Clock Frequency:</u>

The I2C clock on the PIC18F4550 is controlled by the master device through the SCL line. The SSPADD register in the master is used to set the I2C clock frequency.

<u>Buffer Full Flag and Interrupt Flag:</u>

Transmission: After the complete transmission of data/address, the Buffer Full (BF) flag is set. The acknowledgment signal from the slave is received, and then the SSPIF (Serial Port Interrupt Flag) is set.

Reception: During data reception, the Buffer Full (BF) flag is set when a complete byte is received. The device then needs to send an acknowledgment signal. The data is moved from the SSPBUF (Serial Port Buffer) register to the SSPSR (Serial Port Shift Register), and the SSPIF flag is set.

Programming PIC18F4550 I2C:

Initialization:

- Configure PORTB.0 and PORTB.1 as an input pin.
- Configure the SSPSTAT, SSPCON1 and SSPCON2 registers.
- Set frequency of I2C communication by loading value in the SSPADD register in master mode.

```
void I2C_Master_Init(void)        // I2C master initialization
{
  // SSPM3:SSPM0: 1000 = I2C Master mode, clock = FOSC/(4 * (SSPADD + 1))
  TRISB0=1;                   // SCL and SDA are configured as inputs
  TRISB1=1;
   SSPCON1 = 0x28;        // Enable SSP & set SSPM3:SSPM0 bits
   SSPCON2 = 0x00;        // Clear all I2C signal conditions
   SSPADD = ((_XTAL_FREQ/4000)/I2C_BaudRate) - 1;
   SSPSTAT = 0x00;        // Slew rate disabled, other bits are cleared
   PIR1bits.SSPIF = 0;    // Clear SSPIF
}

void I2C_Slave_Init (unsigned char slave_address) {
  // Serial Port Enable & Release clock & 0110 = I2C Slave mode, 7-bit address
   SSPADD = slave_address;         // Set the I2C Slave Device Address
   SSPSTAT = 0x80;                 // 1 = Slew rate control disabled
   SSPCON1 = 0x36;
   SSPCON2 = 0x01;                 // Start Condition Enable
   TRISB0 = 1;                     // SCL Set to Input
   TRISB1 = 1;                     // SDA Set to Input
   INTCONbits.GIE = 1;             // Enable Interrupts
   INTCONbits.PEIE = 1;
```

```
    PIR1bits.SSPIF = 0;
    PIE1bits.SSPIE = 1;
}
```

Check I2C bus is ready:

Check the SSPSTAT register for finding the I2C bus is ready or not.

```
void I2C_Idle() {
    while(SSPSTATbits.BF || (SSPSTATbits.R_nW)|| (SSPCON2 & 0x1F));
    PIR1bits.SSPIF=0;              // Clear SSPIF interrupt flag
}
```

Start Condition on I2C bus:

Send start condition to the slave device by setting a bit in SEN in the SSPCON2 register.

Wait for SEN bit to clear.

Check S bit in SSPSTAT register which indicates the start bit is detected or not.

```
void I2C_Start(void) {
    I2C_Idle();
    SSPCON2bits.SEN=1;             // Release start condition
    while(SSPCON2bits.SEN);        // Wait for completion of start pulse
}
```

Write/Transmit Address/ Data on I2C bus:

Write address/data to the SSPBUF register for transmission and wait for the completion of the transmission.

Check for acknowledgment signal.

```
char I2C_Write(unsigned char add_data) {
     I2C_Idle();
     SSPBUF= add_data;             // Write data to SSPBUF
     return ACKSTAT;               // Return acknowledge bit
}
```

Stop Condition on I2C bus:

After write if we want to Stop I2C communication,

Set the PEN bit in SSPCON2 register and wait for the PEN bit to clear.

Check P bit in the SSPSTAT register which indicates the stop bit is detected.

```
void I2C_Stop() {
   I2C_Idle();
   SSPCON2bits.PEN=1;           // Stop communication
   while(SSPCON2bits.PEN);      // Wait for end of stop pulse
}
```

Read/Receive Data from I2C bus:

Enable receive mode by setting bit RCEN in SSPCON2.

The Buffer flag to set when a complete byte is received and read the buffer immediately.

After reading a byte, send an acknowledge signal if we want to read the next data else send negative acknowledge which tells not to read the next data.

```
char I2C_Read(char flag) {
      char buffer=0;
      I2C_Idle();
      RCEN=1;                        // Enable receive
      // Wait for buffer full flag which when complete byte received
      while(!SSPSTATbits.BF);
      buffer=SSPBUF;                 // Copy SSPBUF to buffer
      I2C_Idle();
      ACKDT = (ak) ? 0 : 1;          //check if acknowledge bit received
      ACKEN = 1;                     // Acknowledge sequence
      return(buffer);
}
```

Acknowledgement/ Negative Acknowledgement on I2C bus:

Send acknowledgment or negative acknowledgment after read to continue or stop reading.

To do this, ACKDT =1 or 0 and ACKEN should be enabled.

```
void I2C_Ack (void) {
  I2C_Idle();
  ACKDT=0;              // Acknowledge data 0: ACK
  ACKEN=1;              // Enable ACK to send
  while(ACKEN);
}

void I2C_Nack(void) {
  I2C_Idle();
  ACKDT=1;              // Acknowledge data 1: NACK
  ACKEN=1;              // Enable ACK to send
  while(ACKEN);
}
```

Algorithm:

Master Device:

1. Define the PIC18 configuration bits using the pragma directive, include xc.h, and set the crystal frequency for _XTAL_FREQ to use the built-in delay function.
2. Configure RB7 as an LED output and set the baud rate for I2C.
3. Initialize the MSSP module for I2C communication in master mode.
4. Generate a Start condition by setting the Start Enable bit, SEN (SSPCON2<0>).
5. Wait until the SSPIF flag is set. The MSSP module will delay before performing any further operations.
6. Load the SSPBUF register with the slave address to be transmitted.
7. Shift out the address from the SDA pin until all eight bits are transmitted.
8. The MSSP module will receive an ACK bit from the slave device and store its value in the SSPCON2 register (SSPCON2<6>).
9. Load the SSPBUF register with eight bits of data to be transmitted.
10. Shift out the data from the SDA pin until all eight bits are transmitted.

11. The MSSP module will receive an ACK bit from the slave device and store its value in the SSPCON2 register (SSPCON2<6>).
12. Release the negative acknowledgment to cancel the data transmission.
13. Generate a Stop condition by setting the Stop Enable bit, PEN (SSPCON2<2>).
14. Toggle the LED port.
15. Repeat steps from step 4.

Slave Device:

1. Define the PIC18 configuration bits using the pragma directive, include xc.h, and set the crystal frequency for _XTAL_FREQ to use the built-in delay function.
2. Configure Port D to receive I2C data.
3. Initialize the MSSP module for I2C communication in slave mode, enable the I2C interrupt, and set the slave address.
4. Halt.

ISR:

1. Check the overflow and write collision flag bits. If set, clear the flags.
2. If the R_nW bit is reset, release the clock and write the SSPBUF value to the LATD register for display.
3. If the R_nW bit is set, write the LATD register value to the SSPBUF register and release the clock.
4. Wait until the Buffer Full (BF) flag is cleared.
5. Clear the SSPIF flag.

Program:

// Transfer data from the Master device to Slave device

/ The master sending data 00H to FFH to the slave; for every transmission an LED at master will be toggle.*

*The slave only receives the I2C data from the master and move it to PORTD. */*

// Master Transmitter:

```
#pragma config PLLDIV = 5, CPUDIV = OSC1_PLL2, USBDIV = 2, FOSC = HS, FCMEN =
```

```
OFF, IESO = OFF
#pragma config PWRT = OFF, BOR = OFF, BORV = 3, VREGEN = OFF, WDT = OFF,
WDTPS = 32768
#pragma config CCP2MX = ON, PBADEN = OFF, LPT1OSC = OFF, MCLRE = ON
#pragma config STVREN = ON, LVP = OFF, ICPRT = OFF, XINST = OFF
#pragma config CP0 = OFF, CP1 = OFF, CP2 = OFF, CP3 = OFF, CPB = OFF, CPD = OFF
#pragma config WRT0 = OFF, WRT1 = OFF, WRT2 = OFF, WRT3 = OFF, WRTC = OFF,
WRTB = OFF, WRTD = OFF
#pragma config EBTR0 = OFF, EBTR1 = OFF, EBTR2 = OFF, EBTR3 = OFF, EBTRB = OFF

#include <xc.h>
#define _XTAL_FREQ 20000000
#define LED LATB7
#define I2C_BaudRate 100                    // I2C Baud Rate = 100 Kbps

void I2C_Master_Init(void);
void I2C_Idle();
void I2C_Wait();
void I2C_Start(void);
char I2C_Write(unsigned char);
void I2C_Stop(void);
void I2C_Ack (void);
void I2C_Nack(void);
void i2c_restart(void);
int i2c_write(unsigned char);

void main ()                        // Main function
{
   unsigned char i=0;
   TRISB7 = 0;                      // RB7 as output port
   LED = 0;                         // Clear LED port
   I2C_Master_Init();               // Calling Master_Init function
   while(1)
   {
      I2C_Start();                  // Releasing I2C Start Condition
      I2C_Write(0x40);              // Writing I2C Slave Device Address + Write mode (0)
```

```
        I2C_Write(i++);              // Sending data
        I2C_Nack();                  // Releasing I2C NACK Condition
        I2C_Stop();                  // Releasing I2C Stop Condition
        __delay_ms(50);
        LED = ~ LED;                 // Toggle LED at RB7
    }
}

void I2C_Master_Init(void)           // I2C master initialization
{
    // SSPM3:SSPM0: 1000 = I2C Master mode, clock = FOSC/(4 * (SSPADD + 1))
    TRISB0=1;                        // SCL and SDA are configured as inputs
    TRISB1=1;
    SSPCON1 = 0x28;                  // Enable SSP & set SSPM3:SSPM0 bits
    SSPCON2 = 0x00;                  // Clear all I2C signal conditions
    SSPADD = (_XTAL_FREQ/(4* I2C_BaudRate *1000))-1;
    SSPSTAT = 0x00;                  // Slew rate disabled, other bits are cleared
    PIR1bits.SSPIF = 0;              // Clear SSPIF
}

void I2C_Idle() {
    while(SSPSTATbits.BF || (SSPSTATbits.R_nW)|| (SSPCON2 & 0x1F));
    PIR1bits.SSPIF=0;                // Clear SSPIF interrupt flag
}

void I2C_Start(void) {
    I2C_Idle();
    SSPCON2bits.SEN=1;               // Release start condition
    while(SSPCON2bits.SEN);          // Wait for completion of start pulse
}

char I2C_Write(unsigned char add_data)  {
     I2C_Idle();
     SSPBUF= add_data;               // Write data to SSPBUF
     return ACKSTAT;
```

```
}

void I2C_Stop(void)   {
   I2C_Idle();
   SSPCON2bits.PEN=1;          // Stop communication
   while(SSPCON2bits.PEN);     // Wait for end of stop pulse
}

void I2C_Ack (void)   {
   I2C_Idle();
   ACKDT=0;                    // Acknowledge data 0: ACK
   ACKEN=1;                    // Enable ACK to send
   while(ACKEN);
}

void I2C_Nack(void)   {
   I2C_Idle();
   ACKDT=1;                    // Acknowledge data 1: NACK
   ACKEN=1;                    // Enable ACK to send
   while(ACKEN);
}

/* ---------------------------------------------------------------------------------*/
// Slave Receiver:
#pragma config PLLDIV = 5, CPUDIV = OSC1_PLL2, USBDIV = 2, FOSC = HS, FCMEN = OFF, IESO = OFF
#pragma config PWRT = OFF, BOR = OFF, BORV = 3, VREGEN = OFF, WDT = OFF, WDTPS = 32768
#pragma config CCP2MX = ON, PBADEN = OFF, LPT1OSC = OFF, MCLRE = ON
#pragma config STVREN = ON, LVP = OFF, ICPRT = OFF, XINST = OFF
#pragma config CP0 = OFF, CP1 = OFF, CP2 = OFF, CP3 = OFF, CPB = OFF, CPD = OFF
#pragma config WRT0 = OFF, WRT1 = OFF, WRT2 = OFF, WRT3 = OFF, WRTC = OFF, WRTB = OFF, WRTD = OFF
#pragma config EBTR0 = OFF, EBTR1 = OFF, EBTR2 = OFF, EBTR3 = OFF, EBTRB = OFF

#include <xc.h>
```

```
#define _XTAL_FREQ 20000000
#define ReceivedData    LATD
void I2C_Slave_Init(unsigned char);

void main(void) {                   // Main function
  TRISD = 0x00;                     // Configure PORTD as output
  ReceivedData = 0x00;
  I2C_Slave_Init(0x40);             // Initiate I2C Slave with slave address 0x40
  while(1);                         // End
}

void __interrupt() ISR(void) {      // ISR for Slave Read operation
unsigned char Dmy;
 if(SSPIF)                          // Check SSPIF is set
 {
  CKP = 0;                          // Hold clock
  if(SSPOV || WCOL)                 //Overflow OR Write Collision Check
  {
  Dmy = SSPBUF;                     // Read the last byte to Clear the Buffer
  SSPOV = 0;                        // Clear Overflow flag
  WCOL = 0;                         // Clear WCOL
  CKP = 1;                          // Release Clock
  }
  if(!D_nA && !R_nW)                // Check valid data & Slave receive
  {
   Dmy = SSPBUF;                    // Read the last byte to Clear the Buffer
   while(!BF);                      // Wait until receive complete
   ReceivedData = SSPBUF;           // Read the Buffer data
   CKP = 1;                         // Release Clock
  }
  else if (!D_nA && R_nW)
   {
   Dmy = SSPBUF;                    // Read the last byte to Clear the Buffer
   BF = 0;                          // Clear BF flag
```

```
      SSPBUF = Dmy;              // Write Data to Buffer
      CKP = 1;                   // Release Clock
      while(BF);                 // wait to write data on I2C bus
   }
SSPIF = 0;
}
}

void I2C_Slave_Init(unsigned char Address) {
   SSPADD = Address;             // Set the I2C Slave Device Address
   SSPSTAT = 0x80;               // 1 = Slew rate control disabled
   // Serial Port Enable & Release clock & 0110 = I2C Slave mode, 7-bit address
   SSPCON1 = 0x36;
   SSPCON2 = 0x01;               // 1 = Clock stretching is enabled
   TRISB0 = 1;                   // SCL Set to Input
   TRISB1 = 1;                   // SDA Set to Input
   GIE = 1;                      // Enable Interrupts
   PEIE = 1;
   SSPIF = 0;
   SSPIE = 1;
}
```

Circuit Diagram:

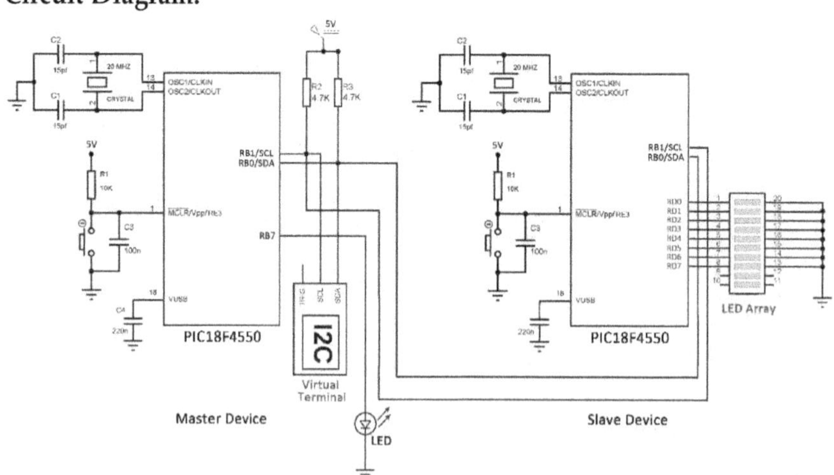

Conclusion:

The interface between two PIC18F4550 Microcontrollers using the I2C protocol has been successfully established. Data transfer between the master and slave devices was observed and verified.

53. INTERFACING RTC USING I2C PROTOCOL

Aim:

Create an embedded system using an RTC and the I2C bus on a PIC18F4550 Microcontroller to display the time and date on an LCD. Verify the output.

Hardware Requirements:

- PIC18F4550 Microcontroller (1), 20 MHz Crystal (1), 15 pF Disc Capacitors (2), 220 nF Disc Capacitor (1), 100 nF Disc Capacitor (1), Resistor 10 K (1), and Push Button (1)
- RTC DS3232 Module and 16x2 LCD module

Software Used:

- IDE: MPLAB X IDE v5.45
- Compiler: XC8 - v2.31

Theory:

RTC DS3232 Module:

The Real-Time Clock (RTC) is an integrated circuit designed for accurate timekeeping. The DS3232, developed by Maxim Integrated, is a precise RTC with an integrated temperature-compensated crystal oscillator (TCXO), eliminating the need for an external crystal. This module includes a 32Kb EEPROM (often the 24C32N) and can maintain accurate timekeeping with a connected 3V CR2032 Lithium Battery, even during power interruptions.

The DS3232 RTC provides seconds, minutes, hours, day, date, month, and year information. It automatically adjusts for months with fewer than 31 days and leap years. It can operate in either 24-hour or 12-hour format with an AM/PM indicator. The RTC communicates via I2C, acting as a slave device on the bus, which is controlled by a master device that generates the serial clock (SCL) and manages the START and STOP conditions.

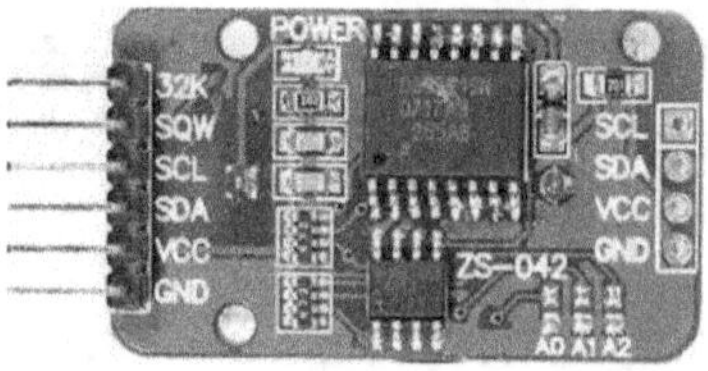

DS3232 is a six terminal device,

VCC	-	Connected to positive of power source (+5V).
GND	-	Connected to ground.
SDA	-	Serial Data pin (I2C interface)
SCL	-	Serial Clock pin (I2C interface)
SQW	-	Square Wave output pin
32K	-	32K oscillator output

The DS3232 requires four connections: SDA, SCL, VCC and GND.

DS3232 RTC

- The write address is 11010000 (0xD0)
- The read address is 11010001 (0xD1)

AT24C32 EEPROM

- The write address is 10101110 (0xAE)
- The read address is 10101111 (0xAF)

The I2C bus conditions are:

- Bus Not Busy: Both data (SDA) and clock (SCL) lines remain high.
- START Condition: Occurs when the data line changes from high to low while the clock line remains high.
- STOP Condition: Occurs when the data line changes from low to high while the clock line remains high.
- Data Valid: Data on the SDA line is considered valid if it remains stable during the high period of the SCL signal. Data should only change during the low period of the SCL signal. Each bit of data is transmitted with one clock pulse.

- Acknowledge: After receiving each byte, the receiving device must generate an acknowledge. The master generates an additional clock pulse for this purpose. To acknowledge, the receiving device pulls the SDA line low during the acknowledge clock pulse.

Data transfer from a master transmitter to a slave receiver:

- Slave Address: The master first sends the slave address. For instance, if the address is 0xD0, it includes the 7-bit address (1101000) followed by the direction bit (R/W), which is 0 for a write operation.
- Acknowledgment: After the slave address is transmitted, the slave (e.g., DS3232) acknowledges by pulling the SDA line low.
- Word Address: The master then sends a word address to the slave. This address sets the register pointer on the slave device. For example, to access the seconds register, the word address might be 0x00 for the seconds register or 0x07 for an alarm register.
- Data Transfer: The master sends the data bytes, which are transferred with the most significant bit (MSB) first. The slave acknowledges each received byte.
- Register Pointer Increment: The register pointer on the slave device increments automatically after each data byte is written.
- STOP Condition: After all data bytes are sent, the master generates a STOP condition to end the data transfer.

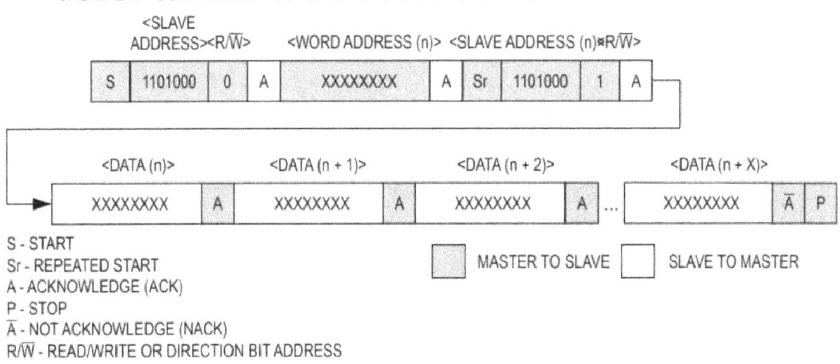

Data transfer from a slave transmitter to a master receiver:

- Slave Address: The master begins by sending the slave address. For example, to read from the DS3232 RTC, the address 0xD1 is used, where the 7-bit address (1101000) is followed by the direction bit (R/W), which is 1 for a read operation.

- Acknowledgment: The slave (DS3232) acknowledges the address by pulling the SDA line low.
- Data Transmission: The slave then transmits data bytes to the master. The master acknowledges each received byte by pulling the SDA line low.
- End of Data: After the last data byte is received, the master sends a not acknowledge (NACK) signal by leaving the SDA line high.
- Start/Repeated Start Condition: Before sending the slave address for reading data, the master generates a START condition or a REPEATED START condition.
- Register Pointer: The RTC DS3232 starts transmitting data from the register pointed to by the previously sent word address.

Algorithm:

1. Define the PIC18 configuration bits using the pragma directive, include xc.h, and define the crystal frequency for _XTAL_FREQ to use the inbuilt delay function.
2. Define PORT D for the 16x2 LCD interface in 4-bit mode.
3. Set the initial values for date and time variables.
4. To set the clock and calendar values of the RTC DS3232:
    - Initialize the PIC18F4550 MCU as a master device for I2C communication.
    - The master device generates a start condition on the I2C bus.
    - The master device sends the DS3232 RTC's device address 0xD0 for the master transmitter.
    - The master device waits for slave acknowledgment.
    - Send the DS3232's register address for seconds (0x00). After the slave acknowledges, the master sends the value for seconds to write in the RTC. The RTC address increments automatically. The master then sends the values for minutes, hours, day, date, month, and year to the slave.

- The master device generates a stop condition to release the I2C bus.

5. To read the time and date values from the RTC DS3232:
   - Start I2C communication by generating a start condition on the I2C bus, followed by sending the slave device address 0xD0 to set the master as a transmitter.
   - The master device waits for slave acknowledgment.
   - Write the DS3232's register pointer (e.g., 0x00 to read from the seconds register).
   - The master device waits for slave acknowledgment.
   - Generate a repeated start condition with the slave address 0xD1 to set the slave as a receiver.
   - The master reads the DS3232's data with acknowledgment from location 0x00.
   - For the last byte, the master reads with a negative acknowledgment (NACK) to indicate the end of data.
   - The master device generates a stop condition to release the I2C bus.

Program:

```
#pragma config PLLDIV = 5, CPUDIV = OSC1_PLL2, USBDIV = 2, FOSC = HS, FCMEN =
OFF, IESO = OFF
#pragma config PWRT = OFF, BOR = OFF, BORV = 3, VREGEN = OFF, WDT = OFF,
WDTPS = 32768
#pragma config CCP2MX = ON, PBADEN = OFF, LPT1OSC = OFF, MCLRE = ON
#pragma config STVREN = ON, LVP = OFF, ICPRT = OFF, XINST = OFF
#pragma config CP0 = OFF, CP1 = OFF, CP2 = OFF, CP3 = OFF, CPB = OFF, CPD = OFF
#pragma config WRT0 = OFF, WRT1 = OFF, WRT2 = OFF, WRT3 = OFF, WRTC = OFF,
WRTB = OFF, WRTD = OFF
#pragma config EBTR0 = OFF, EBTR1 = OFF, EBTR2 = OFF, EBTR3 = OFF, EBTRB = OFF

#include <xc.h>
#define _XTAL_FREQ 20000000
#define RS LATD2                    //Define the LCD pins
#define EN LATD3
#define D4 LATD4
```

```
#define D5 LATD5
#define D6 LATD6
#define D7 LATD7

//Set the current value of date and time variables
unsigned char sec = 00;
unsigned char min = 30;
unsigned char hour = 01;
unsigned char date = 15;
unsigned char month = 12;
unsigned char year = 22;
#include "lcd4bit_head.h"          // Include header files
#include "I2C.h"
#include "DS3232.h"

void main()                        // Main function
{
unsigned char sec_0, sec_1, min_0, min_1, hour_0, hour_1, date_0,
date_1, month_0, month_1, year_0, year_1;
TRISD = 0x00;                      // Make Port D as output port for LCD
lcd_init();                        // To initialize 16x2 LCD in 4-bit mode
I2C_init(100);                     // To initialize I2C Master with 100KHz clock
Set_Time_Date();                   //set time and date on the RTC module
while(1)
{
sec_0 = sec%10;                    //Split the character for the LCD
sec_1 = (sec/10);
min_0 = min%10;
min_1 = min/10;
hour_0 = hour%10;
hour_1 = hour/10;
date_0 = date%10;
date_1 = date/10;
month_0 = month%10;
```

```
month_1 = month/10;
year_0 = year%10;
year_1 = year/10;

//Read the current date and time from RTC module
Update_Current_Date_Time();
lcd_cmd(0x01);          //Display the Time on the LCD screen at line 1
lcd_cmd(0x80);
lcd_display("TIME: ");
lcd_data(hour_1+'0');
lcd_data(hour_0+'0');
lcd_data(':');
lcd_data(min_1+'0');
lcd_data(min_0+'0');
lcd_data(':');
lcd_data(sec_1+'0');
lcd_data(sec_0+'0');
lcd_cmd(0xC0);          //Display the Date on the LCD screen at line 2
lcd_display("DATE: ");
lcd_data(date_1+'0');
lcd_data(date_0+'0');
lcd_data(':');
lcd_data(month_1+'0');
lcd_data(month_0+'0');
lcd_data(':');
lcd_data(year_1+'0');
lcd_data(year_0+'0');
__delay_ms(50);
}
}

/*------------------------------------------------------------------------*/
//#include "I2C.h"          // Header for I2C protocol
//Begin I2C master
```

```
void I2C_init(const unsigned long I2C_BaudRate) {
 TRISB0 = 1;                    //Set SDA and SCL lines as input ports
 TRISB1 = 1;
 //SSPEN=1: Enable synchronous serial port & SSPM0-SSPM3: 1000 for master mode
 SSPCON1  = 0b00101000;
 SSPCON2 = 0x00;                // Clear all I2C conditions
 //Setting Clock Speed
 SSPADD = (_XTAL_FREQ/(4* I2C_BaudRate *1000))-1;
 SSPSTAT = 0x00;                //Clear MSSP Status Register
}

void I2C_MasterWait() {
 while(SSPSTATbits.BF || (SSPSTATbits.R_nW)|| (SSPCON2 & 0x1F));
 PIR1bits.SSPIF=0;              // Clear SSPIF interrupt flag
}

void I2C_StartCondition() {
 I2C_MasterWait ();             // Check I2C bus free
 SEN = 1;                       // Initiate start condition
}
void I2C_StopCondition() {
 I2C_MasterWait ();
 PEN = 1;                       //Initiate stop condition
}

void I2C_MasterWrite(unsigned data) {
 I2C_MasterWait ();
 SSPBUF = data;                 // Write data to SSPBUF
}

unsigned short I2C_MasterRead(unsigned short ak) {
 unsigned short t1;
 I2C_MasterWait ();
 RCEN = 1;                      // Receive enable
 I2C_MasterWait ();
```

```
  t1 = SSPBUF;                      // Read data from SSPBUF
  I2C_MasterWait ();
  ACKDT = (ak) ? 0 : 1;             //check if acknowledge bit received
  ACKEN = 1;                        // Acknowledge sequence
  return t1;
}

/*-------------------------------------------------------------------------*/
//#include "DS3232.h"               //Header for DS3232 RTC module

int  BCD_2_DEC(int c1) {            // Convert BCD to Decimal
  return (c1 >> 4) * 10 + (c1 & 0x0F);
}

int DEC_2_BCD (int c2) {            // Convert Decimal to BCD
  return ((c2 / 10) << 4) + (c2 % 10);
}

void Set_Time_Date()  {             // Setting Time and Date
  I2C_StartCondition ();            // Release start condition
  I2C_MasterWrite (0xD0);           // Write slave address for master transmitter
  I2C_MasterWrite (0);              // Register pointer for seconds
  I2C_MasterWrite (DEC_2_BCD(sec));              //update sec
  I2C_MasterWrite (DEC_2_BCD(min));              //update min
  I2C_MasterWrite (DEC_2_BCD(hour));             //update hour
  I2C_MasterWrite (1);
  I2C_MasterWrite (DEC_2_BCD(date));             //update date
  I2C_MasterWrite (DEC_2_BCD(month));            //update month
  I2C_MasterWrite (DEC_2_BCD(year));             //update year
  I2C_StopCondition();
}

void Update_Current_Date_Time() {
  I2C_StartCondition ();                    // Start condition with slave select
  I2C_MasterWrite (0xD0);
```

```
    I2C_MasterWrite (0);
    I2C_StopCondition();
    //Read Slave data bytes
    I2C_StartCondition ();
    I2C_MasterWrite (0xD1);                        // Initialize master receiver
    sec = BCD_2_DEC(I2C_MasterRead (1));           // Read Time registers
    min = BCD_2_DEC(I2C_MasterRead (1));
    hour = BCD_2_DEC(I2C_MasterRead (1));
    I2C_MasterRead (1);
    date = BCD_2_DEC(I2C_MasterRead (1));          // Read Date registers
    month = BCD_2_DEC(I2C_MasterRead (1));
    year = BCD_2_DEC(I2C_MasterRead (1));
    I2C_StopCondition();
    I2C_StartCondition ();                         //END Reading
    I2C_MasterWrite (0xD1);
    I2C_MasterRead (1);
    I2C_StopCondition();
}
```

Circuit Diagram:

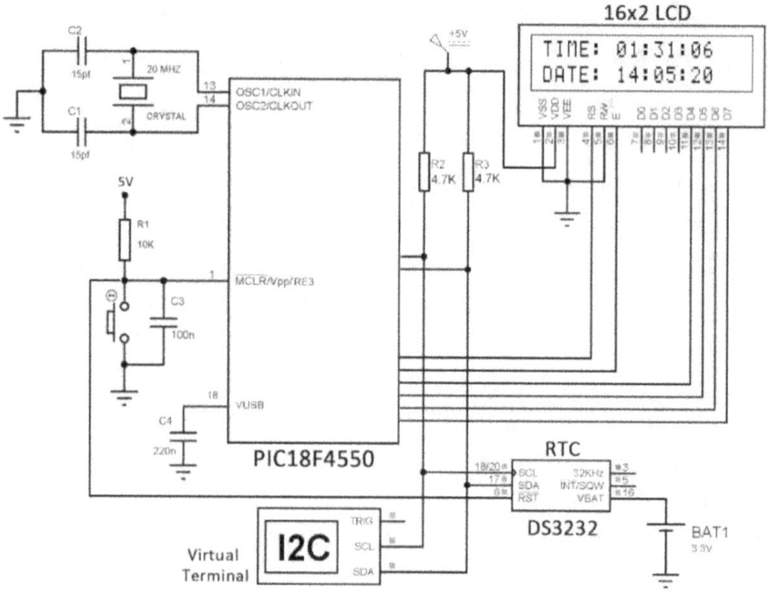

Conclusion:

The embedded system successfully displayed the time and date on an LCD using an RTC with the I2C protocol, a PIC18F4550 microcontroller, and an embedded C program.

54. SPI COMMUNICATION

Aim:

Develop an embedded system to transfer data between two PIC18F4550 microcontrollers using the SPI protocol, with an Embedded C program, and verify its output.

Hardware Requirements:

- PIC18F4550 Microcontroller (1), 20 MHz Crystal (1), 15 pF Disc Capacitors (2), 220 nF Disc Capacitor (1), 100 nF Disc Capacitor (1), Resistor 10 K (1), and Push Button (1)
- LEDs (4) and Resistor 220 (4)

Software Used:

- IDE: MPLAB X IDE v5.45
- Compiler: XC8 - v2.31

Theory:

SPI (Serial Peripheral Interface) is a synchronous serial communication protocol developed by Motorola in the 1970s. It allows for full-duplex communication between a master device and one or more slave devices. The master initiates the communication and provides the clock signal to the slaves.

The Master Synchronous Serial Port (MSSP) module on the PIC18F4550 microcontroller supports both SPI and I2C protocols. For SPI communication, four primary lines are used:

- Serial Data Out (SDO) – RC7/RX/DT/SDO
- Serial Data In (SDI) – RB0/AN12/INT0/FLT0/SDI/SDA

- Serial Clock (SCK) – RB1/AN10/INT1/SCK/SCL
- Slave Select (SS) – RA5/AN4/SS/HLVDIN/C2OUT

The MSSP module includes four key registers for SPI operation:

- MSSP Control Register 1 (SSPCON1)
- MSSP Status Register (SSPSTAT)
- Serial Receive/Transmit Buffer Register (SSPBUF)
- MSSP Shift Register (SSPSR) – Not directly accessible

SSPSTAT: SSP Status Register for SPI mode

7	6	5	4	3	2	1	0
SMP	CKE	D/$\overline{A}$	P	S	R/$\overline{W}$	UA	BF

bit 7 **SMP:** Sample bit
SPI Master mode:
1 = Input data sampled at end of data output time
0 = Input data sampled at middle of data output time
SPI Slave mode:
SMP must be cleared when SPI is used in Slave mode.

bit 6 **CKE:** SPI Clock Select bit(1)
1 = Transmit occurs on transition from active to Idle clock state
0 = Transmit occurs on transition from Idle to active clock state

bit 5 **D/$\overline{A}$:** Data/$\overline{\text{Address}}$ bit
Used in I^2C mode only.

bit 4 **P:** Stop bit
Used in I^2C mode only. This bit is cleared when the MSSP module is disabled, SSPEN is cleared.

bit 3 **S:** Start bit
Used in I^2C mode only.

bit 2 **R/$\overline{W}$:** Read/$\overline{\text{Write}}$ Information bit
Used in I^2C mode only.

bit 1 **UA:** Update Address bit
Used in I^2C mode only.

bit 0 **BF:** Buffer Full Status bit (Receive mode only)
1 = Receive complete, SSPBUF is full
0 = Receive not complete, SSPBUF is empty

SSPCON1: SSP Control Register for SPI mode

7	6	5	4	3	2	1	0
WCOL	SSPOV	SSPEN	CKP	SSPM3	SSPM2	SSPM1	SSPM0

bit 7 **WCOL:** Write Collision Detect bit (Transmit mode only)
1 = The SSPBUF register is written while it is still transmitting the previous word (must be cleared in software)
0 = No collision

bit 6 **SSPOV:** Receive Overflow Indicator bit(1)
SPI Slave mode:
1 = A new byte is received while the SSPBUF register is still holding the previous data. In case of overflow, the data in SSPSR is lost. Overflow can only occur in Slave mode. The user must read the SSPBUF, even if only transmitting data, to avoid setting overflow (must be cleared in software).
0 = No overflow

bit 5	**SSPEN:** Master Synchronous Serial Port Enable bit 1 = Enables serial port and configures SCK, SDO, SDI and $\overline{SS}$ as serial port pins[(2)] 0 = Disables serial port and configures these pins as I/O port pins[(2)]
bit 4	**CKP:** Clock Polarity Select bit 1 = Idle state for clock is a high level 0 = Idle state for clock is a low level
bit 3-0	**SSPM3:SSPM0:** Master Synchronous Serial Port Mode Select bits 0101 = SPI Slave mode, clock = SCK pin, $\overline{SS}$ pin control disabled, $\overline{SS}$ can be used as I/O pin[(3)] 0100 = SPI Slave mode, clock = SCK pin, $\overline{SS}$ pin control enabled[(3)] 0011 = SPI Master mode, clock = TMR2 output/2[(3)] 0010 = SPI Master mode, clock = Fosc/64[(3)] 0001 = SPI Master mode, clock = Fosc/16[(3)] 0000 = SPI Master mode, clock = Fosc/4[(3)]

Operation of PIC18F4550 SPI:

In the PIC18F4550, SPI communication involves 8-bit data transmission and reception in a synchronous manner. Data is transmitted through the SDO (Serial Data Output) line and received through the SDI (Serial Data Input) line. The clock signal (SCK) is generated by the master device and can be configured with one of the following options:

0011: SPI Master mode, clock = TMR2 output/2

0010: SPI Master mode, clock = FOSC/64

0001: SPI Master mode, clock = FOSC/16

0000: SPI Master mode, clock = FOSC/4

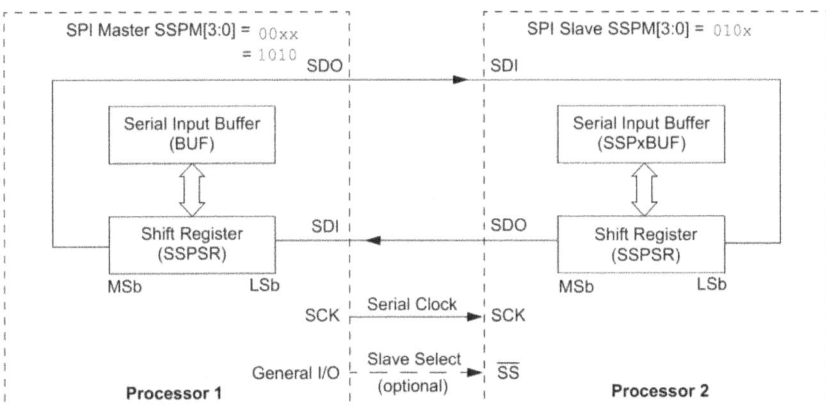

In SPI communication using the PIC18F4550, the Master device controls the data transfer rate and selects the slave device using the SS (Slave Select) line. When multiple slaves are used, GPIO pins of the master are employed to choose the active slave.

Here are the key components and their roles:

- SSPSR (Serial Shift Register): This shift register is used to shift data in and out. It is not directly accessible to users.

- SSPBUF (Serial Buffer Register): This buffer register holds the data bytes for transmission or reception. Data is written to or read from this register.

Data Transmission Process:

Master Device:

- Data to be transmitted is placed in the SSPBUF register.
- The data is then shifted out bit by bit from the SSPSR (Serial Shift Register) on each clock pulse via the SDO line, with the Most Significant Bit (MSB) sent first.

Slave Device:

- Data is shifted in bit by bit via the SDI line into the SSPSR register.
- Once a full byte has been received, it is moved to the SSPBUF register.

Always read the data from SSPBUF before writing new data to avoid buffer overflow. If SSPBUF is not read, the incoming data may be lost. The master transmits the clock and slave select signals. The slave device uses these signals to synchronize and process the SPI data.

The CKP and CKE bits play crucial roles in SPI communication:

CKP (Clock Polarity) determines the idle state of the clock line (SCK). SPI devices must be configured with the same clock polarity for successful communication. If the settings differ, the data exchange may not be meaningful, leading to situations where:

The master sends data while the slave sends dummy data.

The master sends dummy data while the slave sends actual data.

Both the master and slave send data, but the meaning of the data depends on the application's context.

CKE (Clock Edge Select) determines which edge of the clock is used for data transmission and reception. The actual data is latched on the opposite edge of data transmission to ensure synchronization.

SPI Mode	CKP	CKE
0,0	0	1
0,1	0	0
1,0	1	1
1,1	1	0

Master Transmitter and Slave Receiver:

Master Device Initialization

1. Configure the IO pins for SPI Master Mode.
```
TRISB1 = 0;        // SCK -> 0 in master mode
TRISB0 = 1;        // SDI -> Input
TRISC7 = 0;        // SDO -> Output
ADCON1 = 0x07;     // Set PORTA as digital port
TRISA5 = 0;        // SS as a output
```
2. Set the SPI master mode and Set the desired Clock Rate FOSC/64 = 312.5 KBs
```
SSPM3 = 0; SSPM2 = 0; SSPM1 = 1; SSPM0 = 0;
```
3. Enable the Synchronous Serial Port and disable slave select (active low)
```
SSPEN = 1;
RA5 = 1;           // Disable slave select
```
4. Configure the Serial Clock Polarity (Rising edge)
```
CKP = 0;   // 0 = Idle state for clock is a low level
CKE = 0;   // 0 = Transmit occurs on transition from Idle to active clock state
```
5. Configure when the input data is sampled at the Middle
```
SMP = 0;   // 0 = Input data sampled at middle of data output time
```
6. Enable SPI Transmission Interrupts (if needed)
```
SSPIE = 1;    PEIE = 1;    GIE  = 1;
```

Slave Device Initialization

1. Configure the IO pins for SPI Master Mode.
```
TRISB1 = 1;        // SCK -> 1 in slave mode
TRISB0 = 1;        // SDI -> Input
TRISC7 = 0;        // SDO -> Output
```

```
ADCON1 = 0x07;          // Set PORTA as digital port
TRISA5 = 1;             // SS as a input
```

2. Set the MSSP module in SPI Slave Mode

   // 0100 = SPI Slave mode, clock = SCK pin. SS pin control enabled.

   ```
   SSPM3 = 0;    SSPM2 = 1;    SSPM1 = 0;    SSPM0 = 0;
   ```

2. Enable the Synchronous Serial Port and disable slave select

   ```
   SSPEN = 1;
   RA5 = 1;
   ```

3. Configure the Serial Clock Polarity (Rising Edge)

   ```
   CKP = 0;      CKE = 0;
   ```

4. Clear the SMP Bit

   ```
   SMP = 0;
   ```

5. Enable SPI Reception Interrupts (Recommended)

   ```
   SSPIE = 1;    PEIE = 1;    GIE  = 1;
   ```

Algorithm:

// Master Transmitter

1. Define the PIC18 configuration bits using the pragma directive, include xc.h, and set the crystal frequency with _XTAL_FREQ to use the built-in delay functions.
2. Configure the PIC18F4550 as the master device for SPI communication.
3. Activate slave select by setting LATA5 to high.
4. Transmit the data on the SPI bus.
5. Wait for 500 ms.
6. Deactivate slave select by setting LATA5 to low.
7. Repeat steps 3 through 6 as necessary.

// Slave Receiver

1. Define the PIC18 configuration bits using the pragma directive, include xc.h, and set the crystal frequency with _XTAL_FREQ to utilize the built-in delay functions.
2. Configure the PIC18F4550 as a slave device for SPI communication.
3. Set PORTD as an output port.

4. Read data from the SPI bus and transfer the received data to PORTD.
5. Repeat step 4 as needed.

// Header file: "spi1.h"

SPI_Master_Init()

1. Configure the I/O pins for SPI Master Mode: Set the appropriate pins for Serial Data Out (SDO), Serial Data In (SDI), Serial Clock (SCK), and Slave Select (SS).
2. Set the SPI to master mode and configure the clock rate to FOSC/64, which provides a clock speed of 312.5 kHz.
3. Enable the Synchronous Serial Port (SSP) and set the Slave Select (SS) pin to active low.
4. Set the Serial Clock Polarity to rising edge.
5. Configure the SPI module to sample input data in the middle of the clock cycle.
6. Enable SPI transmission interrupts if required.

SPI_Slave_Init()

1. Configure the I/O pins for SPI Slave Mode.
2. Set the MSSP module to operate in SPI Slave Mode.
3. Enable the Synchronous Serial Port (SSP) and set the Slave Select (SS) pin to active low.
4. Configure the Serial Clock Polarity to rising edge.
5. Enable SPI Reception Interrupts (recommended for efficient data handling).

SPI_Write(unsigned char)

1. Clear the write collision detect flag if it is set.
2. Load the data into the Buffer Register (SSPBUF).
3. Wait until the SSPIF (Serial Port Interrupt Flag) is set, indicating that the data transmission is complete.

SPI_ReceiveWait()

Wait until the Buffer Full Flag (BF) is set, indicating that data has been received and is available in the buffer.

SPI_Read()

1. Flush any remaining data in the SSPBUF (if needed).
2. Wait until all bits have been received and the Buffer Full Flag (BF) is set.
3. Return the received data from the Buffer Register (SSPBUF).

Program:

// Master Transmitter

```
#pragma config PLLDIV = 5, CPUDIV = OSC1_PLL2, USBDIV = 2, FOSC = HS, FCMEN =
OFF, IESO = OFF
#pragma config PWRT = OFF, BOR = OFF, BORV = 3, VREGEN = OFF, WDT = OFF,
WDTPS = 32768
#pragma config CCP2MX = ON, PBADEN = OFF, LPT1OSC = OFF, MCLRE = ON
#pragma config STVREN = ON, LVP = OFF, ICPRT = OFF, XINST = OFF
#pragma config CP0 = OFF, CP1 = OFF, CP2 = OFF, CP3 = OFF, CPB = OFF, CPD = OFF
#pragma config WRT0 = OFF, WRT1 = OFF, WRT2 = OFF, WRT3 = OFF, WRTC = OFF,
WRTB = OFF, WRTD = OFF
#pragma config EBTR0 = OFF, EBTR1 = OFF, EBTR2 = OFF, EBTR3 = OFF, EBTRB = OFF

#include <xc.h>
#define _XTAL_FREQ 20000000
#include "spi1.h"                       // Include header file
void main() {                           // Main function
  unsigned char i;
  SPI_Master_Init();                    // Initializing master device for SPI
  while (1) {                           // Forever loop
    LATAbits.LATA5 = 0;                 // Enable slave select
    for(i=0; i<16; i++){
      SPI_Write(i);                     // Write data on SPI bus
      __delay_ms(500);
    }
    LATAbits.LATA5 = 1;                 // Disable slave select
  }
```

```
}
/*---------------------------------------------------------------------------*/
// Slave Receiver
#pragma config PLLDIV = 5, CPUDIV = OSC1_PLL2, USBDIV = 2, FOSC = HS, FCMEN =
OFF, IESO = OFF
#pragma config PWRT = OFF, BOR = OFF, BORV = 3, VREGEN = OFF, WDT = OFF,
WDTPS = 32768
#pragma config CCP2MX = ON, PBADEN = OFF, LPT1OSC = OFF, MCLRE = ON
#pragma config STVREN = ON, LVP = OFF, ICPRT = OFF, XINST = OFF
#pragma config CP0 = OFF, CP1 = OFF, CP2 = OFF, CP3 = OFF, CPB = OFF, CPD = OFF
#pragma config WRT0 = OFF, WRT1 = OFF, WRT2 = OFF, WRT3 = OFF, WRTC = OFF,
WRTB = OFF, WRTD = OFF
#pragma config EBTR0 = OFF, EBTR1 = OFF, EBTR2 = OFF, EBTR3 = OFF, EBTRB = OFF
#include <xc.h>
#define _XTAL_FREQ 20000000
#define output LATD
#include "spi1.h"                    // Include header file
void main() {                        // Main function
  SPI_Slave_Init();                  // Initializing slave device for SPI
  TRISD = 0x00;
  while (1) {                        // Forever loop
    output = SPI_Read();             // Read SPI bus and display it in PORTB
  }
}
/*---------------------------------------------------------------------------*/
// Header file: "spi1.h"
void SPI_Master_Init()
{
//Configure the IO pins for SPI Master Mode.
TRISB1 = 0;          // SCK -> 0 in master mode
TRISB0 = 1;          // SDI -> Input
TRISC7 = 0;          // SDO -> Output
ADCON1 = 0x07;       // Set PORTA as digital port
TRISA5 = 0;          // SS as a output
//Set the SPI master mode and Set the desired Clock Rate FOSC/64 = 312.5 KBs
SSPM3 = 0; SSPM2 = 0; SSPM1 = 1; SSPM0 = 0;
```

```
//Enable the Synchronous Serial Port and disable slave select (active low)
SSPEN = 1;
LATAbits.LATA5= 1;                  // Disable slave select
//Configure the Serial Clock Polarity (Rising edge)
CKP = 0;            // 0 = Idle state for clock is a low level
CKE = 0;            // 0 = Transmit occurs on transition from Idle to active clock state
//Configure when the input data is sampled at the Middle
SMP = 0;            // 0 = Input data sampled at middle of data output time
//Enable SPI Transmission Interrupts (if needed)
// SSPIE = 1;       PEIE = 1;           GIE   = 1;
__delay_ms(100);
}

void SPI_Slave_Init()
{
//Configure the IO pins for SPI Slave Mode.
TRISB1 = 1;                         // SCK -> 1 in slave mode
TRISB0 = 1;                         // SDI -> Input
TRISC7 = 0;                         // SDO -> Output
ADCON1 = 0x07;                      // Set PORTA as digital port
TRISA5 = 1;                         // SS as a input
//Set the MSSP module in SPI Slave Mode
// 0100 = SPI Slave mode, clock = SCK pin. SS pin control enabled.
SSPM3 = 0;      SSPM2 = 1;      SSPM1 = 0;      SSPM0 = 0;
//Enable the Synchronous Serial Port and disable slave select
SSPEN = 1;
LATAbits.LATA5 = 1;
//Configure the Serial Clock Polarity (Rising Edge)
CKP = 0;            CKE = 0;
// Clear the SMP Bit
SMP = 0;
// Enable SPI Reception Interrupts (Recommended)
//SSPIE = 1;        PEIE = 1;           GIE   = 1;
__delay_ms(100);
}
```

```
void SPI_Write(unsigned char Data1)
{
 if (WCOL == 1){                    // Clear write collision detect flag
 WCOL = 0;
 }
 SSPIF = 0;                         // Clear flag
 SSPBUF = Data1;                    // Load Buffer Register
 while(!SSPIF);                     // Wait until set SSPIF
}

static void SPI_ReceiveWait() {
  while ( !BF );                    // Wait for 1 = Receive complete
}

char SPI_Read()                     //Read the received data
{
  SSPBUF=0xff;                      // Copy flush data in SSBUF
  SPI_ReceiveWait();                // wait until the all bits receive
  return(SSPBUF);                   // Return the received data from the buffer
}
```

Circuit Diagram:

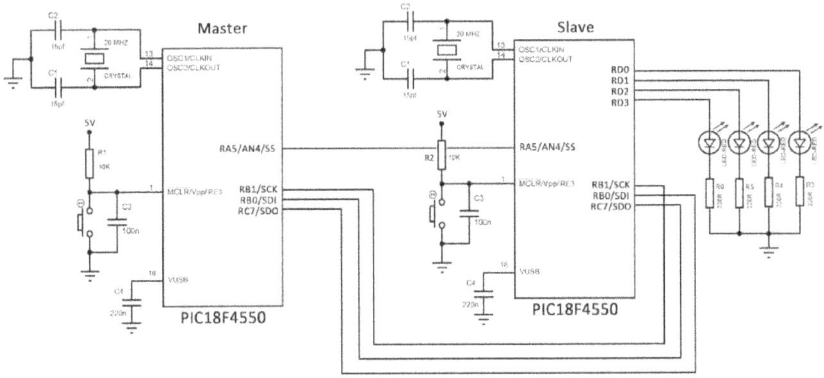

Conclusion:

The Embedded C program for SPI communication between two PIC18F4550 microcontrollers has been successfully implemented and executed. The data sent by the master device was accurately received by the slave device and displayed on PORTB.

55. INTERFACING ESP8266 WIFI MODULE

Aim:

Design an IoT-based temperature monitoring system using the ESP8266 WiFi Module and the PIC18F4550 Microcontroller, and verify its functionality.

Hardware Requirements:

- PIC18F4550 Microcontroller (1), 20 MHz Crystal (1), 15 pF Disc Capacitors (2), 220 nF Disc Capacitor (1), 100 nF Disc Capacitor (1), Resistor 10 K (1), and Push Button (1)
- ESP8266 WiFi Module, Temperature Sensor LM35, Resistor 2K2 (2), Resistor 1K (2), 16x2 LCD (1)

Software Used:

- IDE: MPLAB X IDE v5.45
- Compiler: XC8 - v2.31

Theory:

The ESP8266 is a WiFi module featuring the Cadence Tensilica L106 32-bit MCU, developed by Espressif Systems. It integrates a complete WiFi and TCP/IP stack, enabling easy WiFi connectivity for any microcontroller. The module can be programmed directly without needing an external programmer.

Various third-party manufacturers, including Ai-Thinker, have created custom boards based on the ESP8266 SoC. The Ai-Thinker ESP-01 module, used in this project, has 8 pins:

- VCC: 3.3V power supply

- GND: Ground
- TX: Transmits serial data
- RX: Receives serial data
- RST: Active low reset pin
- CH_PD: Active high chip enable pin
- GPIO0: General Purpose I/O pin 0, used for normal GPIO operations and programming mode
- GPIO2: General Purpose I/O pin 2

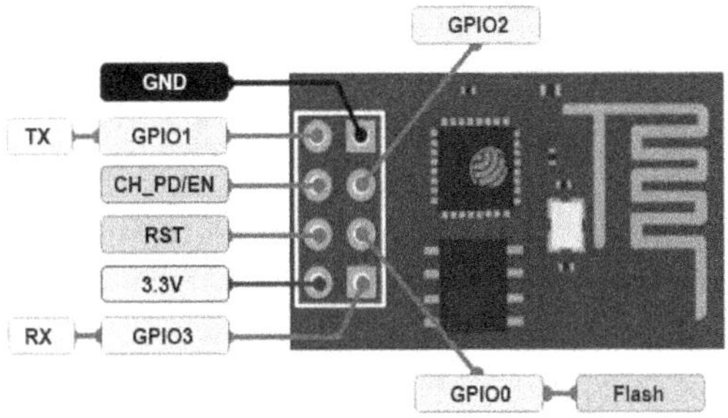

The ESP8266 operates at 3.3V, whereas the PIC18F4550 uses 5V. To ensure proper communication between the two, a voltage level converter circuit is required on the RX line of the ESP8266 module to step down the 5V signals from the PIC to 3.3V. However, this circuit is not needed on the TX line, as the PIC can correctly interpret 3.3V as a logic '1'.

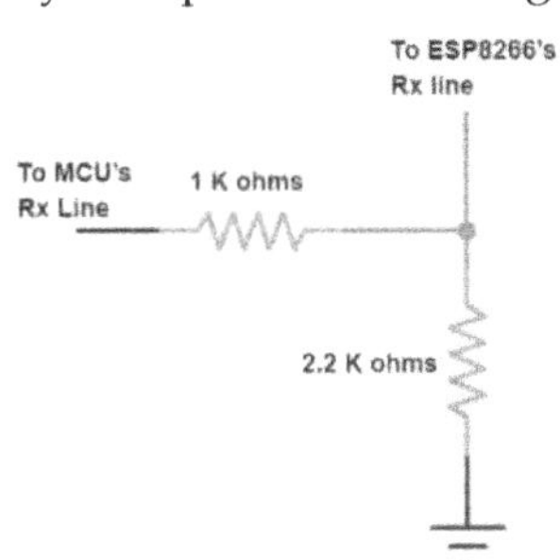

Establishing the PIC16F887 Internet Connection:

The ESP8266 module, which comes with default firmware, can be programmed using AT commands. These commands are sent through a serial communication channel. To establish serial communication between the PIC16F887 microcontroller and the ESP8266 module, the USART

(Universal Synchronous Asynchronous Receiver Transmitter) in the PIC microcontroller is used.

Commonly used AT Commands are,

AT	Test AT startup
AT+RST	Restart module
AT+RESTORE	Factory Reset
ATE	ATE0: Switch echo off
AT+UART_DEF=<baudrate>,<databits>,<stopbits>,<parity>,<flow control>	AT+UART_DEF=115200,8,1,0,0 to make it definite and get it saved in the flash memory
AT+CWMODE_DEF=3	Set the module to "SoftAP+Station mode"
AT+CWJAP_DEF=<ssid>,<pwd>	AT+CWJAP_DEF="abc","0123459"
AT+CWLIF	This command is used to get the IP of stations
AT+CWAUTOCONN	ESP8266 station will connect to AP automatically when power on
Enable/Disable DHCP and save to flash AT+CWDHCP_DEF=<mode>,<en>	AT+CWDHCP_DEF= 2, 1 2 : set both softAP and station 1 : Enable DHCP
Set IP address of ESP8266 station AT+CIPSTA=<IP>[,<gateway>,<netmask>]	AT+CIPSTA="192.168.6.100","192.168.6.1","255.255.255.0"
Set IP address of ESP8266 softAP, save to Flash AT+CIPAP_DEF=<IP>[,<gateway>,<netmask>]	AT+CIPAP_DEF="192.168.5.1","192.168.5.1","255.255.255.0"
Start SmartConfig AT+CWSTARTSMART	AT+CWMODE=1 AT+CWSTARTSMART
Stop SmartConfig AT+CWSTOPSMART	AT+CWSTOPSMART
AT-CIPMUX=0	Enables single connection mode
Establish TCP connection or register UDP port, start connection AT+CIPSTART=<type>,<remote IP>,<remote port>[,<UDP local	AT+CIPSTART="TCP","192.168.101.110",1000

port>,<UDP mode>][,<TCP keep alive>]	
Send data AT+CIPSEND=<length>	AT+CIPSEND=4 // set date length which will be sent, such as 4 bytes
Close TCP or UDP connection AT+CIPCLOSE=<link ID>	AT+CIPCLOSE=0 // Delete NO.0 connection.
Configure as TCP server AT+CIPSERVER=<mode>[,<port>]	AT+CIPSERVER=1,80 The '1' creates a server and listens to port 80.

The ESP8266 Wi-Fi module is used to connect the MCU to a Wi-Fi network and upload temperature data to ThingSpeak. ThingSpeak is an open-source IoT application and API that allows for the collection, storage, analysis, and visualization of data from connected devices over the Internet.

To use ThingSpeak:

1. Sign in at www.thingspeak.com and create your own channel by defining a field.
2. After saving the channel, you will receive a channel ID and two API keys: a write API key for uploading data and a read API key for retrieving data.

In this setup, temperature data from an LM35 sensor is fed to pin RA0 (pin 2) of the PIC16F887 microcontroller. This data is then sent to the ESP8266 Wi-Fi module, which transmits it to the ThingSpeak Cloud platform. The temperature data can be accessed remotely through the ThingSpeak website on devices like smartphones or laptops. Additionally, an LCD is used to display the circuit's status and the temperature data as a user interface.

ThingSpeak API – Keywords:

- Channel: Identified by a numerical Channel ID, this is where data is inserted or retrieved within the ThingSpeak API.
- Field: One of up to eight specific locations within a channel for storing data. Each field is identified by a number between 1 and 8

and can store numeric data from sensors or alphanumeric strings from devices.

- Status: A brief message that can be added to the data in a channel for additional context.
- Location: The latitude, longitude, and elevation of the data source.
- Feed: The collective term for all data within a channel, including field data, status updates, and location information.
- Write API Key: A 16-digit code used to write data to a channel.
- Read API Key: A 16-digit code used to read data from a channel.

ThingSpeak - Addresses and Locations:

- Regular URL: http://api.thingspeak.com
- Secure URL: https://api.thingspeak.com
- IP Address: http://184.106.153.149
- Cross-domain XML: http://api.thingspeak.com/crossdomain.xml

Algorithm:

1. Define the PIC18 configuration bits using the pragma directive. Include xc.h and set the crystal frequency for _XTAL_FREQ to utilize the built-in delay functions.
2. Initialize PORTD for interfacing with a 16x2 LCD.
3. Include the lcd4bit_head.h header file for LCD functions.
4. Declare global variables: value[50], pos, and sec.
5. Define a function for creating delays (unsigned int delay).
6. Implement the interrupt service routine (ISR) for serial port reception (Rx).
7. Define the transmit(unsigned char) function for sending serial data.
8. Define the transmit_string(unsigned char) function for sending strings.
9. Implement the delay1sec() function for one-second delays.
10. Define the lcd_write function to display strings at specified character addresses on the LCD.

Main function:

1. Set PORTD as an output port.
2. Configure TRISC for Tx and Rx pin directions.
3. Enable the serial port receive interrupt.
4. Configure the USART for asynchronous communication.
5. Set up the ADC for analog readings at AN0.
6. Initialize the 16x2 LCD in 4-bit mode.
7. Display "IOT TEMP Monitor" on the LCD screen.
8. Send the "AT" command to the ESP8266.
9. Verify the response from the ESP8266.
10. If the response is "OK," proceed; otherwise, retry.
11. Send the "ATE0" command to the ESP8266.
12. Verify the response from the ESP8266.
13. If the response is "OK," proceed; otherwise, retry.
14. Send the command "AT+CWMODE=3" to configure the ESP8266 for station mode.
15. Verify the response from the ESP8266.
16. If the response is "OK," proceed; otherwise, retry.
17. Send the command "AT+CIPMUX=1" to configure the ESP8266 for multiple connections.
18. Verify the response from the ESP8266.
19. If the response is "OK," proceed; otherwise, retry.
20. Send the command AT+CWJAP="TP-LINK_A6A8","password" to connect the ESP8266 to the Wi-Fi network.
21. Verify the response from the ESP8266.
22. If the response is "OK," proceed; otherwise, retry.
23. Start ADC conversion with the LM35 sensor connected to RA0/AN0.
24. Wait until the conversion is complete.
25. Display the ADC result on the LCD.
26. After 30 seconds, clear the LCD screen and display "Uploading."
27. Send the IP address of ThingSpeak.com (184.106.153.149) to the ESP8266.
28. Verify the response from the ESP8266.
29. If the response is "OK," proceed; otherwise, retry.
30. Set the data length for sending to ThingSpeak.com.

31. Verify the response from the ESP8266.
32. If the response is "OK," proceed; otherwise, retry.
33. Update the ThingSpeak channel using the Write API Key.
34. Transmit the ADC value to the cloud.
35. Close the channel.
36. Repeat steps from 23 onward.

Program:

```
#pragma config PLLDIV = 5, CPUDIV = OSC1_PLL2, USBDIV = 2, FOSC = HS, FCMEN =
OFF, IESO = OFF
#pragma config PWRT = OFF, BOR = OFF, BORV = 3, VREGEN = OFF, WDT = OFF,
WDTPS = 32768
#pragma config CCP2MX = ON, PBADEN = OFF, LPT1OSC = OFF, MCLRE = ON
#pragma config STVREN = ON, LVP = OFF, ICPRT = OFF, XINST = OFF
#pragma config CP0 = OFF, CP1 = OFF, CP2 = OFF, CP3 = OFF, CPB = OFF, CPD = OFF
#pragma config WRT0 = OFF, WRT1 = OFF, WRT2 = OFF, WRT3 = OFF, WRTC = OFF,
WRTB = OFF, WRTD = OFF
#pragma config EBTR0 = OFF, EBTR1 = OFF, EBTR2 = OFF, EBTR3 = OFF, EBTRB = OFF

#include <xc.h>
#define _XTAL_FREQ 20000000
#define RS       LATD2                    // RD2 is named as RS
#define EN       LATD3                    // RD3 is named as EN
#define D4       LATD4                    // 4-bit mode (RD4-D4, RD5-D5
#define D5       LATD5                    // RD6-D6, RD7-D7)
#define D6       LATD6
#define D7       LATD7
#include "lcd4bit_head.h"                 // Include header file
#include<string.h>
unsigned char value[50], pos;
unsigned char sec;

void delay(unsigned int a)  {             // Delay subroutine
  while(a--);
}
```

```
__interrupt() void Serial(void)              // ISR
{
if(RCIF==1&&pos<28)
{
value[pos]=RCREG;
pos++;
RCIF=0;
}
}

void transmit(unsigned char x)               // Serial data transmit 1
{
TXREG = x;                         // Transmit the recived character
while(TXSTAbits.TRMT ==0);
PIR1bits.TXIF=0;                   // Clear transmit flag
}

void transmit_string(char *tx_str)           // Serial data transmit 2
{
unsigned char ch;
pos=0;
transmit(0x0d);
transmit(0x0d);
while(*tx_str != 0x00)   {
 ch = *tx_str;                     // Get the charcter from a string
 TXREG = ch;              // Transmit to the serial port one by one
 while(!(TXSTAbits.TRMT));
 PIR1bits.TXIF=0;                  // Clear TXIF
 tx_str++;                         // Increment pointer
 delay(100);
}
transmit(0x0d);
transmit(0x0a);
delay(60000);
```

```
}

void clearVAL() {                    // Clear the values
char i;
for(i=0;i<30;i++)
value[i]=' ';
}

void delay1sec()                     // Delay function for 1 sec
{
char i;
for(i=0;i<20;i++) {
TMR1H=0x3a;
TMR1L=0xbb;
TMR1ON=1;
while(TMR1IF==0);
TMR1ON=0;
TMR1IF=0;
}
sec++;
}

void lcd_write(char *p,unsigned char x)            // LCD write function
{
 int hj=0;
 if(x!='0')
 lcd_cmd(x);
   while(p[hj]!='\0')
    {
    lcd_data(p[hj]);
    hj++;
    }
}
```

```
void main()                     // Main function
{
char i,x,flag;
unsigned int adc_val;
TRISD=0x00;                     // Set PORTD as output port
T1CON=0x00;                     // Clear T1CON
TRISC=0X80;                     // Set the direction for Tx and Rx pins
delay(60000);
GIE=1;                          // Enable serial receive interrupt
RCIE=1;
PEIE=1;
SPBRG=0x19;                     // Set Baudrate (9600)
TXSTA=0x26;                     // Configure USART for receive and
transmit
RCSTA=0x90;
TRISA = 0x01;                   // Analog pin AN0 as Input port
ADCON0 = 0x81;                  // Channel AN0, ADC Clock FOSC/64 & Turn ON ADC
ADCON1 = 0xCE;                  // Right justified, AN0 Analog port & VDD and VSS Ref.
delay(1000);
lcd_init();                     // Initializing 16x2 LCD
delay(60000);
lcd_write("IoT TEMP Monitor",0x80);
delay(60000);
delay(60000);
delay(60000);
lcd_cmd(0x01);                  // Clear LCD screen

//Sending AT Commands
clearVAL();                     //AT
lcd_write("AT",0x80);
transmit_string("AT");
while(1)
{
x=strstr(&value,"OK");          // Check the returns from ESP8266
```

```
if(x-32<0)
  { lcd_write("ERROR1",0xc3);}
else
  { lcd_write("OK1   ",0xc3); break; }
}
delay(60000);

clearVAL();                         //ATE0
lcd_write("ATE0",0x80);
transmit_string("ATE0");
while(1)  {
x=strstr(&value,"OK");              // Check the returns from ESP8266
if(x-32<0)
  { lcd_write("ERROR2",0xc3);}
else
  { lcd_write("OK2   ",0xc3); break; }
}
delay(60000);

clearVAL();                         //AT+CWMODE=3
lcd_write("AT+CWMODE=3",0x80);
transmit_string("AT+CWMODE=3");
while(1)  {
x=strstr(&value,"OK");              // Check the returns from ESP8266
if(x-32<0)
  { lcd_write("ERROR3",0xc3);}
else
  { lcd_write("OK3   ",0xc3); break; }
}
delay(60000);

clearVAL();                         //AT+CIPMUX=1
lcd_write("AT+CIPMUX=1",0x80);
transmit_string("AT+CIPMUX=1");
```

```
while(1)
{
x=strstr(&value,"OK");                        // Check the returns from ESP8266
if(x-32<0)
  { lcd_write("ERROR4",0xc3);}
else
  { lcd_write("OK4   ",0xc3); break; }
}
delay(60000);

clearVAL();                                   //AT+CWJAP
lcd_write("connecting...",0x80);
value[0]='\0';

//Connect to WIFI network
strcat(value,"AT+CWJAP=\"TP-LINK_A6A8\",\"password\"");
transmit_string(&value);
while(1)  {
x=strstr(&value,"OK");                        // Check the returns from ESP8266
if(x-32<0)
  { lcd_write("ERROR/WAIT",0xc3);}
else
  { lcd_write("OK5   ",0xc3); break; }
}
delay(60000);
lcd_cmd(0x01);
delay(2000);
lcd_write("TEMP:-",0x80);                     // Send "TEMP" to line1 of LCD
lcd_write("Upload after:",0xc0);              // Send "Upload after" to LCD line2
sec=0;

while(1)
{                                   // forever loop
GO=1;                                         // Start AD conversion
```

```
while(GO==1);                          // Wait until the conversion over
adc_val=((ADRESH<<8)+ADRESL)*4.88;
lcd_cmd(0x87);                         // Display the ADC value on LCD
lcd_data((adc_val/1000)+48);
lcd_data(((adc_val%1000)/100)+48);
lcd_data(((adc_val%100)/10)+48);
lcd_data('.');
lcd_data((adc_val%10)+48);
lcd_data('C');
adc_val=adc_val/10;
delay(20000);
delay1sec();
lcd_cmd(0xce);
lcd_data((30-sec)/10+48);
lcd_data(((30-sec)%10)+48);

if(sec==30)   {
   lcd_cmd(0x01);                      // Clear screen
   delay(1000);
   delay(60000);
   lcd_write("Uploading...",0x80);     // Display "Uploading" on LCD
   clearVAL();
   value[0]='\0';
   //IP Address: http://184.106.153.149 to Thingspeak.com
   strcat(value,"AT+CIPSTART=4,\"TCP\",\"184.106.153.149\",80");
   transmit_string(&value);
   sec=0;
   delay(60000);
   delay(60000);
   delay(60000);
   delay(60000);
   while(1)
   {
     x=strstr(&value,"OK");            // Check the returns from ESP8266
```

```
    if(x-32<0)
        { lcd_write("Error",0xc3); flag=0; break;}
    else
        { lcd_write("OK6  ",0xc3);flag=1; break; }
    }
    delay(10000);

if(flag==1)  {
  clearVAL();
  value[0]='\0';
  //Send No. of characters
  strcat(value,"AT+CIPSEND=4,46");     //Set data length which will be sent
  transmit_string(&value);
  delay(60000);
  delay(60000);
  delay(60000);
  while(1)
   {
    x=strstr(&value,">");                // Check the returns from ESP8266
    if(x-32<0)
        { lcd_write("ERROR",0xc3); flag=0; break;}
    else
        { lcd_write("OK7   ",0xc3);flag=1; break; }
    }
    delay(60000);
    delay(60000);

  if(flag==1)
  {
  clearVAL();
  value[0]='\0';
  lcd_write("GET DATA",0xc0);
  //Update Channel using Write API Key
  strcat(value,"GET /update?key=xxxxxxxxxxxx&field1=");
```

```
transmit_string(&value);
lcd_data('1');
transmit((adc_val/1000)+48); lcd_data('1');
transmit(((adc_val%1000)/100)+48);lcd_data('1');
transmit(((adc_val%100)/10)+48);lcd_data('1');
transmit((adc_val%10)+48);lcd_data('1');
transmit(0x0d);
transmit(0x0a);
delay(40000);
lcd_data('1');
delay(10000);
lcd_cmd(0x01);
delay(2000);
lcd_write("CIPLCOSE",0x80);
clearVAL();  //AT+CIPCLOSE=0
value[0]='\0';
delay(3000);
strcat(value,"AT+CIPCLOSE");                    //Close Channel
transmit_string(&value);
lcd_cmd(0x01);
delay(1000);
}
}
lcd_cmd(0x01);
delay(1000);
lcd_write("TEMP:-",0x80);
lcd_write("Upload after:",0xc0);
sec=0;
}
}
}
//-----------------------------------------------------------------------------------------------------
#include "lcd4bit_head.h"                    // Include header file
//-----------------------------------------------------------------------------------------------------
```

Circuit Diagram:

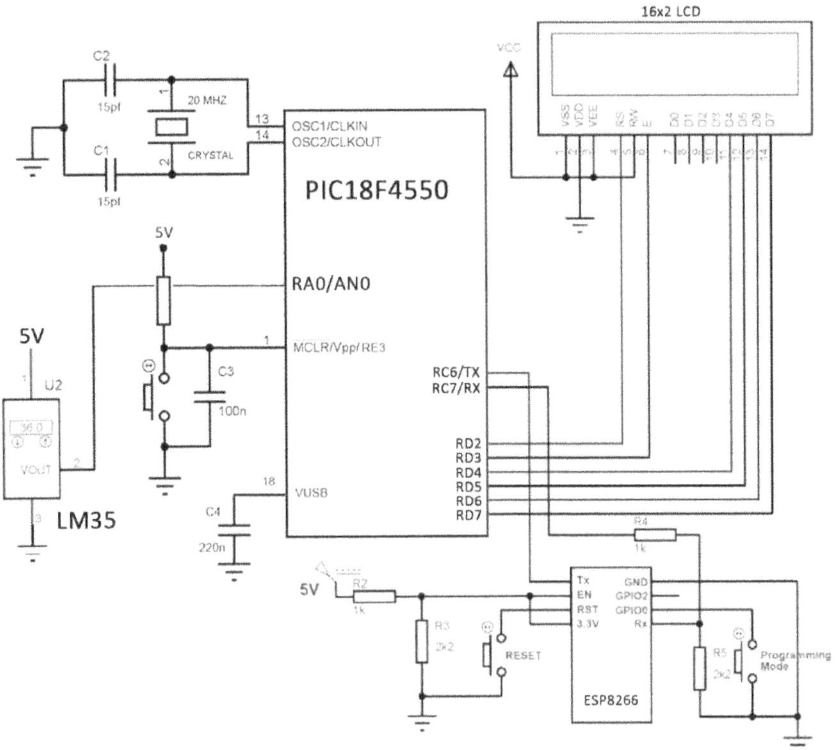

Conclusion:

The IoT-based temperature monitoring system has been successfully designed using the ESP8266 WiFi module and the PIC16F887 microcontroller. The system has been tested and its output verified, demonstrating effective integration and data transmission capabilities.

………………………………………………………………………………

www.ingramcontent.com/pod-product-compliance
Lightning Source LLC
Chambersburg PA
CBHW062133160726
48282CB00027B/810
9789334105094